# A Step-by-Step Guide to Your Sewing Machine

## OTHER BOOKS IN THE CREATIVE MACHINE ARTS SERIES, AVAILABLE FROM CHILTON:

*Claire Shaeffer's Fabric Sewing Guide*

*The Complete Book of Machine Embroidery,*
by Robbie and Tony Fanning

*Creative Nurseries Illustrated,*
by Debra Terry and Juli Plooster

*Creative Serging Illustrated,* by Pati Palmer,
Gail Brown, and Sue Green

*Distinctive Serger Gifts and Crafts,*
by Naomi Baker and Tammy Young

*The Fabric Lover's Scrapbook,*
by Margaret Dittman

*Friendship Quilts by Hand and Machine,*
by Carolyn Vosburg Hall

*Innovative Serging,* by Gail Brown
and Tammy Young

*Innovative Sewing,* by Gail Brown
and Tammy Young

*Know Your Bernina,* 2nd edition, by Jackie
Dodson

*Know Your Brother,* by Jackie Dodson
with Jane Warnick

*Know Your Elna,* by Jackie Dodson
with Carol Ahles

*Know Your New Home,* by Jackie Dodson
with Judi Cull and Vicki Lyn Hastings

*Know Your Pfaff,* by Jackie Dodson
with Audrey Griese

*Know Your Sewing Machine,* by Jackie Dodson

*Know Your Singer,* by Jackie Dodson

*Know Your Viking,* by Jackie Dodson
with Jan Saunders

*Know Your White,* by Jackie Dodson
with Jan Saunders

*Owner's Guide to Sewing Machines, Sergers,
and Knitting Machines,* by Gale Grigg Hazen

*Petite Pizzazz,* by Barb Griffin

*Sew, Serge, Press,* by Jan Saunders

*Sewing and Collecting Vintage Fashions,*
by Eileen MacIntosh

*Simply Serge Any Fabric,* by Naomi Baker
and Tammy Young

## OTHER BOOKS* IN JAN SAUNDERS' TEACH YOURSELF TO SEW BETTER SERIES, AVAILABLE FROM CHILTON:

*A Step-by-step Guide to Your Bernina*

*A Step-by-step Guide to Your Viking*

*A Step-by-step Guide to Your New Home*

*More to come in the future

*Teach Yourself to Sew Better*

# A STEP-BY-STEP GUIDE
# TO YOUR SEWING MACHINE

**Jan Saunders**

**Chilton Book Company**

**Radnor, Pennsylvania**

Published in Radnor, Pennsylvania 19089, by Chilton Book Company

Designed by Kevin Culver and Teddi Jensen

Illustrations by Pamela Poole

Photography by Lee Phillips

Manufactured in the United States of America

Library of Congress Cataloging in Publication Data
Saunders, Janice S.
    A step-by-step guide to your sewing machine / Jan Saunders.
      p.  cm. — (Teach yourself to sew better)
    Includes bibliographical references and index.
    ISBN 0–8019–8013–5 (pbk.)
    1. Machine sewing.  2. Sewing machines.  I. Title.  II. Series.
TT713.S258    1990
646.2′044 – dc20                     89–45964
                                         CIP

1 2 3 4 5 6 7 8 9 0    9 8 7 6 5 4 3 2 1 0

# CONTENTS

**Preface**

**Foreword**
*by Robbie Fanning*

*Part One:*
# MEET YOUR MACHINE .............. 1

## Chapter One: Meet Your Machine.....................3

Have you wanted to know how your sewing machine works without having to go to school to become a mechanic? What about those gadgets that came with your machine? This is a crash course to clear up misunderstandings you may have about threading your machine, tension adjustments, needle and thread selection; simple care and maintenance information, and how to use the basic presser feet and stitches. Also see how various tools can make sewing easier and a lot more fun.

*Part Two:*
# THE WORLD OF SEWING ..........33

## Chapter Two: Sew Fashion.........................37

Learn the proper stitches and presser feet to sew woven and knit fabrics by making a pair of woven pull-on shorts and a knit top with ribbing. Once you've completed this project, you'll have the basic skills to tackle more challenging ones.

## Chapter Three: Sew Embellishments—
## Machine Appliqué and Embroider ...................61

Practice the basics of machine appliqué and embroidery by making a Compass Tote Bag. Embellish a pocket for your shorts and knit top made in Chapter 2.

**Chapter Four:  Sew for Your Home** ................83

Make Envelope Placemats and matching "Lapkins" to master buttonholes, mitered corners, and professional edge finishes.

**Chapter Five:  Sew a Quilt** .........................95

Stitch a small quilt to perfect free-machine quilting, piecing, borders, straight-stitch quilting, and tying a quilt.

**Chapter Six:  Sew Toys** ........................109

Create stuffed fabric blocks and a hobbyhorse while mastering thread fringe, yarn fringe, gusset insertion, gathering over a cord, and more.

**Chapter Seven:  Sew Gifts** ......................125

Surprise your family and friends with quick-to-stitch key rings, and a fabric gameboard and pouch.  At the same time you'll learn zipper insertion, edgestitching and topstitching techniques, and new ways to use your decorative stitches.

*Part Three:*

# STITCH & PRESSER FOOT ENCYCLOPEDIA
.................143

**Chapter Eight:  Encyclopedia of Stitches** .......145

See both practical and decorative stitch applications for common stitches available on most machines made within the last 15 years.  The stitches introduced here are cross-referenced throughout the projects in Part II, and with the Encyclopedia of Presser Feet.

**Chapter Nine:  Encyclopedia of Presser Feet** ...180

See both practical and decorative presser foot applications for presser feet common to most sewing machines.  The presser feet applications are cross-referenced throughout the projects in Part II, and with the Encyclopedia of Stitches.

**Sources of Supply** ...................203

**Bibliography** ...........................207

**Index** .................................209

# PREFACE

In most sewing books the word "sewing" means making garments. Such books spend pages showing you how to measure yourself, choose patterns, lay out fabric, cut, and mark.

This book is different. To me, the word "sewing" implies using your sewing machine to its fullest potential. You may want to use your machine to make garments, but that's only part of the World of Sewing. In this book you'll learn to use your machine wisely not only to make clothing, but also for appliqué and embroidery, home decoration, quilt making, toys and games, and gifts.

For this reason, *Teach Yourself to Sew Better* takes a broad look at sewing. In **Part I**, Meet Your Machine, you will take a look at the parts of the machine, at tools necessary for respectable results, and at basic stitches. You will also preview the way the projects in Part II are constructed, by completing three simple exercises.

**Part II**, The World of Sewing, is divided into six chapters—like spokes in a wheel, with the sewing machine at the hub.

*1.*
**Sew Fashion**

*2.*
**Sew Embellishments— Machine Appliqué and Embroidery**

*3.*
**Sew for Your Home**

*4.*
**Sew a Quilt**

*5.*
**Sew Toys**

*6.*
**Sew Gifts**

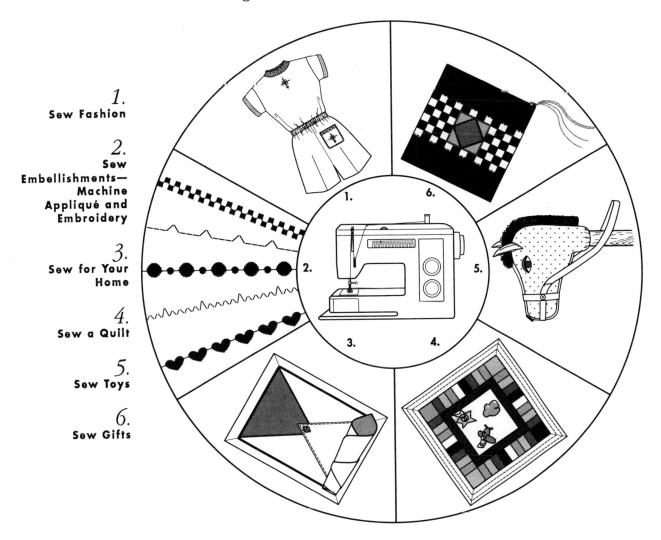

You may wonder how "The World of Sewing" can be covered in one book. I don't pretend to cover each area in infinite detail. But just as you don't need to know every landmark to follow directions to a place you've never been before, you don't need to know everything about one area of sewing to complete the project. Each chapter covers how to use some part of your sewing machine and guides you step by step through a project. The projects were selected and designed to appeal to almost anyone, regardless of age or gender. Instructions for many projects are written as a "master recipe." The variations for each project should enable you to tailor it to your needs. Even if you don't plan to make a project, read through the directions and make the project in your mind. You will learn many valuable techniques that can be transferred to other projects in this book and others. Look for **Transferable Learnings** as a checklist of what you have learned by making the project, and as a chapter review.

Also look for the **Sew-How** tips sprinkled throughout the book. Think of them as a sewing smorgasbord: keep what you like and discard the rest. **Sew-How** tips are designed to give you insight into a particular technique—a kind of "did you know?" or "don't forget" department. Other **Sew-How** information should enhance your knowledge and understanding of sewing.

 Don't think I've ignored the benefits of using the serger for fast professional results. However, I couldn't cover everything about serging in this book. If there is a particular technique or step that could be completed as well on the serger as on your conventional sewing machine, you will see a serger symbol in the margin.

**Part III** is an encyclopedia of the undiscovered treasures available for your machine—stitches and presser feet. Each major stitch and foot is illustrated. The text explains settings and uses, and the projects in Part II are cross-referenced to both stitch and presser feet encyclopedias in Part III.

This book is for anyone who wants to sew...better. Whether you're a beginner or have been sewing for years, whether you need a refresher course or an advanced look at your machine, this book shows you how to sew more efficiently by learning to use your machine better. Some of the information you may know already; some may be enlightening. My hope is that you'll sew more (and encourage others to do the same) by enjoying your machine, stitches, and presser feet as much as I do.

**Jan Saunders**
Columbus, Ohio

# FOREWORD

It had been a long, hard, hot day at work—interruptions, backtracking, emergencies, deadlines. I came home at 6 pm, pooped. But within an hour, I was rejuvenated, relaxed, peaceful. Why? Because I was machine-piecing a quilt for my daughter. You see, I truly love to sew. Like a kid's blankie, sewing is my Best Thing. (And best of all is to listen to recorded books as I sew.)

But I was lucky. My mother sewed as we grew up and we learned by osmosis. Later came seventh grade home ec and some sewing classes at the local fabric store.

Today, people are not as lucky as me. Sewing is rarely taught in home ec and many stores do not have classes. (Thank heavens for 4-H, where teaching sewing is still strong.) At the same time that fabrics have improved, machines have become easier to use, and speedy techniques have revolutionized sewing, fewer people know how.

Jan's book should help. For each of the six main sewing areas, it contains simple projects for any age. She then explains how the skills learned in each chapter can be transferred to more ambitious projects. The more experienced sewer will appreciate Jan's "Encyclopedia of Stitches and Presser Feet" in Part III.

Still, I propose you take one further step: share your love of sewing with someone else. You don't need teaching credentials to do this. Simply challenge yourself to help someone else learn to sew. It may be as simple as inviting a neighborhood child in to help you thread your machine. If he or she wants to run the machine, use the warm-up exercises in Chapter 1.

There are many other imaginative ways to share our mutual love of sewing. Set up a machine at work and let interested people use it on lunch breaks. Join 4-H and learn to teach sewing. Take your machine to a local school and show the students what you have made. Volunteer to teach sewing costumes to community theater. Demonstrate sewing at the church bazaar or county fair. Spend a day in the children's ward of a hospital, machine-embroidering patients' initials on bean bags.

As Diana Davies, a member of the Minneapolis chapter of the American Sewing Guild, suggested, "Each one teach one."

Jan and I would like to hear about your experiences. Please write us at the address below.

**Robbie Fanning**
*Series Editor, Creative Machine Arts*

*Are you interested in a quarterly newsletter about creative uses of the sewing machine, serger, and knitting machine? Write to The Creative Machine, PO Box 2634, Menlo Park, CA 94026.*

...............................

# ACKNOWLEDGMENTS

When you read a book, you remember the subject matter and maybe the author. You may also recognize the name of those quoted on the back cover and the editor. But there are many other people who selflessly lend their knowledge and expertise so a book—this book—can be the best it can be.

I wish to acknowledge and thank the following people who are very much a part of this book: Audrey Griese, Marsha Fredrickson, Ron and Barbara Goldkorn, Janet Penwell, Kathy Thompson, and Ann Williams for their candid comments on their businesses and their retail customers; Carol Ahles, Sue Bagley, Sandra Betzina, Gail Brown, Clotilde, David Coffin, Louise Garigk, Lois Gotwals, Sue Hausmann, Carl Jorden, Kathy Embry, Nancy Rice, Cheryl Robinson, Jane Schenck, Ann Wallace, and Nancy Zieman for their insightful comments on our industry at large, and their interest in and love for sewing in their own lives.

Also, a big thanks to the McCall Pattern Company for use of their patterns and pattern graphics, and V.W.S., Inc., for use of their sewing machines.

A special thanks goes to Pam Poole for her willingness to make each drawing as clear and understandable as possible, even at the expense of many corrections.

As always, thanks to Robbie Fanning for crafting this book, polishing my writing style, and helping me when I really needed it.

# MEET YOUR MACHINE

● *Chapter One: Meet Your Machine*

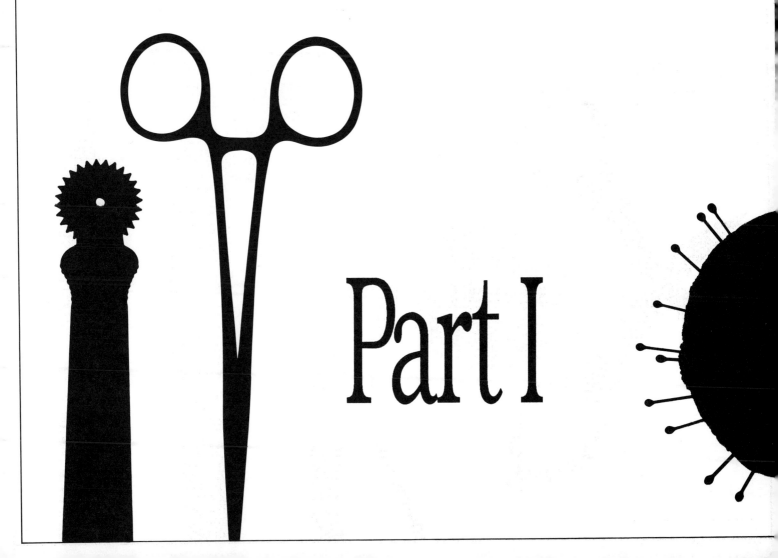

Part I

# MEET YOUR MACHINE

**Chapter 1: Meet Your Machine** .......................3

Step One: Identify the Parts of Your Machine.............................4
Step Two: Assemble Your Tools................................................14
Step Three: Learn the Basic Stitches .......................................22

# MEET YOUR MACHINE

- *Step One: Identify the Parts of Your Machine*

- *Step Two: Assemble Your Tools*

- *Step Three: Learn the Basic Stitches*

EVERYTIME I SIT DOWN TO SEW, I want my machine to perform perfectly. But it can't take care of itself. This section will acquaint you with the common parts of your machine and briefly explain their function. You will also brush up on how to take care of your machine, so it takes care of you.

I have found that instruction manuals sometimes leave too much to the imagination. To help you understand the basics of your machine, I've designed this section as a workbook to accompany your instruction manual. If your manual has disappeared, call your local dealer to get another one (or see the Sources of Supply). You will also make stitch samples, so have a variety of fabrics such as cotton kettle cloth, T-shirt knit, and light- and medium-weight wovens, cut into 7" (18 cm) squares. To keep your samples straight, buy a large three-ring binder and clear pocket-type pages to document your successes and failures. Why keep your failures? So you don't make the same mistake twice.

*Step One:*

# IDENTIFY THE PARTS OF YOUR MACHINE

Regardless of the model or sophistication, sewing machines have many parts in common. Review Fig. 1.1 and compare it with your machine and with the diagram of your sewing machine in your instruction manual.

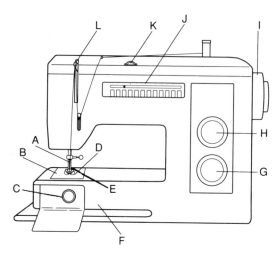

| A. | Needle | E. | Presser foot | I. | Flywheel |
|---|---|---|---|---|---|
| B. | Needle plate | F. | Free-arm | J. | Stitch selector |
| C. | Bobbin and bobbin case | G. | Stitch length | K. | Top tension |
| D. | Feed dogs | H. | Stitch width | L. | Take-up lever |

A. The **needle** is the most important part of the machine.

---

**Sew-How:** *To prevent skipped stitches and snagging, use a new needle for each garment or project. Use a fine needle for fine fabric, heavier needles for heavier fabric (see Table 1.1, Fabric, Needle, Thread, and Presser Foot Guide).*

---

B. The **needle plate**, sometimes referred to as a throat plate, rests on the bed of the machine over the feed dogs and has a round or oblong hole for the needle to pass through.

---

**Sew-How:** *Use the needle plate with the oblong hole for most of your sewing. If the fabric puckers and you are using the appropriate needle and stitch length for the fabric, decenter the needle to the far left or right. This offers support around three sides of the needle and often solves a puckering problem. If the puckering continues, use the needle plate with the round hole (but only for straight stitching).*

---

C. The **bobbin** and **bobbin case** are necessary to make a stitch. The bobbin holds thread necessary for sewing; the bobbin case holds the bobbin and is positioned in the front, side, or top of the machine in the race area. When top and bobbin threads lock, a stitch is formed.

## Table 1.1 Fabric, Needle, Thread, and Presser Foot Guide

| Type of Fabric | | Machine Needle | | | Thread | | | | Presser Foot |
|---|---|---|---|---|---|---|---|---|---|
| | | U.S. Size 15 x 1 | Eur. Size 130/705 | Style | Mercerized Cotton | All-purpose Cotton-covered Polyester | Polyester | Nylon | |
| Knits | Lightweight: Tricot | 9, 10 | 65 HS, 70 H | Universal | Yes | | No | Yes | Teflon/metal |
| | Medium Weight: Interlock, Qiana®, swimsuit fabric, Spandex™ | 11-14 | 75-90 HS | Universal | Yes | Yes | No | Yes | Teflon/metal |
| | Heavyweight: Double knit, velours | 12-14 | 80-90 H | Universal | Yes | Yes | Yes | No | Teflon/metal |
| | Fake Furs & Furlike Fabrics | 14-16 | 90-100 H | Universal | Yes | Yes | Yes | No | Roller or even-feed foot |
| Wovens | Very Sheer: Lace, net, chiffon, voile | 8 | 60 H | Universal | Yes | Yes | No | Yes | Teflon/metal |
| | Sheer: Qiana®, lawn, taffeta, gingham, crepe, organdy | 10 | 70 H | Universal | Yes | Yes | No | No | Teflon/metal |
| | Medium: Wool, linen, piqué, brocade, velvet, velveteen, terry cloth, nylon (outerwear) | 12 | 80 H | Universal | Yes | Yes | No | No | Embroidery |
| | Heavy: Denim, corduroy, sailcloth, duck | 14 | 90 HJ | Jeans | Yes | Yes | Yes | Yes | Teflon/metal |
| | Extra Heavy: Canvas, upholstery, awning, drapery fabric | 14-16 | 90 HJ, 90-110 H | Jeans or Universal | Yes | Yes | Yes | Yes | Teflon/metal |
| Leather | Ultrasuede, Ultraleather | 11 | 75 HS | Stretch | Yes | Yes | No | No | Teflon foot |
| | Vinyls | Leather 14-18 | NTW 90-110 | Wedge-point | Yes | Yes | Yes | No | Roller or even-feed foot |
| | Light to Medium Weight: Leathers and Suedes | Leather 14 | NTW 90 | Wedge-point | Yes | Yes | Yes | No | Roller or Teflon foot |
| | Vinyl Fabric with Knit Backing | Leather 14-16 | NTW 90-100 | Wedge-point | Yes | Yes | Yes | No | Roller or even-feed foot |
| | Heavy | Leather 14-16 | NTW 90-100 | Wedge-point | Yes | Yes | Yes | No | Roller or Teflon foot |
| Decorative Stitching | Machine Embroidery | 14 | 90 HS | Stretch | Yes* | No | No | No | Varies/Embroidery |
| | Topstitching with Heavier Thread | 14 | Topstitching 90 N | Universal large eye | No | No | Yes | No | Teflon or embroidery foot |
| | Twin Needles | Distance btwn. needles:<br>1.6mm<br>2.0mm<br>2.5mm<br>2.7mm<br>3.0mm<br>3.0mm<br>4.0mm<br>4.0mm | Size: U.S./Eur.<br>10/70 H<br>12/80 H<br>12/80 H<br>12/80 H<br>11/75 HS<br>14/90 H<br>11/75 HS<br>14/90 H | Universal<br>Universal<br>Universal<br>Universal<br>Stretch<br>Universal<br>Stretch<br>Universal | Yes<br>"<br>"<br>"<br>"<br>"<br>"<br>" | Yes<br>"<br>"<br>"<br>"<br>"<br>"<br>" | Yes<br>"<br>"<br>"<br>"<br>"<br>"<br>" | Yes<br>"<br>"<br>"<br>"<br>"<br>"<br>" | Teflon, embroidery, or pin tuck foot |

*Use 100% cotton mercerized embroidery or 100% rayon machine embroidery thread in size 40 or 50. See Sources of Supply.

**Table 1.1**

D. **Feed dogs** are the teeth or pads under the presser foot that move the fabric through the machine.

---

*Sew-How: Keep the lint cleaned out from under the feed dogs to prevent skipped stitches (see Care and Maintenance later in this chapter).*

---

E. The **presser foot**, sometimes incorrectly referred to as the pressure foot, holds the fabric firmly against the feed dogs for proper stitch formation. There are many types of presser feet, each designed for specific purposes (see Chapter 9, Encyclopedia of Presser Feet).

---

*Sew-How: To determine the use of a presser foot, examine its underside. Even if you have lost your instruction manual, you may understand its intended use just by looking.*

---

F. The **free-arm**, often called an open arm, enables you to stitch tubular areas, such as cuffs, arm holes, or pant legs, without ripping out a seam.

G. **Stitch length** used to be calibrated in stitches per inch (spi); now it is more commonly calibrated in millimeters (mm). In the *Machine Readiness Checklist* throughout this book, stitch length is described both in millimeters (mm) and stitches per inch (spi). The following chart shows you what stitch length really means:

| setting in mm | stitches per inch (spi) |
| --- | --- |
| 0.5 | 60 |
| 1 | 24 |
| 2 | 13 |
| 3 | 9 |
| 4 | 6 |
| 5 | 5 |
| 6 | 4 |

**Sew-How:** *Instead of adjusting thread tensions, remember this rule for selecting the proper stitch length:*

*If the fabric **puckers** when you sew, **shorten** the stitch length. Shortening the length adds thread to the stitch allowing the fabric to relax and eliminating puckers.*

*If the fabric **waves out of shape** as you sew, **lengthen** the stitch. Lengthening the stitch eliminates thread from the stitch, preventing the thread from pushing the fabric out of shape.*

H. **Stitch width** is what gives the sewing machine its creative possibilities. Add width to a straight stitch to get a zigzag stitch.

I. The **flywheel**, also called a hand wheel, is found on the right side of the machine and turns as you are sewing. The flywheel either helps drive the machine or coordinates needle swing with the action of the feed dogs to create a stitch. Move the flywheel by hand to place the needle exactly where you want it for stitch-by-stitch control.

J. The **stitch selector** indicates stitches available on your machine. Rather than creating a variety of stitches manually, most machines have a way of selecting built-in stitches with a dial, lever, push button, or touch pad.

K. **Top thread tension** is one of the most misunderstood parts of your machine. I prefer the term "thread control." Thread control is necessary on both top and bobbin for proper stitch formation. On most machines, both can be changed without damaging your machine to create many interesting effects (see Part II, The World of Sewing).

L. The **take-up lever** is what pulls the thread through the upper tension as the stitch is being formed.

---

**Sew-How**: *Prevent your machine from unthreading the needle by stopping with the take-up lever at the highest position.*

---

## THREADING

### Upper Threading

Although every machine threads a little differently, each follows a similar threading procedure. From the spool, threading usually follows this order (Fig. 1.2). Note there may be a thread guide or two between one or more of the following:

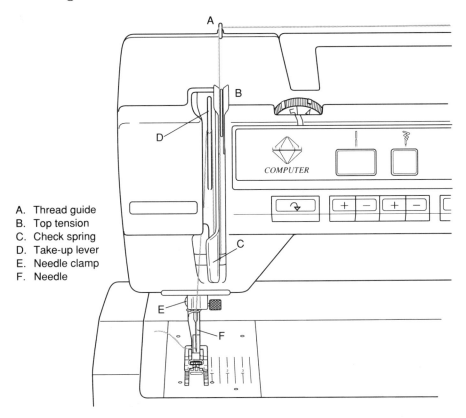

A. Thread guide
B. Top tension
C. Check spring
D. Take-up lever
E. Needle clamp
F. Needle

**Fig. 1.2**
Upper threading.

### Bobbin Winding and Threading

Bobbin winding varies from brand to brand, so check your instruction manual.

---

**Sew-How:** *Machines with removable bobbin cases should be threaded so that when the thread is pulled, the bobbin turns clockwise. This prevents the bobbin thread from backlashing, which can cause uneven tension and thread breakage.*

---

## THREAD CONTROL (TENSION)

What do you think when you hear the word "tension"? A tension headache? I remember a sign in the home ec room that read "Don't Touch the Tension!" and my shoulders automatically tightened up. That's why I prefer to call thread tension "thread control."

If you have a removable bobbin case, set your bobbin tension first, then adjust the upper tension to it.

1. Place bobbin in bobbin case. When you pull the thread, the bobbin should turn clockwise.

2. Some bobbin cases have one scew on the side of the bobbin case to adjust tension. Others have two screws on the side of the bobbin case. If yours has two screws, locate the one closest to the thread. This screw is used to adjust bobbin tension. With the tiny screwdriver that came with your machine, carefully loosen this screw on the side of the case, without removing it, so there is no drag on the thread. When you pull the thread, it should pull out easily.

3. By quarter turns, tighten the screw until the thread supports the weight of the bobbin and bobbin case, but there is still a little bit of slipping when you jerk on the thread (Fig. 1.3).

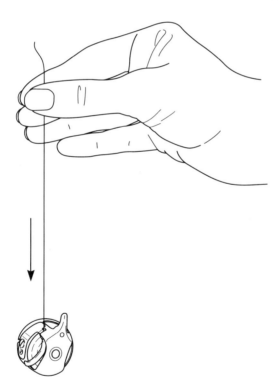

**Fig. 1.3**
For proper bobbin tension, tighten screw until thread supports the weight of the bobbin and bobbin case, then tighten screw another quarter to half turn.

4. Tighten screw *another* quarter to half a turn.
For balanced thread control, top and bobbin thread should lock in the middle of the fabric. It's easier to check if you use one color thread in the top and a different color in the bobbin. (Make sure they are the same weight and brand.) To test this, set your straight stitch on a 2.5–3 (10–12 spi) length and sew on the bias, using a double thickness of

medium-weight fabric. Pull stitch on the bias. Thread should break on both top and bobbin side of the stitch.

If the top thread breaks, loosen the upper tension. If the bobbin thread breaks, tighten the upper tension. Now stitch a 3 length (9 spi), 3 width zigzag stitch. Turn the fabric over. Stitches should lock perfectly on one side of the stitch. A slight loop on the other side of the stitch is permissible (Fig. 1.4).

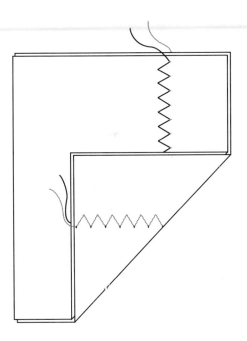

**Fig. 1.4**
Zigzag stitch should lock between the two layers of fabric on one side.

## PRESSURE

Pressure is the amount of force the presser foot exerts against the fabric and feed dogs. Most sewing is done with full pressure. However, lighter pressure is advisable when sewing certain delicate fabrics and for decorative treatments.

## NEEDLE SELECTION

The purpose of the needle is to poke a hole in the fabric big enough for the thread to pass through without fraying. Choose your thread to match the weight of fabric; the needle to match the size of the thread; and the point of the needle to match the type of fabric. (Review Table 1.1.)

The best needle for any project is a new one. For the sewer, a new needle for every project is like a clean, sharp scalpel for each operation for the surgeon. New needles prevent skipped stitches, snags, puckering, and unnecessary holes in your fabric.

Needles are sized by the European or American systems and are identified by numbers and letters. The number identifies the size; the letters, the type of point. Tables 1.2 and 1.3 will help you in selecting your needles. Needle sizes and types are listed in the *Machine Readiness Checklists* for each project in Part II.

**Table 1.2**

European and American Needle Sizes

| European | American | Suggested Fabrics |
|----------|----------|-------------------|
| 60 | 8 | silk organza, chiffon, georgette, sheers |
| 70 | 10 | blouse and lightweight dress fabrics |
| 75 | 11 | available in "stretch" needle type only—knit interlock, Lycra®, swim wear, knit sheers, Ultrasuede™, and other synthetic leathers and suedes |
| 80 | 12 | suit-weight silks, linens, and wool |
| 90 | 14 | denim, topstitching with topstitching thread, heavy duck cloth, real leather |
| 100 | 16 | use only if the size 90/14 breaks |
| 110 | 18 | use only if the size 100/16 breaks |
| 120 | 20 | hemstitching |

**Table 1.3**

Needle Point Types

| H | **Universal:** cross between a sharp and ball point tip; use on most knits and wovens. |
|---|---|
| H-S | **Stretch:** sharper point than a universal needle with a deeper scarf, which aids in stitch formation to prevent skipped stitches. Recommended for swim wear knits and synthetic suedes. |
| H-J | **Jeans:** sharp point to penetrate closely woven fabrics easily without breaking the needle. Recommended on denim, corduroy, and upholstery fabric. Sometimes colored blue to avoid confusion with the other size 14/90 needles. |
| N | **Topstitching:** eye is twice the size of a normal 90/14 needle to accommodate heavy topstitching thread. |
| NTW | **Wedge:** large-eyed needle with a wedge point to penetrate genuine leather. The point slices into leather rather than perforating it. |

## TWIN NEEDLES

Twin needles, also called double needles, have one shank and two needles fixed to a crossbar. They are sized by two numbers and a letter. For example, a 2.0/80(12)H means the needles are 2mm apart, are size 80/12, and have a universal point; a 4.0/90(14)H, means the needles are 4mm apart, are size 90/14, and have a universal point.

## RULES FOR THREAD SELECTION

When selecting thread, read the label and unwrap a little, then take a close look at it. It should have a smooth, even appearance.

Throughout this book, you will see a *Machine Readiness Checklist* for each technique. One of the following thread types is recommended.

- 100% cotton sewing
- all-purpose sewing
- cotton embroidery
- rayon embroidery
- nylon monofilament

**One hundred percent cotton sewing thread** works well for most garment construction provided it is colorfast and mercerized against shrinkage. It has a lot of sheen, so it can also be used for embroidery, topstitching, and buttonholes. Cotton fibers are long and smooth, so you shouldn't experience tension problems. Cotton thread is not as strong as cotton-wrapped polyester or 100% polyester; however, if used with the correct stitch for the fabric, cotton thread is strong enough for most projects. The only other disadvantage with cotton thread is that it is not as readily available as the others. Look for these brand names: D.M.C., Mettler Metrosene, Zwicky.

**All-purpose cotton-wrapped polyester thread**, referred to in the *Machine Readiness Checklist* as "all-purpose" thread, is also colorfast and mercerized and is recommended for garment construction. All-purpose thread has slightly less sheen than the 100% cotton thread. It is also stronger and stretches more than the all-cotton thread because of its polyester core, and so it requires some tension adjustments. All-purpose thread is widely available. Look for these brand names: J. P. Coats (Dual Duty), Mettler Metrosene, Zwicky.

**Cotton embroidery thread** is finer than the cotton sewing thread, so it is not generally recommended for construction of seams. However, it is great for machine blind hemming, and for machine embroidery. It is recommended for blind hemming because, when used with a fine needle and a loosened top tension, the stitches become almost invisible. Cotton embroidery thread is also colorfast, mercerized, and fills in a design smoothly and with less bulk than the all-cotton sewing thread. Look for these brand names: D.M.C., Mettler Metrosene, Zwicky.

Rayon is not as strong a fiber as cotton or polyester, but it has a lot of shine. Therefore, **rayon embroidery thread** is not recommended for construction, but is beautiful for machine embroidery. To prevent the thread from shredding and breaking, use a size 90/14 stretch needle and a loosened top tension. Look for these brand names: Natesh, Paradise, Sulky.

**Nylon monofilament thread** looks like very fine fish line, and blends with any color—helpful because you don't have to rethread your machine when using different color fabrics in the same project. It can also be used on the bobbin so that to change thread color you need only rethread the top. However, some kinds of nylon monofilament thread are wiry, won't hold a knot, and may irritate sensitive skin. See Sources of Supply for newer, softer forms.

Buy your thread at the fabric store or your sewing machine dealer, and stick with the major brands (see Sources of Supply). Buying five spools for a dollar is not a bargain when the thread breaks, fuzzes, and causes the fabric to pucker. Remember, match your thread to the weight of your fabric. If you're sewing on lightweight woven fabric, for example, you want the thinnest thread possible—machine embroidery thread.

## STANDARD PRESSER FEET AND ACCESSORIES

Do you know where the accessories are that came with your machine? Do you know what each item is for? The following information may refresh your memory. Specific techniques and usage for these and extra accessories are covered thoroughly in Chapter 9, Encyclopedia of Presser Feet.

Most machines come with the metal zigzag, embroidery (appliqué), buttonhole, blind hem, and zipper foot. Others may also include the button sewing foot and quilting or edge guide. Before describing each one, dump out your feet and match them with those pictured in Fig. 1.5. Your instruction manual probably illustrates the standard feet and accessories. **Note:** A presser foot for each technique is also recommended in the *Machine Readiness Checklists* throughout the book.

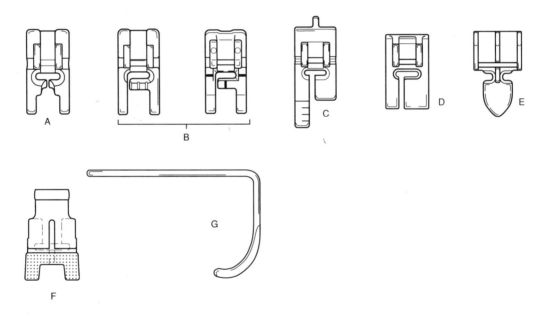

**Fig. 1.5** Standard sewing machine accessories— A, standard zigzag foot; B, embroidery (appliqué) foot; C, buttonhole foot; D, blind hem foot; E, zipper foot; F, button sewing foot; G, edge (quilting) guide.

A. The **metal zigzag foot** is used for general straight seams and topstitching of lightweight and heavy fabrics. The needle hole is oblong, and the underside is smooth and flat to keep the needle from pulling the fabric up and down with each stitch.

B. The **embroidery (appliqué) foot** can be made of metal but is often transparent, allowing you to see what's going on under it. The underside has a wide channel behind the needle so it rides smoothly over decorative stitching. It's also great for seaming medium-weight and bulky fabrics such as sweater knits, stretch terry cloth, and velour.

C. The **buttonhole foot** usually differs with the brand because each company has a unique buttonhole function. However, buttonhole feet generally have two narrow channels on the underside behind the needle. This way, the foot rides over the first row of stitching, so the two sides of the buttonhole are parallel.

D. The **blind hem foot** also may differ with the brand, but usually has a guide or wide toe on the right that may or may not be adjustable. The underside is higher on the left for easier guiding.

E. The **zipper foot** adjusts by a screw or clamp or can be snapped off and moved to sew both sides of the zipper without riding over the coil.

F. The **button sewing foot** has short toes and may have a rubber sleeve or pad to hold the button in place while stitching.

G. The **quilting** or **edge guide** usually slides behind the foot and rides over a row of stitching, or next to an edge so that successive rows of stitching are evenly spaced.

## CARE AND MAINTENANCE

### Cleaning

Next to changing the needle with each project, cleaning the lint from the area under the feed dogs and the bobbin race area is most important (Fig.1.6). (Remember, the race is the area that houses the bobbin and bobbin case.)

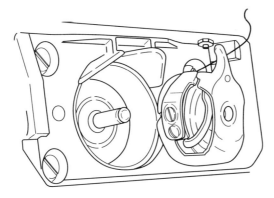

**Fig. 1.6**
Sewing machine race
for front loading
bobbin.

1. Remove your bobbin, bobbin case, presser foot, needle, and needle plate. Some machines have a removable race; others don't. Check your manual. If the race is removable, snap off the race cover, and memorize how the hook fits into the assembly; then remove the hook so you can see under the feed dogs. If your race is not removable, proceed to the next step.

2. Fluff your lint brush. This way, each bristle will reach into a lint-infested area and pull the lint out. Dust the big chunks out of the race with the brush. Finish the job by blowing out the finer particles with canned air (brand names Dust-Off® or Tac Air Blast) or your vacuum cleaner rather than with your breath. The moisture from your breath may cause parts to rust.

### Oiling

Check your manual or with your local dealer to find out if your machine requires oil. Newer electronic and computerized machines don't; however, older mechanical machines should be oiled after about every eight to twelve hours of sewing time or once a month. This keeps your machine running smooth and quiet.

If you can't remember when you last oiled your machine, rub your finger on the needle bar—you should always get a little oil on your finger. If it's dry, oil it with **sewing machine oil**, which is fine, pure, and won't "gum up" the parts. To oil:

1. Unplug machine. Remove the bobbin, bobbin case, presser foot, needle, and needle plate. Remove the top cover and race.

2. Dust out the lint from race.

3. Turn the flywheel by hand, and put a drop of oil on every metal part that moves against another metal part. Repeat for the race area. **Note:** If your machine is a flatbed model, tip it back in the cabinet or carrying case. Turn the flywheel and oil every metal part that moves against another metal part. **Don't** oil nylon gears or the belt on the flywheel.

4. Put race back together. Plug machine in and run it without the needle for a couple of minutes until the oil has a chance to work in. Wipe off excess oil from bed of machine.

5. Put in new needle and stitch on a scrap to check if oil comes off on the fabric. If it does, stitch until stitches are dry; then don't use as much oil the next time.

*Step Two:*

# ASSEMBLE YOUR TOOLS

Besides your sewing machine, you will need a few tools and notions to measure, cut, mark, sew, and press your completed projects (Fig. 1.7). I refer to many of these throughout the book, so refresh your memory and check your sewing inventory. Note that the bulleted items are essential. Besides the items below, there are hundreds of other notions to make sewing easier. See the Sources of Supply for mail-order companies.

## MEASURING TOOLS

• Use a **tape measure** so pattern pieces are cut on-grain and for other quick measurements as you lay out a pattern. Choose one that is made of paper or plastic-coated fabric, so it won't stretch with continued use. Most tapes are 5/8" (1.5mm) wide—the width of a standard seam allowance.

---

**Sew-How:** *Wear your tape measure around your neck while sewing, for ready reference.*

---

• A **sewing gauge** has a sliding guide for measuring hem depth, button and buttonhole spacing, trim placement, and pleat width; ear length and eye spacing for toys and appliqués; and more. A must for anyone who mends or sews.

Fig. 1.7
Measuring,
cutting, marking, and
sewing tools.

• A **see-through cutting ruler** is thick enough to cut against using the rotary cutter. The O'Lipfa™ ruler is 24" (61cm) long and 1/8" (3mm) thick and has a lip edge. This lip hangs off the edge of the cutting mat and is used like a T-square. It is 5" (12.5cm) wide and is marked every 1/2" (1.3cm) the length of the rule.

---

**Sew-How:** *For accuracy, use the same rule to measure and cut all quilting strips and borders.*

---

## CUTTING TOOLS

• **Shears** have a thumb hole and an oblong hole for two or more fingers. They are designed for the best grip and extended usage, so you can cut for long periods of time without straining your hand. The bend provides a place to rest your index finger and allows you to cut without raising the fabric off the table.

Shear blades are made of hot-forged steel, stainless steel, or aluminum. Steel blades can be resharpened more often than their aluminum counterparts, but are heavier to use.

Some shears are joined by a rivet; others, by a screw and nut. Generally, riveted shears cannot cut as heavy a fabric as those joined by a screw and nut. When purchasing a pair of shears, test them by cutting through at least two thicknesses of medium-weight fabric. They should cut to the tip.

• **Scissors** have a thumb and finger hole and are used for smaller jobs such as trimming and clipping. There are specific scissors for specific jobs. For general-purpose sewing, use 5" (12.5cm) scissors with one pointed and one round-tipped blade. This way you are less likely to snip a hole where it isn't wanted, or to push scissors through the fabric while pushing out a collar or pocket point.

• A **rotary cutter** and **mat** are for the more serious home sewer. They are more expensive than shears, and you still need shears for cutting intricate designs and pattern pieces. However, the cutter cuts through multiple layers of fabric at one time—great for cutting quilt blocks, strips, and long, straight pattern pieces—but it must be used with a special mat to protect the layout surface.

Rather than sharpening the cutter, you change the blade. If you're looking for a faster way of cutting, this is it.

## HOLDING TOOLS

• **Pattern weights** speed up the layout and cutting process. Rather than pinning the pattern pieces to the fabric, weights have pin-like tacks on the underside to hold the pattern tissue and fabric while cutting. If you are using a fabric that snags easily, use the weights with the smooth side down.

• **Pins** are necessary for sewing. If your pins are a collection scavenged from men's dress shirts or the floor of the home ec room at school, buy some new ones.

My favorites are fine, glass-headed quilting pins. They are extra long, and the glass heads won't melt if pressed over. They are also easy to find when accidentally dropped on the floor or carpet.

• A **pin cushion**, or magnetic Grab-It™ is an ideal home for your pins. I use a wrist pin cushion while sewing. A Grab-It sits on the table and on the ironing board during layout, cutting, and pressing. This way, I have a place for my pins, no matter where I am in the construction process.

• **Tweezers** are handy for grabbing too-short threads when you have to rip something out, removing tear-away stabilizer, and retrieving a needle or pin that accidentally fell into the workings of your machine. They also help you hold threads, appliqué edges, and tricky seam allowances, and can be used to remove lint and broken threads from the race and bobbin area. My favorite tweezers are those that came with my serger. They have a sharp nose which is bent at a slight angle for easy use and visibility. If you don't have a serger, purchase a pair of tweezers through your local serger dealer.

## MARKING TOOLS

• **Dressmaker's chalk** or a sliver of soap marks well on dark fabrics, but is sometimes difficult to remove. I like Clo-Chalk (see Sources of Supply) because it marks well, comes with its own sharpener, and disappears in five days on its own or immediately when washed or ironed. Use chalk to transfer pattern markings.

• A **water-erasable marker** is like a felt-tipped marker for fabric and marks well on light-colored fabrics. Marks erase with clear water.

---

**Sew-How:** *Use the water-erasable marker to transfer pattern markings by resting the tip on the pattern tissue. The ink bleeds through the tissue, first layer of fabric, then second layer of fabric for an accurate mark.*

---

• **Vanishing marker** is similar to the water-erasable marker, except the mark disappears within 24 to 48 hours, depending on the humidity. Mark darts and dots, transfer an appliqué pattern, or copy a monogram on the right side of the fabric. If you make a mistake, the ink disappears, and no one is the wiser.

• **Transparent tape** is another handy marking and basting tool. Stitch next to it for straight topstitching, to sew a straight dart, or to stitch in a zipper. Stick a button or appliqué in place before stitching. Just remember to hide your supply from your family, or it may disappear like the vanishing marker.

---

**Sew-How:** *I like the type of tape that has a cloudy appearance because it is less sticky and easier to see on dark fabrics than the shiny type.*

---

## SEWING TOOLS

• "As s/he sews, so must s/he rip." A **seam ripper** is essential for fixing mistakes or "unsewing." The point picks the stitch out of the seam, while the blade cuts the thread. Like pins and needles, a ripper wears out occasionally, so replace it when it dulls. The best quality I've found is available through your local sewing machine dealer. Look for the little arrow etched on the blade.

• Rather than tying off threads or backstitching, use a **liquid fabric sealant** to prevent threads from fraying and coming unstitched. The brand available in most fabric stores is Fray-Check™ (see Sources of Supply).

---

**Sew-How:** *Use sealant on the edge of ribbons, trims, and lace to prevent raveling.*

---

• A **glue stick** is a basting aid. Use it to stick a button, appliqué, lace, or trim in place before sewing.

• As much as I like to stitch everything by machine, a **hand needle** and **thimble** are necessary in your sewing stash. Use a needle for pulling threads through to the wrong side of the fabric before tying them off, to sew on hooks, eyes, snaps, and other odds and ends. Use a thimble on the middle finger of your right or left hand, to push the needle comfortably through the fabric.

---

**Sew-How:** *There is nothing more annoying than hunting for a hand needle when you need one, so store your needles on one end of your wrist pin cushion away from the pins or make yourself a needle case.*

---

• A **large-eye tapestry needle** is used to pull heavier threads and cord to the wrong side of the fabric before tying it off. Thread cord end from a corded buttonhole through the large eye of the needle, then pull cords between the facing and garment front to tie them off (see Fig. 8.13).

• A **needle threader** is helpful not only for threading hand and machine needles, but also for pulling threads, embroidery floss, and pearl cotton cord to the wrong side of the fabric so it can be tied off.

• A **spring hoop** holds the fabric taut to minimize puckering for free-machine embroidery, free-machine quilting, and appliqué. It is also narrow enough to fit under the foot without removing the needle.

• **Waxed paper** is used to make alterations, redraw a pattern, and to trace off patterns. Use an old, dry ballpoint pen or a tracing wheel to transfer the marks onto the waxed paper. Make a roll of waxed paper part of your sewing supplies.

## PRESSING TOOLS

The art of pressing is essential to the art of sewing, so you need a few pressing tools (Fig. 1.8).

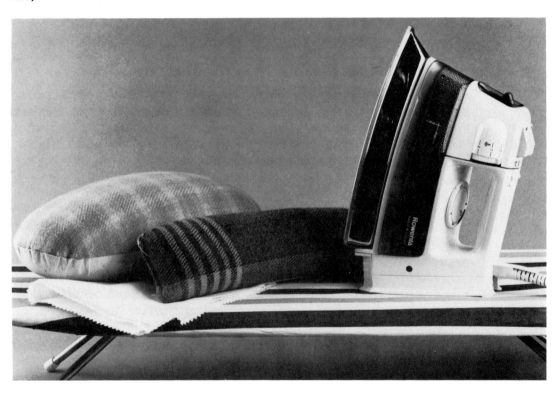

**Fig. 1.8**
Pressing tools.

• A **hand iron** is used to smooth yardage that has been preshrunk before cutting, to press seams and darts, and for countless other uses in the world of sewing.

---

**Sew-How:** *If your iron has a rough, uneven surface, clean it with hot iron cleaner, available through your local fabric store. After cleaning, put a piece of brown paper on your ironing board, then a piece of waxed paper over it. Run the warm iron over the waxed paper to restore the shine and smoothness to the soleplate.*

---

• An **ironing board** is essential for pressing. A muslin cover works better for shaping and pressing a project than the heat-reflective type.

---

**Sew-How:** *If the pad under your ironing board cover is flattened, make another one, as Sara Bunje of San Mateo, California, did. She used the old pad as a pattern and cut a new pad from an army blanket.*

---

• To prevent shine and overpressing, place a **press cloth** over the fabric before pressing or ironing on the right side of the fabric. Use a piece of 100% cotton unbleached muslin or a press cloth, available through your fabric store or mail-order source (see Sources of Supply).

• A **tailor's ham** is a curved, stuffed cushion used to press curved areas. A good ham has cotton drill cloth on one side and wool on the other. The cotton side is used to press cotton, cotton blends, and linens that require higher temperatures. The wool side is for wool, silk, and wool blends and, if used properly, will minimize shine.

## FABRIC STABILIZERS

• **Interfacing** is used to stabilize areas in a garment that are likely to stretch out and wear—armholes, necklines, front tabs, plackets, cuffs, collars, and waistbands, to name a few. Fusible interfacing is applied to the fabric with heat, moisture, and pressure. Sew-in interfacing is usually hand- or machine-basted into place. To select the appropriate interfacing, refer to Table 1.4.

• **Paper-backed fusible web** is a stabilizer and adhesive used in appliquéing. With adhesive side against the wrong side of fashion fabric, iron with a dry iron. Draw the appliqué shape on the paper backing, cut out shape, remove paper, and the shape is ready to fuse to the base fabric. See Chapter 3 for specific application and use. There are many brands, but I almost always use Wonder-Under™.

• **Plastic-coated freezer wrap**, available through your local grocery store, is generally used to rewrap food for storage in the freezer. It's also ironed to the wrong side of fabric to stabilize it for embroidery, appliqué, or quilting, so you rarely need a hoop. Remove wrap after stitching by peeling it off the back of the fabric.

• **Tear-away stabilizer** is used to stabilize fabric and to minimize puckering in machine embroidery and monogramming. Use it on top of or under the work and remove after stitching.

• **Water-soluble stabilizer** is a plastic film and is clamped in the hoop with the fabric either on top or underneath. It can be drawn on and is removed by rinsing with warm water.

# Table 1.4 Interfacing Selection Chart

| Fabric Type | Interfacing "Hand" | Recommended Interfacing | Fusible or Sew-In | Other Information | Colors |
|---|---|---|---|---|---|
| Sheer to light-weight fabrics, such as chiffon, georgette, crepe de chine, charmeuse, voile, batiste, gauze, lace, silk broadcloth | Sheer | Self-fabric<br>Organza<br>Pellon #906F<br>Bridal illusion, netting, or veiling<br>Pellon sheer weight #905<br>HTC Sheer D'Light™ Featherweight<br>Armo® Sheer-Shape™<br>Pellon #905 | S<br>S<br>F<br>S<br>S<br>F<br>S<br>S | Matches color and hand<br>Available in many colors<br>Light, crisp hand, nonwoven,<br>Adds crispness, won't show through<br>Nonwoven, softer than 906F<br>Crosswise give; soft and drapable<br>Soft and drapable<br>Soft and drapable | —<br>—<br>Wht, bge, chrcl<br>—<br>Wht, bge<br>Wht, chrcl<br>Wht<br>Wht, bge |
| Featherweight to midweight wovens, such as gingham, challis, tissue faille, jersey, polyester, silk crepe<br>Knits: cotton and cotton blend interlocks, jersey, lightweight sweater knits | Soft | Pellon Sof-Shape®<br>Armo® So-Sheer™<br><br>Stacy Easy-Knit®<br>Dritz Knit Fuze™<br>HTC Fusi-Knit™<br>J & R Quick Knit™<br><br>Armo® Intra-Face™ Bias Featherweight<br>Pellon #910 Featherweight<br>HTC Sew Shape™ Featherweight<br><br>Armo® Press Soft<br>Pellon #910 Featherweight | F<br>F<br><br>F<br>F<br>F<br>F<br><br>S<br><br>S<br>S<br><br>S<br>S | Nonwoven, all-bias<br>Nonwoven<br><br>Nylon tricot knits with crosswise stretch and lengthwise stability. Use on knits and wovens.<br><br>All-bias for knits and wovens<br><br>Crosswise stretch, lengthwise stability<br>Gentle control on lightweight knits and wovens<br>Soft shaping for lightweight wovens<br>All-bias gentle support | Wht, chrcl<br>Wht, bge, chrcl<br><br>Wht, bge, blk<br>Wht, bge, blk<br>Wht, ivy, blk, gry<br>Wht, bge, blk, gry<br><br>Wht<br><br>Wht<br>Wht<br><br>Wht<br>Wht |
| Other feather-weight to midweight wovens: shirtings, broad-cloth, oxford, muslin, seersucker, chambray, poplin, pincord, madras, lightweight linen<br>(Heavier) knits: double knits, stretch terry, velour, regular weight and heavy sweatshirt fleece | Firm | Armo® PressSoft<br>Pellon #911FF<br><br>Stacy Shape-Flex®<br><br>Armo® Uni-Stretch® Lightweight<br>HTC Sheer D-Light™ Lightweight | S<br>F<br><br>F<br><br>F<br>F | Woven, permanent press<br>All bias; soft supple shaping for midweight knits and wovens.<br>Woven<br><br>Crosswise give, stretch & recovery for knits and stretch-wovens. | Wht<br>Wht, gry<br><br>Wht<br><br>Wht<br>Wht, chrcl |
|  | Crisp | Pellon Shapewell® (#70)<br>Dritz Shape Maker™<br><br>Pellon ShirTailor® (#905F)<br>Armo®Shirt-Shaper™<br>Dritz Shirt Maker™<br>J & R Shirt Bond™ | S<br>S<br><br>F<br>F<br>F<br>F | 100% cotton; crisp shaping for oxford cloth, poplin, calico and other light to medium weight dress & blouse fabrics.<br><br>For shirt collars, cuffs and other details where firmness is desirable for a crisp tailored look. | Wht<br>Wht, blk<br><br>Wht<br>Wht<br>Wht<br>Wht |
| Skirt, pants, or suiting fabrics, such as gabardine, chino, linen, linen blends, wool and wool-like crepe, duck, cotton and cotton blends, faille, velvet, velveteen | Soft | Armo® PressSoft<br>Pellon Sof-Shape®<br><br>Stacy Easy-Knit®<br>Armo® Whisper Weft™<br>Pellon Shapewell® (#70F)<br><br>Pellon Easy-Shaper®<br>Dritz Shape-Up Lightweight™<br>HTC Sheer D'Light™ Medium Weight<br>J & R Stretch 'N Shape™ | S<br>F<br><br>F<br>F<br>F<br><br>F<br>F<br>F<br><br>F | Woven, permanent press<br>For tailoring loosely woven light- to midweight fabrics<br><br>Knit<br>Weft insertion<br>100% cotton; use in lightweight wovens for soft shaping<br><br>Soft supple controlled shaping for light and midweight knits and wovens | Wht<br>Wht, chrcl<br><br>Wht, bge, blk<br>Wht, bge, gry<br>Wht<br><br>Wht, chrcl<br>Wht, chrcl<br>Wht, chrcl<br><br>Wht, blk |

## Interfacing Selection Chart (cont.)

| Fabric Type | Interfacing "Hand" | Recommended Interfacing | Fusible or Sew-In | Other Information | Colors |
|---|---|---|---|---|---|
| Other skirt, pants, or suiting fabrics: denim, poplin, flannel, wool, mohair, coating, corduroy | Crisp | Stacy Shape-Flex® Universal<br>HTC Form-Flex™ Universal<br>J & R Classic Woven | F<br>F<br>F | 100% cotton, use in light- to midweight wovens for crisp support | Wht, blk<br>Wht, blk<br>Wht |
| | | Dritz Suitmaker ™<br>J & R Tailor Fuse™ | F<br>F | Lengthwise and crosswise stability and bias give like a woven. Use in mid- to heavyweight tailoring projects. | Natural<br>Wht, blk |
| | | HTC® SRF™<br>Pellon Stretch-Ease (#921F) | F<br>F | Stretch and recovery for midweight knits, wovens, and stretch wovens | Wht, chrcl<br>Wht, chrcl |
| | | Armo® Uni-Stretch® Suitweight | F | Use for collars, lapels and cuffs | Wht |
| | | Pellon #930<br>Armo® Press Firm | S<br>S | Firm to very firm shaping of medium- to heavyweight knits and wovens. | Wht<br>Wht |
| | | HTC Sta-Form™ Durable Press<br>HTC Veri-Shape™ Durable Press<br>Dritz Sew-In DuraPress™<br>J & R Woven Form™ | S<br>S<br>S<br>S | Crisp shaping in midweight wovens, stable knits. | Wht, blk<br>Wht<br>Wht<br>Wht |
| Heavy, tailoring-weight wools and wool coating. | Tailored | HTC Fusible Acro<br>Armo® Weft<br>Pellon #931 TD Midweight (MVI) | F<br>F<br>F | Washable hair canvas<br>Weft insertion<br>For firm support in midweight knits | Natural<br>Wht, bge, blk, gry<br>Wht |
| | | Pellon Pel-Aire® (#881F)<br>Dritz Shape-Up Suitweight™ | F<br>F | Textured surfaces and heavier adhesive coating provides better adhesion to suit and coat-weight fabrics for tailoring. | Natural, gry<br>Wht, chrcl |
| | | HTC (Armo) Acro | S | Washable hair canvas for medium to heavy tailoring: 52% rayon/ 43% polyester/ 5% goathair | Natural |
| | | HTC (Armo) Fino II | S | Hair canvas for fine couture tailoring: 35% wool/35% rayon/ 15% polyester/ 15% goathair | Natural |
| | | HTC P-26 Red Edge | S | Economy hair canvas: 57% cotton/ 32% rayon/ 11% goat hair | Natural |
| | | Pellon Sewer's Choice™ (#90H) | S | Traditional hair canvas: 43% cotton/ 36% rayon/ 21% goat hair | Natural |
| Fur, fake fur, fleece | Stabilizing | Armo® Press Firm<br>HTC (Armo) Acro<br>Pellon Sewer's Choice™ | S<br>S<br>S | Woven, permanent press<br>Washable hair canvas<br>Traditional hair canvas | Wht<br>Natural<br>Natural |

Pellon® and Stacy® are registered trademarks of The Pellon Company, a division of Freudenberg Nonwovens Limited Partnership. The Stacy® products listed were purchased by Pellon when Stacy Industries went out of business. Armo® is a registered trademark of Crown Textile Company; Handler Textile Corporation (HTC) sells Armo products to the home sewing market.

| Colors Legend: | White = Wht<br>Black = Blk<br>Grey = Gry | Ivory = Ivy<br>Beige = Bge<br>Charcoal = Chrcl |
|---|---|---|

*Step Three:*

# LEARN THE BASIC STITCHES

By now you have cleaned and oiled your machine. You have changed the needle. You have wound a bobbin, threaded it in the bobbin case, completed the upper threading, and balanced top and bobbin tensions. You have also assembled your tools, important notions, and supplies, so let's look at some basic stitches, and sew something.

## STRAIGHT STITCH

---

**New Sewer's Note:** *If you have never operated a sewing machine before, you may want to practice sewing straight lines, pivoting corners, and sewing curves with an unthreaded machine, stitching on paper. Paper will dull the needle, so be sure to put in a new one when you switch to fabric. (If you have done a similar exercise in the past, or simply need to brush up on your skills, advance to the next exercise.) If you use waxed paper, you can hang it up in a window, for pretty patterns of light. To practice, enlarge the designs in Fig. 1.9 to two hundred percent at your local copy center. Trace the lines, rectangle, circles, and triangle on a piece of tracing paper. Press two sheets of waxed paper together with a moderately hot iron. This way the paper is stiff and easier to maneuver. Place waxed paper over tracing paper so you see the stitching lines. Tape corners together with transparent tape.*

---

**Fig. 1.9**
Enlarge designs to twice the size shown. Then stitch lines, rectangle, circles, and triangle to practice sewing straight, pivoting, and sewing curves.

## WARM-UP EXERCISES

### Supplies

- waxed paper (optional)
- tracing paper
- water-erasable marker

1. Set the stitch length to 2.5 (10–12 spi), the most common stitch length used in sewing. Put the standard metal foot on your machine. Place edge of paper under the foot and put the needle into the work. The needle is unthreaded.

2. Lower the presser foot and start sewing.

3. To pivot a corner, turn the flywheel by hand so the needle is in the waxed paper. Lift the presser foot, pivot, then lower presser foot to continue.

4. To sew inside and outside curves, slow down and guide the fabric by using your fingers like the center point in a compass.

5. Press over waxed paper again to flatten and set the holes. Put this sampler in your notebook, or hang it in a window. Now you're ready for the first exercise.

## EXERCISE 1: PRESSED FABRIC LEAVES

The best part of fall is its color. Whether or not it's fall in your neck of the woods, create colorful leaves any time of year while perfecting straight stitching, sewing inside and outside curves, and pivoting. This time, use thread and fabric.

### Machine Readiness Checklist

| | |
|---|---|
| **Stitch:** | straight |
| **Stitch length:** | 2–4; 6–13 spi |
| **Stitch width:** | 0 |
| **Foot:** | standard metal zigzag |
| **Needle:** | 80/12 universal |
| **Thread:** | 100% cotton or all-purpose one shade darker than fabrics |
| **Fabric:** | sheers (e.g., organdy, organza, batiste) in colors you like. (I used light pink, blue, lavender, and peach) |
| **Accessories:** | tear-away stabilizer or tracing paper, water-erasable marker, waxed paper, iron |

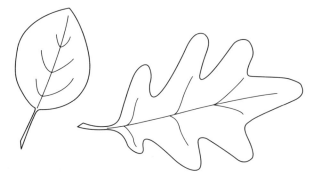

1. Enlarge leaf patterns in Fig. 1.10 to two hundred percent at your local copy center. Trace leaf patterns on tracing paper or tear-away stabilizer. Cut two small leaves and one oak leaf.

2. Layer two or three colors of sheer fabric, and pin them together so stabilizer with leaf pattern is on top.

3. Stitch around the leaf, including the veins, one complete time. Practice using a short stitch length (2; 13 spi) on the curves, and longer stitch length 3–4 (6–9 spi) on the veins.

4. Repeat sewing around the leaf three or more times, practicing curves and pivots and changing the stitch length.

5. Remove the stabilizer. Cut out leaf and clip threads close to the fabric.

6. Repeat for other small leaf and oak leaf.

---

**Sew-How:** *For variation in color, trim away one or more underlayers from various sections of each leaf.*

---

7. Arrange and sandwich leaves between two pieces of waxed paper.

8. Press over leaves and waxed paper with a moderately hot iron. Pressing means moving the iron in an up-and-down motion, lifting the iron off the paper, then putting it down next to where you just pressed. After pressing, iron over the piece to eliminate wrinkles and creases. Ironing means sliding the iron back and forth with a long, smooth motion.

Hang your creation in a window to see the colors made by layering sheer fabrics.

### Variations on Exercise

Layer two or three sheer fabrics and stitch geometric shapes, your initials, flower petals, or any other shape. Arrange shapes, add glitter, crayon shavings, and/or dried flowers, then press between waxed paper.

## AUTOMATIC STITCHES

Adding width to the straight stitch creates the zigzag stitch. To achieve this with your machine, you may have to select the zigzag stitch by moving a dial or lever, or by touching a button or pad.

On a double layer of medium-weight fabric, stitch a sample for your notebook using the embroidery foot and zigzag stitch on a 1 length (24 spi) and 1 width. Stitch another row on a 2 length (13 spi) and a 2 width; the next row on a 3 length (9 spi) and 3 width, and so on.

Next stitch rows of zigzag stitches, keeping the stitch length on 0.5 (60 spi) and changing only the width. Start on a 1 width, then sew rows using a 2, 3, 4, and 5 width zigzag. This is called a satin stitch. It is used around appliqués, on napkin edges, in cut work, and in many other decorative ways (Fig. 1.11).

**Fig. 1.11**
Satin stitch sampler showing various stitch widths.

---

**Sew-How:** *If your fabric tunnels under the satin stitch, loosen the upper tension slightly. If tunneling continues, iron plastic-coated freezer paper to the wrong side of the fabric.*

---

Finally, set the width on 4 and change only the stitch length. Start on a 1 length (24 spi) and work your way through a 2, 3, and 4 stitch length (6, 9, 13 spi).

This exercise demonstrates the difference between width and length as it affects the zigzag stitch. You can also create designs by moving the width as you sew. However, it's almost impossible to stitch an even pattern with the unpracticed hand.

**Automatic stitches** are variations on the zigzag and are controlled by the machine. Examples are the blind hem, stretch blind hem, three-step zigzag, ball, diamond, and scallop (Fig. 1.12). Once selected, with the proper stitch width and length set, the machine stitches them automatically.

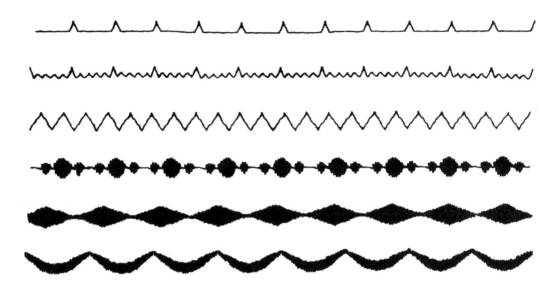

**Fig. 1.12**
Automatic stitches—blind hem, stretch blind hem, three-step zigzag, ball, diamond, and scallop.

## FORWARD AND REVERSE FEEDING STITCHES

Another type of stitch available on most machines is called a forward and reverse feeding stitch. Not only does the needle zigzag from side to side, but the feed dogs move the fabric forward and back at the same time, creating tracery patterns such as the overlock, double overlock, stitch-and-overcast, honeycomb, clover, and daisy (Fig. 1.13).

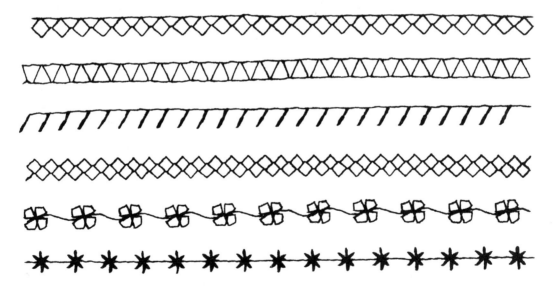

**Fig. 1.13**
Forward and reverse stitches—overlock, double overlock, super stretch, honeycomb, clover, and daisy stitch.

The following exercise will familiarize you with what is available on your machine, as well as help you practice upper threading, winding a bobbin, and threading it.

## EXERCISE 2: STITCH SAMPLER

A good way to become familiar with the stitches on your machine is to make a sampler. In this exercise, your sampler will feature automatic and forward and reverse feeding stitches. Then you'll turn it into a pin cushion.

## Machine Readiness Checklist

**Stitch:** automatic; forward and reverse stitches

**Length:** automatic stitches—0.5–2; 24–60 spi
forward and reverse feeding stitches—varies

**Width:** 3–widest

**Foot:** embroidery

**Needle:** 80/12 universal

**Thread:** 100% cotton or all-purpose in coordinating color to fabric

**Fabric:** striped cotton or cotton/poly blend with a white stripe
(pillow ticking works well)

**Accessories:** lightweight fusible interfacing, ruler, vanishing marker, hand
needle, polyester fiberfill (used to stuff toys), coffee mug, and
rubber band.

1. Cut striped fabric 10" x 5" (25.5 x 12.5cm), so the stripes are going the short way. Fuse lightweight interfacing to wrong side of fabric.

---

**Sew-How:** *For the interfacing to bond permanently, use heat, moisture, and pressure. Place fabric on ironing board, wrong side up. Cut interfacing a little smaller than fabric so it will not stick to the ironing board. Place interfacing fusible (rough) side down. Use the cotton setting on your iron.*

---

With a very damp press cloth over the work, firmly press 10 to 20 seconds in one spot. Let the steam escape, then press again for a few seconds. Lift up the iron and press again, overlapping iron on previously fused section. Repeat this bonding technique the length of your fabric until the interfacing has been applied (Fig. 1.14).

**Fig. 1.14**
To fuse interfacing, use a damp press cloth, set iron on cotton setting, then press for 10 to 20 seconds in one spot. Lift iron, then press, overlapping iron on previously fused section.

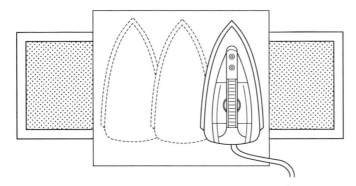

2. Decide which stitches you want on your sampler. Some machines have an almost unlimited number to select from, so find your favorites.

3. Stitch a different automatic stitch on every other light stripe. Remember, for automatic stitches, the fabric feeds through the machine in one direction.

4. On the remaining light stripes, stitch a different forward and reverse feeding stitch. For extra color, change the top thread and slightly loosen top tension. (The bobbin thread shouldn't show.)

5. Place the sampler in your notebook or finish it as explained below.

## FINISHING

### Easiest Pin Cushion

1. Cut your sampler in half to make two 5" (12.5cm) squares. Overcast the four edges of each piece with the three-step zigzag stitch on a 1–1.2 length (20–24 spi) and the widest stitch width. Guide the raw edge so the needle stitches just off the edge at the right. Put one sampler piece in your notebook.

2. Wrap a small handful of fiberfill with the second half of your sampler and put a rubber band around the bottom to keep stuffing in place.

3. Stick the fabric-covered stuffing in a coffee mug, rubber band side down (Fig. 1.15). **Note:** If the stuffed sampler gets pushed down too far in the mug, stuff with more fiberfill. Set your pin cushion next to your machine, on the cutting table, or on the ironing board.

**Fig. 1.15**
Wrap fiberfill with stitch sampler and put rubber band around the bottom. Set stuffed sampler in a coffee mug and use as a pin cushion.

## BUTTONHOLES

Contrary to popular opinion, buttonholes are not difficult and you don't have to avoid a pattern because it calls for them.

Each machine company keeps improving the method by which its machine makes buttonholes. If you are sewing on a new machine, or the machine is new to you, take a few minutes to read your instruction manual and see how truly easy it is. The next project is designed to help you practice.

## EXERCISE 3: BUTTONHOLE SAMPLER

As with the automatic and forward and reverse feeding stitches, you will make a buttonhole sampler. As before, you can stitch it and put it in your notebook or finish it by making a paperweight.

**Machine Readiness Checklist**

| | |
|---|---|
| **Stitch:** | zigzag or buttonhole |
| **Length:** | 0.4–0.8; 55–60 spi |
| **Width:** | widest |
| **Foot:** | buttonhole |
| **Needle:** | 80/12 universal |
| **Thread:** | all-purpose in four or five primary and secondary colors |
| **Fabric:** | white medium-weight cotton or cotton/poly blend, cut 6" (15cm) square |
| **Accessories:** | Wonder-Under cut 6" (15 cm) square, cardboard, small glass ashtray or paperweight globe (available at cross-stitch shops), craft glue, colorful buttons (optional), vanishing marker |

1. Wind bobbins for each thread color.

2. Fuse Wonder-Under on wrong side of fabric square.

---

**Sew-How:** *Place fabric wrong side up on the ironing board. Place Wonder-Under with rough side down, paper side up. Set dry iron on cotton and press for three seconds.*

---

3. On the right side of the fabric, stitch four or five different sized buttonholes in each color all over your fabric square. (The Wonder-Under paper acts as a stabilizer on the underside of the sampler.) Space buttonholes far enough apart so that your foot will not ride on another buttonhole. Place sampler in your notebook or finish it as explained below.

## FINISHING

1. Place the ashtray upside down on the right side of sampler, and trace its outline with the vanishing marker.

2. Cut out ashtray shape from sampler.

3. Remove the Wonder-Under paper from the wrong side of sampler. Now it's ready to fuse to the cardboard.

4. Fuse the cut sampler to the cardboard using a dry iron on wool setting. After the cardboard cools, cut out the cardboard in the shape of the ashtray.

5. Place a few colorful buttons of varying sizes over the sampler (optional). They are loose, not sewn. Drop a few beads of craft glue on the rim of the ashtray and smooth it around. Lay ashtray, upside down, over sampler so buttonholes are seen through the glass. Place a heavy book over paperweight and let the glue dry for 24 hours (Fig. 1.16).

**Fig. 1.16**
Buttonhole sampler
paperweight.

If you don't want to make a paperweight, use this patch as a pocket and stitch it to a T-shirt or sweatshirt.

# TRANSFERABLE LEARNINGS

The information and techniques you have learned in this chapter have given you the skills to sew other projects. You have learned:

• **Pressing vs. ironing**—when you pressed your leaves between the waxed paper, you used both an up-and-down pressing motion and a side-to-side ironing motion. Pressing helps give a project a finished, professional look during construction. Ironing is done to smooth out wrinkles after the project is complete.

• **Straight stitching**—necessary for sewing seams and topstitching. Standard stitch length is 2.5mm (10–12 spi).

• **Inside and outside curves**—necessary for sewing any curve at a neckline, armhole, collar, pocket, or seam.

• **Pivoting**—necessary for turning any corner at a pocket, collar, seam, or for topstitching.

• The **satin stitch** is used to appliqué, finish napkin edges and cutwork, and for other decorative techniques.

• **Stitch length** and **stitch width** must be adjusted for both decorative and practical stitches.

• **Fusible interfacing** is used in many areas to add stability and increase wear. Proper bonding and application is important so interfacing stays put once a project is washed or cleaned.

• **Sewing in a straight line** is important. If you can sew a straight line by stitching accurately between the stripes, you can seam or topstitch almost anything.

• **Buttonholes** are seen everywhere on clothing, crafts, and gifts. After practicing, you are ready to make buttonholes whenever the pattern calls for it.

• **Wonder-Under** paper-backed fusible web is used to bond appliqués so they don't shift when stitched. You will use this product and technique again for machine appliqué and for many other projects in this book.

---

Now that you have gotten to know your machine a little better, understand what many sewing notions and tools are for, and have practiced some basic stitches, let's see how this applies to the World of Sewing.

Part II walks you chapter by chapter through six World of Sewing categories—you will "Sew Fashion," "Sew Embellishments—Machine Appliqué and Embroider," "Sew for Your Home," "Sew a Quilt," "Sew Toys," and "Sew Gifts." Stitch through each in order, or skip to the one of most interest. Happy sewing!

# THE WORLD OF SEWING

- *Chapter Two: Sew Fashion*

- *Chapter Three: Sew Embellishments—Machine Appliqué and Embroider*

- *Chapter Four: Sew for Your Home*

- *Chapter Five: Sew a Quilt*

- *Chapter six: Sew Toys*

- *Chapter Seven: Sew Gifts*

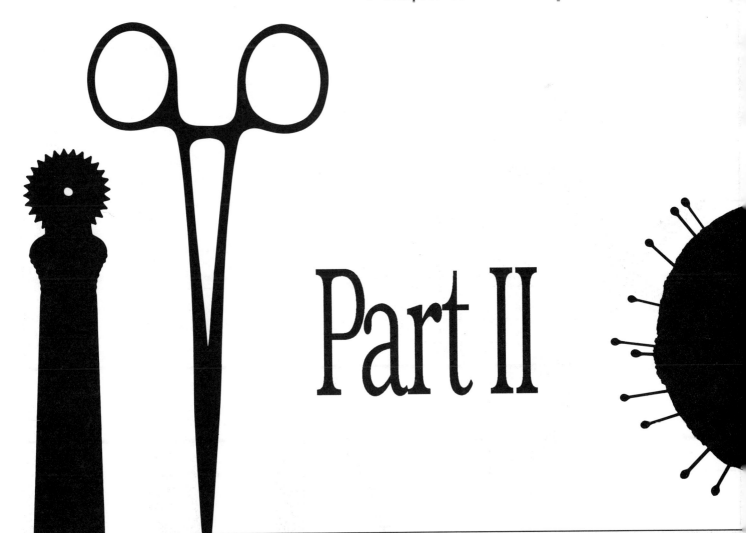

Part II

# THE WORLD OF SEWING

**Chapter 2: Sew Fashion** ........................**37**

Step One:  Plan Your Projects ........................37
Step Two:  Sew Woven Pull-on Shorts ........................43
Step Three:  Sew a Knit Top with Ribbing ........................53
Step Four:  Project Variations—Instant T-shirts ........................59

**Chapter 3: Sew Embellishments—
Machine Appliqué and Embroider** ........................**61**

Step One:  Plan Your Project ........................62
Step Two:  Compass Tote ........................64
Step Three:  Project Variations—
                Pocket and T-shirt Embellishment ........................80

**Chapter 4:  Sew For Your Home** ........................**83**

Step One:  Plan Your Project ........................83
Step Two:  Envelope Placemats ........................85
Step Three:  Project Variation—Envelope "Lapkins" ........................91

**Chapter 5:  Sew a Quilt** ........................**95**

Step One:  Plan Your Project ........................96
Step Two:  Quilted Wall Hanging ........................98

**Chapter 6:  Sew Toys** ........................**109**

Step One:  Plan Your Projects ........................109
Step Two:  Sew Jumbo Fabric Blocks ........................110
Step Three:  Make a Hobbyhorse ........................114

**Chapter 7:  Sew Gifts** ........................**125**

Step One:  Plan Your Projects ........................125
Step Two:  Sew Three Key Rings ........................126
Step Three:  Sew a Fabric Game Board and Pouch ........................130

# THE WORLD OF SEWING

THIS PART OF THE BOOK EXPLORES six areas of sewing. Although you may know something about each area, you may not know the best way to complete a project using the stitches, presser feet, and features of your sewing machine. Rather than making stitch samples, the objective here is to complete a project using all the tools available, so you can apply the techniques and shortcuts to any other project you attempt in the World of Sewing.

Each chapter has a series of steps. The first step helps you with fabric selection, layout, cutting, marking—the all-important preliminaries. The next steps take you step-by-step through each project and show you shortcuts and professional finishing techniques not usually covered in the pattern instructions. You also learn how to customize the basic project to your skill level, age, and gender.

At the end of each chapter you'll find **Transferable Learnings**, a review of what you've learned and a guide to how you can use the techniques in other areas of sewing.

If you have never sewn before, pay attention to **New Sewer's Notes**. This should help you avoid common pitfalls so your experience is fun and the projects are successful.

## ORGANIZE YOUR WORK SPACE

Before starting, however, let's organize some efficient work space for the three functions in sewing—cutting, sewing, and pressing.

### CUTTING AREA

The cutting area can be as simple as a cardboard cutting board on a bed or dining room table, or as fancy as a cutting table designed specially for the area or room you sew in. Some people like to cut on the floor. To save the carpet and your back, cutting is a lot easier if the table is at least 30" (76cm) high and you can get around all four sides of it.

On or near the cutting area, have a yardstick or straightedge of some kind, and a tape measure. This way you can check grainlines, measure and mark strips and quilt blocks, check fabric width and length, plan your pattern layout—the list goes on—without hunting for measuring tools.

An extra station for pins is also helpful. I load my Grab-It™ with pins in case I use all those in my wrist pin cushion.

One of my best investments was a tall wastebasket. It's large enough to hold a lot of pattern and fabric scraps, I empty it less, and it's close enough to the height of the table to brush scraps into it without dropping them all over the floor. My family also understands it's not for the disposal of food or unfinished drinks. (I never know when I'll have to dig through it for a scrap or something that fell into it by mistake.)

### SEWING AREA

Set your machine accessory box to the right of your machine so you don't have to hunt for a presser foot when you need it. A sewing caddy with marking tools, threads, extra scissors, and accessories is also helpful. If you don't have a caddy, empty checkbook boxes are a good substitute.

To me, a pattern is like toothpaste—once it's out of the envelope, it's almost impossible to put back. Tape a gallon-size resealable plastic bag on the table to the right of your machine for pattern storage. Keep the envelope, extra pattern pieces, and the pattern pieces that come off your fabric in this bag. Everything fits, and you can find your pattern pieces easily.

If you teach, have students put their names on all pattern pieces before cutting them apart. This way a student won't end up with another student's pattern piece.

---

**Sew-How:** *Fold tissue pattern pieces so the name and number of each is on the outside. This way if you need to find it again, you don't have to fish around and unfold every one. It's also easier to get pattern pieces back in the envelope when they are folded.*

---

You'll need a place for pattern instructions. If your sewing machine faces a wall, you can tape pattern instructions to the wall or tack them to a bulletin board in front of you. Nancy Zieman, president of Nancy's Notions, Ltd., recommends taping an acetate sheet to the table and slipping the pattern instructions underneath. If you don't have an acetate sheet, try a dry cleaner bag instead.

Finally, have another wastebasket near your sewing machine for threads and fabric clippings.

## PRESSING AREA

Here you'll need an ironing board, iron, tailor's ham, and press cloth. Position your ironing board to one side of your machine and lower it so you can press while seated. This way you don't have to get up and down from your machine each time you press. Store the ham, iron, and press cloth at the wide end of the board.

---

**Sew-How:** *If your press cloth is damp, store it in a resealable plastic bag pinned to the wide end of the ironing board.*

---

Are you ready to make something? The first project is a pair of woven, elastic-waist shorts. After completing them, you'll have the skills to make a pair of pants, culottes, skirt, or sweatshirt. Let's get started.

# SEW FASHION

- *Step One: Plan Your Projects*

- *Step Two: Sew Woven Pull-on Shorts*

- *Step Three: Sew a Knit Top with Ribbing*

- *Step Four: Project Variations—Instant T-Shirts*

- *Transferable Learnings*

---

*Step One:*

# PLAN YOUR PROJECTS

## A TRIP TO THE FABRIC STORE

Once you have mastered the skills to make a pair of woven shorts and a knit top, you can use those skills to make a pair of woven pants, culottes, or elastic waist skirt; as well as a knit shirt, sweatshirt or knit dress. The style and fabric will be up to you. Before shopping for your fabric and pattern, however, take some measurements to determine your pattern size.

Dress in your underwear or a leotard. Tie a piece of elastic around your waist to find your natural waistline, and ask a friend or spouse to take your measurements, filling in the chart on the following page (Table 2.1). When taking circumference measurements, the measuring tape should be loose enough to get a finger between the tape and your body. Once you have taken measurements, determine your pattern category.

| Table 2.1 | Measurement and Ease Chart | | | |
|---|---|---|---|---|
| **WOMEN** | | Your Measurement | Ease to be Added | Tissue Paper Measurement to Seam Line |
| **Bodice** | High bust | | 3-5" | |
| | Bust | | 3-5" | |
| | Center front bodice length | | 1/2" | |
| | Length of center back, neck to waist | | 3/4" | |
| | Back shoulder width | | 1/2" | |
| **Sleeves** | Upper arm circumference | | 2-3" | |
| | Arm length, shoulder to elbow | | — | |
| | Arm length, shoulder to wrist | | — | |
| | Wrist circumference | | 3/4" | |
| **Skirt** | Waistline | | 3/4" | |
| | High hip, 3" below waist | | 3/4" | |
| | Hips at fullest part, parallel to floor | | 2-3" | |
| | Waist to fullest part of hips | | — | |
| | Thighs, parallel to floor | | 2-3" | |
| | Shirt length, waist to desired length | | — | |
| **Pants** | Waistline | | 3/4" | |
| | Thigh circumference | | 2"+ | |
| | Calf circumference | | 2"+ | |
| | Inseam | | — | |
| | Crotch depth (sitting) | | 1" | |
| | Crotch depth (standing) | | 1" | |
| **MEN** | | | | |
| **Upper body** | Neck | | 1/2" | |
| | Chest | | 3-5" | |
| | Center front waist length | | 1/2" | |
| | Center back waist length | | 1/2" | |
| | Back width | | 1" | |
| | Shoulder width | | — | |
| **Sleeves** | Shirt sleeve length | | — | |
| | Upper arm circumference | | 2-3" | |
| | Arm length | | — | |
| | Wrist circumference | | 3/4" | |
| **Lower body** | Waist | | 3/4" | |
| | Waist to fullest part of hips | | — | |
| | Hips (seat) | | 1-2" | |
| | Thigh | | 1-2" | |
| | Trouser outseam (side length) | | — | |
| | Trouser inseam | | — | |
| | Waist to knee length | | — | |
| | Crotch depth (sitting) | | 3/4" | |
| | Crotch depth (standing) | | 2-3" | |

Table 2.1
Measurement Chart.

In the back of the pattern catalog you will find different figure types (Fig. 2.1). Find the one most like yourself or the person you are sewing for. Then, look at the pattern you have chosen in the pattern catalog and find the size that most closely fits your measurements. Other information to help you find the right size is in the descriptive paragraph found on the catalog page or on the back of the pattern (Fig. 2.2). This often tells you if the garment is "fitted," "loose fitting," or "very loose fitting," which indicates how much ease is allowed in the pattern.

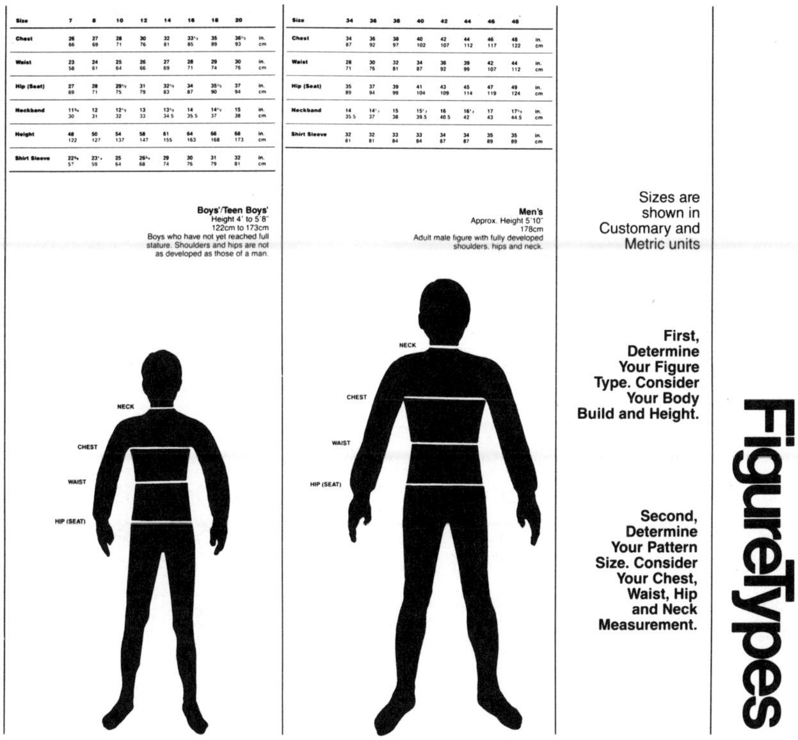

| Size | 7 | 8 | 10 | 12 | 14 | 16 | 18 | 20 | |
|------|---|---|----|----|----|----|----|----|---|
| Chest | 26 66 | 27 69 | 28 71 | 30 76 | 32 81 | 33½ 85 | 35 89 | 36½ 93 | in. cm |
| Waist | 23 58 | 24 61 | 25 64 | 26 66 | 27 69 | 28 71 | 29 74 | 30 76 | in. cm |
| Hip (Seat) | 27 69 | 28 71 | 29½ 75 | 31 79 | 32½ 83 | 34 87 | 35½ 90 | 37 94 | in. cm |
| Neckband | 11½ 30 | 12 31 | 12½ 32 | 13 33 | 13½ 34.5 | 14 35.5 | 14½ 37 | 15 38 | in. cm |
| Height | 48 122 | 50 127 | 54 137 | 58 147 | 61 155 | 64 163 | 66 168 | 68 173 | in. cm |
| Shirt Sleeve | 22½ 57 | 23½ 59 | 25 64 | 26½ 68 | 29 74 | 30 76 | 31 79 | 32 81 | in. cm |

| Size | 34 | 36 | 38 | 40 | 42 | 44 | 46 | 48 | |
|------|----|----|----|----|----|----|----|----|---|
| Chest | 34 87 | 36 92 | 38 97 | 40 102 | 42 107 | 44 112 | 46 117 | 48 122 | in. cm |
| Waist | 28 71 | 30 76 | 32 81 | 34 87 | 36 92 | 39 99 | 42 107 | 44 112 | in. cm |
| Hip (Seat) | 35 89 | 37 94 | 39 99 | 41 104 | 43 109 | 45 114 | 47 119 | 49 124 | in. cm |
| Neckband | 14 35.5 | 14½ 37 | 15 38 | 15½ 39.5 | 16 40.5 | 16½ 42 | 17 43 | 17½ 44.5 | in. cm |
| Shirt Sleeve | 32 81 | 32 81 | 33 84 | 33 84 | 34 87 | 34 87 | 35 89 | 35 89 | in. cm |

**Boys'/Teen Boys'**
Height 4' to 5'8"
122cm to 173cm
Boys who have not yet reached full stature. Shoulders and hips are not as developed as those of a man.

**Men's**
Approx. Height 5'10"
178cm
Adult male figure with fully developed shoulders, hips and neck.

Sizes are shown in Customary and Metric units

First, Determine Your Figure Type. Consider Your Body Build and Height.

Second, Determine Your Pattern Size. Consider Your Chest, Waist, Hip and Neck Measurement.

**FigureTypes**

NECK

CHEST

WAIST

HIP (SEAT)

NECK

CHEST

WAIST

HIP (SEAT)

**Fig. 2.1**
Figure types found in the back of pattern catalogs. (Courtesy of the McCall Pattern Company)

GIRLS'  CHUBBIE  YOUNG JUNIOR TEEN  MISS PETITE  MISSES  HALF-SIZE  WOMEN'S

Sizes are shown in Customary and Metric units

First, Determine your Figure Type. Consider Your Height, Back Waist Length and Bust Position

Second, Determine Your Pattern Size. Consider Your Bust, High Bust, Waist and Hip Measurement

**FigureTypes**

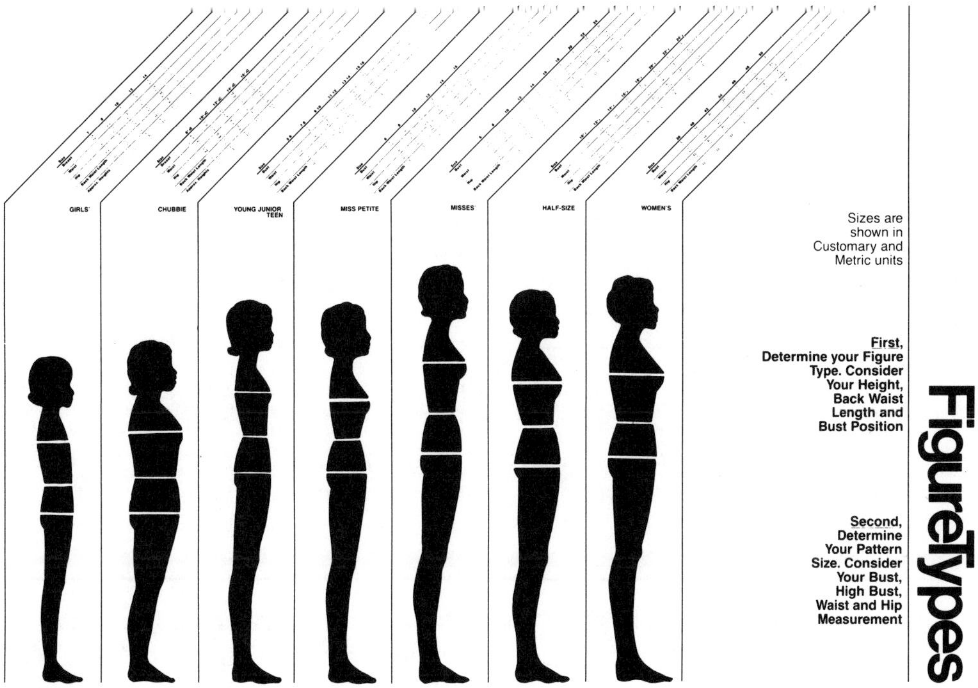

**Fig. 2.2**
Descriptive paragraph found on the catalog page and back of pattern. Find the fabric width on back of pattern to determine how much fabric to buy. (Courtesy of the McCall Pattern Company)

**GIRLS' OR BOYS' CARDIGAN, TOP, PANTS AND SHORTS – CARDIGAN AND TOP – FOR STRETCH KNITS ONLY:** Cardigan has extended shoulders, long sleeves, patch pockets and front button opening. Pullover top has extended shoulders, short sleeves and patch pocket. Pants with or without elasticized ankle and pull-on shorts in two lengths have elasticized waistline.

---

**Sew-How:** *Even a fitted garment has 2" (5cm) of ease in its circumference. Loose fitting or very loose fitting garments usually have more than 2" (5cm) of ease and are subject to your interpretation of the words "loose" and "very loose."*

---

## FABRIC SELECTION

Which comes first, the pattern or the fabric? Judging from my personal stockpile, it must be the fabric. Besides, selecting the fabric is the part I like the best—it's like eating dessert first.

For the shorts, choose a medium-weight woven fabric, such as poplin, weaver's (kettle) cloth, or duck. For easy care and comfort, choose fabric that is a cotton and polyester blend. It won't shrink or wrinkle as much as 100% cotton, and it's easy to sew. Have fun while you're in the store: look at and feel a lot of fabric. Then choose one without a nap (see New Sewer's Note). If you need help, the salespeople will gladly show you different fabrics appropriate for your pattern.

---

**New Sewer's Note:** *Plaids, stripes, one-way prints, and pile fabrics such as corduroy and velvet all have a nap. They are laid out and cut so the pattern or design matches, or the pile or one-way design runs in one direction. This requires more yardage than fabrics without a nap. See back of pattern envelope for "with" and "without nap" yardage requirements.*

---

For the top, choose an all-cotton or cotton/polyester T-shirt interlock knit to coordinate with your shorts fabric. Choose one that does not curl or run. To check for running and curling, pull the fabric across the grain at the cut end.

---

**New Sewer's Note:** *In a woven fabric, warp yarns are placed in the lengthwise direction on a loom. Filler or weft yarns are woven across the warp to create a piece of fabric. The lengthwise grain is parallel to the warp or lengthwise yarns, the crosswise grain is parallel to the weft or filler yarns.*

---

Grainlines, as discussed in pattern directions and illustrated on the tissue pattern piece as a line with an arrow head on either end, indicate yarn direction (Fig. 2.3). Most pattern pieces are laid out so the length of the pattern piece follows the lengthwise grain. Lengthwise yarns are stronger than the crosswise yarns so the pattern piece is less likely to stretch out of shape or distort when laid out this way.

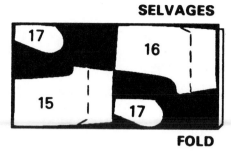

A knit fabric is made with a series of interconnecting loops. Although the fabric isn't stronger in the lengthwise direction, a knit is generally stable on the lengthwise grain and stretches across the grain.

## PRESHRINKING

Care and washing instructions should be written on the bolt end for most fabrics. Some stores include care labels with your purchase (ask when you pay). If not, copy the information from the bolt end. It is important to preshrink washable fabrics, trims, and elastics before cutting so they won't shrink and so the colors won't run after the project is completed. Preshrinking also removes the sizing or finish put on some fabrics. Sizing gives fabric body, but can cause skipped stitches if it is not washed out of the fabric before sewing.

---

**Sew-How:** *As soon as you walk in your door from the fabric store, preshrink your washable fabric, elastic, interfacing, zippers, and trims in the manner in which you intend to care for the project after construction. For example, if your fabric is a dark blue print and is a cotton/polyester blend, preshrink in cold water and dry on the permanent press setting in your dryer. Read your notes from the bolt end for care instructions.* **Note:** *If the interfacing is fusible, immerse it in warm water, wring it out by hand, then dry it on the line. Don't ever put fusible interfacing yardage in the dryer.*

---

When the fabric is dry, clip off a small square from a corner and tape or glue it to a piece of paper, along with its care instructions, fiber content, cost, where you bought it, and the pattern number. Store the paper in your notebook.

How much fabric to buy? You'll find out next when selecting the pattern.

## PATTERN SELECTION

For the shorts project, select a pattern recommended for woven fabrics, with elastic in a fold-over casing for the waistline, and a back patch pocket. For the top, select a pattern recommended for knits, with a crew neck, raglan, or set-in sleeve, and a straight hem (Fig. 2.4).

Fig. 2.4
Recommended
patterns for woven
shorts and knit top.
(Courtesy of the
McCall Pattern
Company)

---

**New Sewer's Note:** *For the top, select a pattern marked "for knits only." You may find an ease chart printed on the pattern back to help you determine how stretchy a knit is, and whether the pattern is appropriate for your fabric. For this project, choose a knit in which when stretched across the grain, 4" (10cm) stretches to 5" (12.5cm), but not more than 8" (20.5cm). For the top, select a pattern with either a raglan sleeve or sleeve bands. You may find both top and shorts in one pattern—look in the pattern catalog under "coordinates" or "sportswear." If you are a new sewer, a pattern for a specific size rather than one that includes several sizes, is easier to read and understand because there are fewer cutting lines to follow.*

---

Children and teens may enjoy using KidSew™ or Kids Can Sew™ patterns, or To Sew Kits (see Sources of Supply). The instructions are well written, and easy to understand. The styling is also simple and fashionable, so young people enjoy immediate success and are proud to wear and display their creations.

To buy the correct yardage, you need to know the width of the fabric. Fabric width is printed on the bolt end and is commonly 45" (1.1m) or 60" (1.5m). Read the back of the pattern for the correct width to determine how much fabric to buy (Fig. 2.2). Also check the list of notions and other supplies you'll need, to save another trip to the store later.

To make the shorts, you'll need elastic and thread. The easiest elastic to use has a knitted construction. When stretched, the holes open up and the elastic doesn't narrow. Knit elastic is comfortable to wear and doesn't stretch out, even when stitched through.

How much elastic to buy? Enough to fit comfortably around your waist, with a little extra for experimenting. I usually buy enough at a time for two waistlines.

Select a thread color one shade darker than the fabric. If you are using a print, thread color should match the background or the most dominant color. See Table 1.1, Fabric, Needle, Thread, and Presser Foot Guide on page 5.

The knit top also requires ribbing. Ribbing is usually knitted in a tube and priced by the inch. See pattern back for yardage requirements. Sometimes fabric stores put ribbing bolts in a different place than regular knits. Ask for help finding it.

---

**Sew-How:** *If you can't find ribbing to match your knit fabric, you can often use the same knit fabric for bands. Cut and stitch as described on pages 57-58 for the knit ribbing neckband.*

---

If the fabric is a jacquard knit, the right and wrong sides look different but obviously are made with the same colored yarn. For a contrasting band, use the wrong side of the fabric. This trick also works with stretch terry cloth and velour.

*Step Two:*

# SEW WOVEN PULL-ON SHORTS

---

**New Sewer's Note:** *Before starting, remove and unfold the pattern instructions from the pattern envelope. On the instruction sheet you should find a list of common pattern symbols as shown in Fig. 2.5. Besides the explanation on your instruction sheet, I will also explain what the symbols mean as we go along.*

---

**Fig. 2.5**
Pattern symbols you need to know to read and understand a pattern. (Courtesy of the McCall Pattern Company)

**FOLD LINE:** Lay and pin Fold Line directly on fabric fold. Never cut on fold line.

**SEAM LINE:** Broken line showing where to sew. Seam lines do not appear on multi-size patterns.

**SEAM ALLOWANCE:** Distance between sewing and cutting lines.

**CUTTING LINE:** Thickest black line around pattern tissue showing where to cut.

**NOTCHES**: Wedges cut outward, used to match one piece to another correctly.

**CIRCLES:** Also used for matching pattern pieces.

## LAYOUT AND CUTTING

If a garment is cut off-grain, perfect sewing technique and all the pressing in the world will not correct the mistake, so let's start off on the right foot.

1. Unfold the pattern instructions and pattern tissue. Find the correct layout for the width of your fabric on the pattern instructions and circle it for easy reference. Your pattern instructions also lists the pattern pieces needed for a particular view. They are identified by name and a number or letter (e.g., Pants Back B). Cut the pattern tissue apart between the pieces. You can either cut on the black cutting lines or cut in the plain areas between the pieces. Put aside the pattern pieces you need. Put the rest in the pattern envelope. If you have selected a multisized pattern, trim away surrounding tissue to the proper size.

---

**Sew-How:** *Fold extra pattern pieces so the number and name of each is visible. This way, when you use a pattern piece again, you can find it easily. Since it's difficult to refold patterns small enough, you may want to store your pattern pieces in a larger envelope, pinning the original pattern envelope to the outside.*

---

2. If the fabric needs it, iron it flat, then, if appropriate for the layout, fold it in half the long way so the selvages are even. If you need to straighten the grain, unfold your fabric and pull it on the bias to square it up (Fig. 2.6). Iron your pattern smooth with a hot, dry iron.

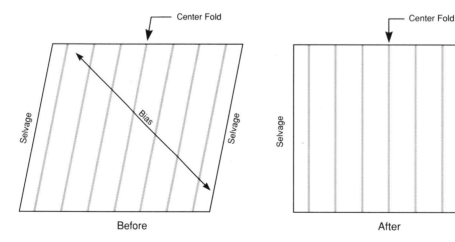

**Fig. 2.6**
If the fabric is off-grain, unfold it and pull on the bias to square it up

---

**New Sewer's Note:** *Selvages are finished edges that run parallel to each other and with the lengthwise grain.*

---

**Sew-How:** *Even after preshrinking, the center crease may be difficult to press out on some fabrics. Either refold the fabric and lay out the pattern to avoid the crease or use a mixture of half white vinegar, half water on a press cloth to press out the crease. The vinegar/water mixture can also be used for setting creases in pants and pressed-in pleats.*

---

3. Follow the layout so pattern pieces are laid out on the straight of grain (Fig. 2.3). This means the grainline arrow on the pattern tissue runs parallel with the fold and/or selvage edge. When the distance from the printed grainline to one selvage is the same everywhere along the grainline, your layout is correct.

**Sew-How:** *Before pinning pattern to the fabric, push a pin straight through one arrow head of the grainline so pattern piece pivots around the pin. This way, you can pivot the pattern piece one way or the other so the grainline is parallel with the selvage edge or fold. Check that the entire grainline is parallel to the selvage or fold, measuring with your tape measure.*

4. Pin tissue pattern pieces to the fabric or use weights to hold pattern pieces in place. Cut fabric, following the solid black cutting line on the pattern tissue and using your shears or rotary cutter and mat.

**Sew-How:** *Notches on the cutting line are usually numbered and indicate where the pattern pieces match up to one another during construction. Single notches are usually found on front pattern pieces; double notches on back pattern pieces; triple notches when front and back pieces are put together. Instead of cutting around every notch, cut across them. Then use the point of your shears and snip into the seam allowance 1/8" (3mm) to 1/4" (6mm) at each notch (Fig. 2.7).*

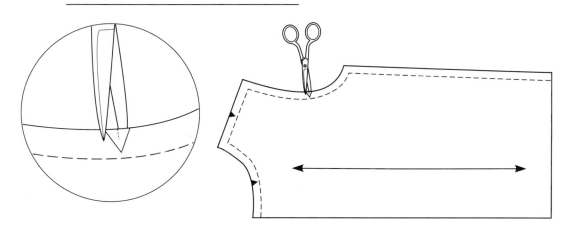

**Fig. 2.7**
Use the tips of your shears or scissors to snip notch 1/8–1/4" (3mm–6mm) at each notch on cutting line.

## MARKING

The best time to mark your pattern is before removing the pattern tissue. An easy way to mark a light- to medium- colored fabric is with a water-erasable or a vanishing marker. If you plan to work on a project right away, use the vanishing marker; otherwise, use the water-erasable marker. We will mark the pocket position and the waistline casing line.

Hold the point of the marker over the pattern tissue at a dot. Let the ink from the marker bleed through the tissue pattern piece, through one layer of fabric, then to the other layer of fabric. In a few seconds, both fabric layers are accurately marked.

Mark darker fabrics this way: from the pattern side, use a fine head pin and push it through the dot. Turn fabric over and push another pin through to the other side. Pull pattern pieces apart and mark pin placement with a soap sliver or disappearing dressmaker's chalk (Clo-Chalk; see Sources of Supply).

If the fabric looks the same on both sides and the shapes of the pattern pieces look similar, identify them before removing the pattern tissue. On the wrong side of the fabric, label each pattern piece with masking tape. It's easy to write on and won't melt if accidentally pressed over. **Note:** Before using masking tape, test tape on a scrap of your fabric to be sure it will not mark or damage the fabric when removed.

---

**New Sewer's Note:** *In addition to labeling the pattern pieces with masking tape, you may also want to indicate the top of each piece by drawing an arrow (Fig. 2.8).*

---

**Fig. 2.8**
On the wrong side of the fabric, label pattern pieces with masking tape. The arrow indicates the top of each piece.

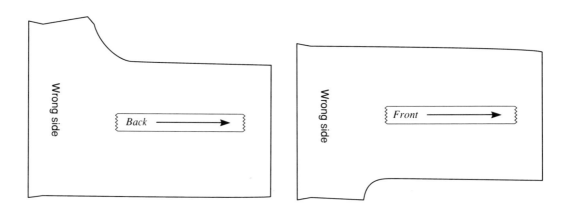

## CONSTRUCT PULL-ON SHORTS

Most of us who sew a lot don't follow the pattern instructions to the letter because we've learned easier, faster ways. I construct a project by utilizing the best stitches and presser feet, as well as shortcuts I've learned. Here's how:

### PRESS-AS-YOU-SEW

Pressing each seam as you go is as important as using the proper sewing techniques. Throughout this project and the others in this book, you will be directed to press as you sew.

The correct way to press a seam is first to press it flat and together to set or blend the stitches into the fabric. Then, from the wrong side, press seams open with steam, using an up-and-down *pressing* motion rather than a side-to-side *sliding* motion.

To prevent shine on the right side of the fabric, use a press cloth between the fabric and iron. This is called top pressing.

### SEAMS AND SEAM FINISHES FOR WOVEN FABRICS

Seam allowances on patterns are usually 5/8" (1.5cm). Depending on the project and the fabric, I generally use 5/8" (1.5cm) seam allowances on a woven and 1/4" (6mm) seam allowances on a knit. On the knit seam allowances, I usually trim to 1/4" (6mm) after stitching, which I'll explain later in the chapter (see page 54).

To give the inside of the shorts a finished look and to prevent the fabric from ravelling, overcast the raw edges using the three-step zigzag (see Figs. 8.41 and 9.38). After finishing raw edges, steam press edges flat on the right side.

---

**New Sewer's Note:** *Overcast the inseam, out seam, and crotch of the shorts. The waistline and hem edge will be finished later.*

---

## POCKETS

Most experienced sewers don't follow pattern instructions. Putting on a patch pocket is a classic example. Here are two ways to put them on, using your machine to its fullest capability.

| Machine Readiness Checklist |
| --- |

| | |
| --- | --- |
| **Stitch:** | straight |
| **Length:** | 2.5; 10–12 spi |
| **Width:** | 0 |
| **Foot:** | standard metal zigzag |
| **Needle:** | 80/12 universal |
| **Thread:** | all-purpose sewing |
| **Tension:** | normal |

### Patch Pocket (for New Sewers)

1. Fold down pocket hem of pattern tissue. Fold fabric right sides together perpendicular to the lengthwise grain; entire pocket is cut on a double layer. Lay out and cut pocket so the top is on the fold (Fig. 2.9).

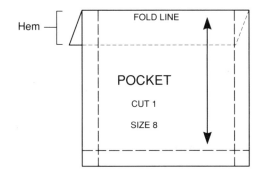
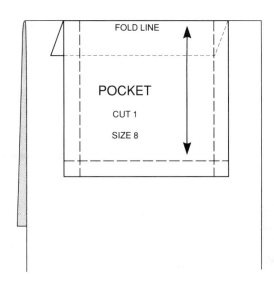

**Fig. 2.9**
Fold down pocket hem. Cut pocket on lengthwise grain so top is on the fold.

2. With right sides together and the fold at the top, stitch around three sides of the pocket on the 5/8" (1.5cm) seam allowance, leaving a 1" (2.5cm) opening at the bottom.

---

**Sew-How:** *For sharp corners, take one tiny stitch across the corner.*

---

3. Trim and clip corners as shown (Fig. 2.10). Backstitch or tie off threads on either side of the opening on the bottom of the pocket. Turn pocket right side out. Gently push a point turner or the tip of blunt-nosed scissors into each corner of pocket. Once corners have been squared, top press the pocket, using a press cloth and steam.

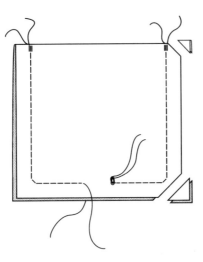

**Fig. 2.10**
Stitch pocket leaving a 1" (2.5cm) opening at the bottom. For sharp corners, take one tiny stitch across the corner. Trim and clip corners.

4. Pin pocket on shorts back. Align edge of pocket with the right edge of presser foot and topstitch with a 3 length (9 spi) straight stitch.

---

**Sew-How:** *When topstitching 1/4" (6mm) from the edge, the distance from the needle in the center position to the right edge of the foot is generally 1/4" (6mm) (see Fig. 2.11). To be sure, measure your foot by placing the needle on the 1" (2.5cm) mark of your tape measure with the end to your right. Lower the foot. Does the right side of the foot rest on the 3/4" (2cm) mark?*

---

### Curved Patch Pocket (for Intermediate and Advanced Sewers)

1. Cut unlined pocket and lightweight fusible interfacing following the pattern instructions. Trim interfacing seam allowances to 1/8" (3mm) and fuse to the wrong side of pocket.

**Sew-How:** *Use heat, moisture, and pressure to bond interfacing permanently to the fashion fabric. Heat iron to cotton setting. Place rough side of interfacing to wrong side of pocket. Using a very damp press cloth over the pocket, press over interfacing and press cloth with even pressure for about 10 seconds. Let the steam escape, then press again until the fabric is dry (see Fig. 1.14).*

2. Overcast pocket hem edge. With right sides together, stitch sides of pocket hem at the 5/8" (1.5cm) seamline. Trim and clip corner. Turn hem right side out, and top press pocket, using a press cloth.

3. Starting 1" (2.5cm) above each curve, easestitch "plus" 1/4" (6mm) from the raw edge (See Fig. 8.4).

4. Place pocket on shorts back so there is a little slack and topstitch 1/4" (6mm) from the edge. The slack enables wearer to put things in the pocket without putting stress on the stitches.

**Sew-How:** *Put on the transparent embroidery foot and set your machine on a 0.5 length (60 spi), 2 width zigzag. Satin stitch 1/4" (6mm) at each corner for extra reinforcement (Fig. 2.11). Pull threads to the wrong side and tie them off. If your machine has an automatic tie-off, use it instead.*

**Fig. 2.11**
Place pocket on shorts back so there is a little slack and topstitch. Satin stitch 1/4" (6mm) at each corner.

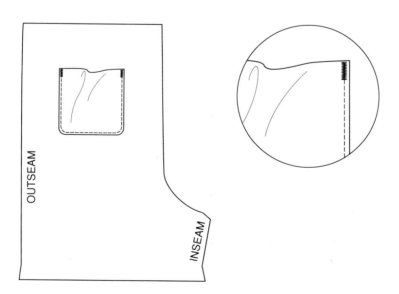

## CONSTRUCT ONE LEG AT A TIME

**New Sewer's Note:** *To make the shorts fit, baste them together first (see explanation on page 148).*

You can construct a pair of shorts or pants in two ways. One way is to stitch the front of the pants, the back of the pants, then stitch the inside and outside leg seams. The other way is to construct each leg individually, then stitch legs together at the crotch seam. For pull-on garments, the one-leg-at-a-time method is easier to alter, and results in a better fit.

### Machine Readiness Checklist

| | |
|---|---|
| **Stitch:** | straight |
| **Length:** | 2.5; 10–12 spi |
| **Width:** | 0 |
| **Foot:** | standard metal zigzag |
| **Needle:** | 80/12 universal |
| **Thread:** | all-purpose sewing |
| **Tension:** | normal |

1. Find a front and back leg piece. Place and pin right sides together, matching notches so pins are perpendicular to the seamline. Stitch the inseam and outside seam at the 5/8" (1.5cm) seamline, removing pins before stitching over them. Repeat for other leg.

**Sew-How:** *You may have been told your machine can sew over pins. This is not a good practice. When the needle hits a pin, the broken ends may fall into the workings of your machine or hit you in the face. It also dulls the needle or creates burrs, which may snag on your fabric.*

Press seams flat and together, then press them open.

**Sew-How:** *Sometimes a seam that is pressed open leaves a ridge on either side of the seamline. To prevent this, Press seams open over a seam roll—a stuffed cushion about the size and shape of a rolling pin, but without the handles. Seam rolls are available at fabric stores.*

2. Turn one leg right side out. Slip it inside the other leg, right sides together. Match notches, pin, and stitch the long front and back seam at the 5/8" (1.5cm) seamline.

3. Press open center front and center back seam from notches to waistline. Turn shorts, right side out, and try them on. Tie or pin a piece of elastic around your waist. Remember, the top of the shorts have a casing that folds down over elastic, so place elastic where the finished waistline will be. Adjust gathers and check the fit.

---

**Sew-How:** *If seams need to be adjusted, pin from the right side. If adjustments are made with the garment inside out, adjustments are made for the wrong side of the body (most of us are lopsided). After pinning, remove the garment and use a fabric marker to transfer pin marks on the wrong side by gently separating the fabric and marking where each pin enters the fabric.*

---

4. Once shorts fit, trim crotch seam, notch to notch, to 3/8" (1cm) and overcast seam allowances together with the three-step zigzag (length 1 (24 spi), width 4–5).

## ELASTIC APPLICATION

Do you use a large safety pin or bodkin to pull elastic through a casing? Did either one hang up in the seam allowances or pull off the end before the elastic was all the way through the casing?

This one-step method takes about the same amount of time as pulling elastic through a casing, but eliminates the frustration.

1. Cut elastic 3" (7.5cm) to 5" (12.5cm) shorter than waistline measurement. Before cutting it to length, check that elastic fits over your hips. (You wouldn't want to get the elastic stitched in, then be unable to pull your pants up over your hips.) Join elastic into a circle by overlapping the ends. Stitch using a three-step zigzag on a 1 length (24 spi), 4 width. **Note:** Overlapping the join eliminates bulk and evenly distributes stress on the stitches.

2. Overcast raw edge of fabric casing using the three-step zigzag on a 1 length (24 spi) and a 4–5 width. Fold down to the inside and press casing the width of elastic plus 5/8" (1.5cm). Edgestitch 1/8" (3mm) from fold (see Fig. 8.5).

3. Pin elastic circle inside casing, pinning under and parallel to the elastic (Fig. 2.12). Elastic should pull freely around the top of the shorts.

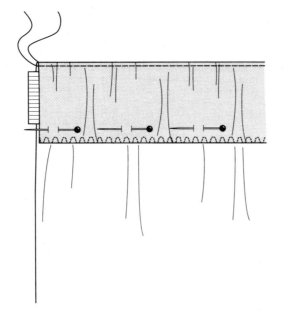

**Fig. 2.12**
Pin elastic in casing, under fold, pinning parallel to elastic. Elastic should pull freely around the top of shorts.

## Machine Readiness Checklist

| | |
|---|---|
| **Stitch:** | straight |
| **Length:** | 2–2.5; 10–12 spi |
| **Width:** | 0 |
| **Foot:** | transparent embroidery |
| **Needle:** | 80/12 universal |
| **Thread:** | all-purpose or 100% cotton |

4. With wrong side up, place casing under the foot so the needle does not stitch through elastic. Smooth fabric casing in front and behind the needle so the elastic is relaxed and the fabric is flat.

---

**Sew-How:** *Use a mark on your needle plate to guide the edgestitched fold. For example, if your elastic is 1" (2.5cm) wide, casing should be 1-1/4" (3cm) wide so that elastic moves freely in the casing. Therefore, guide the fold at the 1-1/4" (3cm) mark on the needle plate. If elastic is too wide to guide by a mark in the needle plate, use the edge guide (see Fig. 9.29) or put a piece of masking tape on the bed of your machine. (Remove it after stitching or it will become gummy.)*

---

5. Stitch a short distance, stop with the needle in the fabric, raise the foot, then pull elastic toward you so the casing fabric in front of the foot is smoothed flat (Fig. 2.13). Stitch a short distance, then repeat. This way, the elastic is stitched flat and in one step...no more pins or bodkins.

YELLOW

BLACK

■ *Teaching yourself to sew means more than making just garments. You can sew a hobby horse (Chapter 6) and practice machine quilting on a wall quilt (Chapter 5).*

- *Once you learn to construct a knit top and woven pull-on pants (Chapter 2), you can embellish the pants pocket with your machine (Chapter 3).*

- *Make a fabric gameboard and pouch (Chapter 7) and a Compass Tote Bag (Chapter 2) for a day at the beach.*

■ *Master buttonholes, mitered corners, and professional edge finishes on the Envelope Placemats and matching "Lapkins" (Chapter 4).*

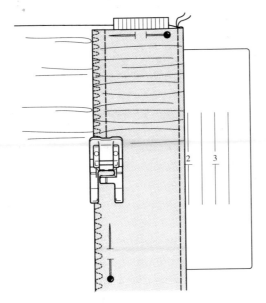

**Fig. 2.13**
Stitch a short distance,
stop with the needle in
the fabric, raise the
foot, then pull elastic
toward you so the
casing is smoothed flat
in front of the foot.

6. Try on the shorts and adjust the fullness around the waist as desired. Then stitch-in-the-ditch at the center front, center back, and side seams through the casing and width of elastic, to prevent elastic from rolling (see Fig. 8.7).

## HEMMING

1. Even raw hem edge, and overcast with the three-step zigzag on a 1 length (24 spi) and a 4–5 width (see Fig. 8.41).

2. Pin up leg hem desired depth, with pins perpendicular to the hem edge. Press hem without pressing over the pins.

3. Blind hem each leg hem using the blind hem stitch and foot (see Figs. 8.29, 8.30, 9.12, and 9.13).

*Step Three:*

# SEW A KNIT TOP WITH RIBBING

Layout, cutting, and marking are similar to the shorts—let's review:

1. Lay out top pattern so the center front and center back are cut on the fold. The lengthwise grainline will be parallel to fold and selvage edge. When laid out this way, the stretch goes around the body—necessary for proper fit and ease (Fig. 2.14).

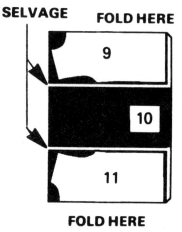

SELVAGE

**Fig. 2.14**
Lay out top pattern so center front and center back are cut on the fold and with the most stretch around the body. (Courtesy of the McCall Pattern Company)

2. Cut pattern and fabric on solid black cutting line, using a pair of shears or rotary cutter and mat.

---

**Sew-How:** *Do not cut a knit with pinking shears. The notched blades snag the fabric.*

---

3. Snip 1/8" (3mm) into seam allowance to mark notches, as you did for the shorts.

4. Mark dots on pattern pieces with vanishing or water-erasable marker.

5. Label pattern pieces with masking tape (optional).

## CONSTRUCT THE KNIT TOP

As with the pull-on shorts, the following construction and stitching sequence makes the best use of your sewing machine.

## SEAMS AND SEAM FINISHES FOR KNIT FABRICS

It's difficult to press open a 5/8" (1.5cm) seam on most knits. Therefore, we will use 1/4" (6mm) seams, and press them to one side. Rather than trimming the seam allowance to 1/4" (6mm) before stitching, however, leave the 5/8" (1.5cm) seam allowance to allow for fitting. In most cases, the seam also looks better when trimmed to 1/4" (6mm) after stitching. Exceptions are those areas where ribbing is applied at a neck edge or at a cuff and when making lingerie with nylon tricot. In these cases, it is generally easier to trim the seam allowance to 1/4" (6mm) and stitch.

### Shoulder Seams

Because forward and reverse "stretch" stitches are tough to rip out, speed-baste knit projects together to check fit (see Fig. 8.26). Here are two ways to stitch a 1/4" (6mm) seam, depending on the stitches built into your machine. If your pattern calls for 5/8" (1.5cm) seams, trim them to 1/4" (6mm) after stitching is complete.

## 1/4" (6mm) Seam, One-Step Method
## Using Forward and Reverse Stitches

Test for the appropriate forward and reverse stitch on a double layer of knit (for suggestions, see Figs. 8.49, 8.50, 8.54, and 8.55). Place test samples in your notebook. Identify the stitch and stitch setting on each sample.

---

**Sew-How:** *When testing for the right stitch, remember this principle. If the fabric waves out of shape, lengthen the stitch. If the fabric puckers, shorten the stitch length.*

---

**New Sewer's Note:** *If your shirt has raglan sleeves, pin each sleeve right sides together, to front and back, matching notches. Double notches indicate the back of the shirt; single notches, the front of the shirt. You may find it helpful to lay the shirt on a large table to do this (Fig. 2.15).*

---

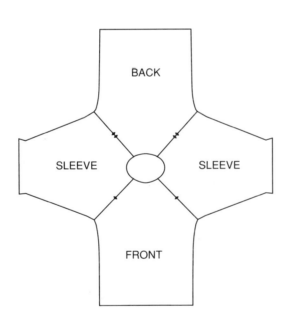

**Fig. 2.15**
Pin shirt, right sides together, matching notches. You may find it helpful to lay shirt on a large table to do this and to label the pieces with tape.

---

**Intermediate and Advanced Sewer's Note:** *To prevent cross-grain shoulder seams from stretching out of shape, place a double strand of elastic thread or a length of preshrunk twill tape under the foot. Sew across the grain without pulling elastic thread or tape (see Fig. 8.55).*

---

1. For all seams, pin right sides together so pins are perpendicular to the seamline. Guiding by the 5/8" (1.5cm) seamline, stitch seam with the best forward and reverse feeding stitch tested above.

2. Trim excess seam allowances up to the stitch. Press seam to one side.

.......

---

**Sew-How:** *If seam is trimmed to 1/4" (6mm) before seaming, guide fabric so the stitch falls over the raw edge on the right (see Fig. 8.49).*

---

## 1/4" (6mm) Seam, Two-Step Method

If you don't have one of the above-mentioned forward and reverse feeding stitches, stitch 1/4" (6mm) seams in two steps. If your pattern calls for 5/8" (1.5cm) seams, trim them to 1/4" (6mm) after stitching is complete.

| Machine Readiness Checklist | |
| --- | --- |
| **Stitch:** | tiny zigzag |
| **Length:** | 1.5–2; 10 spi |
| **Width:** | 1 |
| **Foot:** | transparent embroidery |
| **Needle:** | 75/11 stretch |
| **Thread:** | all-purpose |

1. For all seams, pin right sides together so pins are perpendicular to the seamline. Sew the tiny zigzag 5/8" (1.5cm) from raw edge, removing pins before sewing over them.

2. Using the three-step zigzag on a 1 length (24 spi) and a 4–5 width, stitch to the immediate right of the tiny zigzag. Trim excess seam allowance up to the stitch (Fig. 2.16).

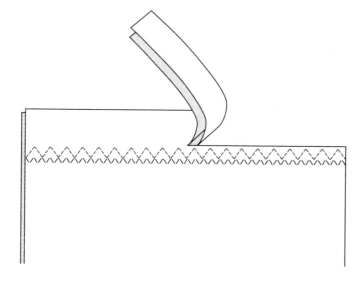

**Fig. 2.16**
Two-step 1/4" (6mm) seam finish using the tiny zigzag and three-step zigzag.

## Set-in Sleeves and Side Seams

Set-in sleeves generally must be eased into each armhole—some sleeves more than others. The flatter the curve of a sleeve, the less fabric is eased into the armhole. If the knit you are working with will not stretch enough for the sleeve to fit into the armhole, use this method. This technique also works on woven fabrics.

1. Snip the notch at the top of the sleeve cap. Easestitch "plus" each sleeve from back notches to front notches, stitching 1/2" (1.3cm) from the raw edge (see Fig. 8.4).

---

**Sew-How:** *If the sleeve hasn't eased enough, rip out first stitches and this time tighten upper tension as you easestitch "plus."*

---

2. Open shirt flat and pin sleeve into armhole, right sides together, matching notches and with the garment body on top. The snipped notch at the sleeve cap should match the shoulder seam of the top. Speed-baste sleeve in place so sleeve is down against the feed dogs. The action of the feed dogs helps ease in the fullness of the sleeve cap. After sleeve is basted so the seam is smooth, and without tucks, final stitch each sleeve using one of the two methods described above for a 1/4" (6mm) seam finish.

3. For the side seams, start at the bottom of the sleeve and use a 1/4" (6mm) seam finish. Press side seams toward the front. At the break of the hem, twist the seam allowance and press the rest of the seam toward the back. This way, when the hem is turned up, there is less bulk at the seam and it is easier to stitch over without distorting the stitch.

## Neck Band

Neck band or ribbing patterns are often the wrong length for the openings. The following measuring and stitching techniques have never failed me. *Remember, cut bands with the most stretch around the body.*

1. To determine the proper band *length* for a crew neck or waistband, cut band two-thirds the circumference of the opening so the stretch goes around the body.   To determine the proper band *width*, double the finished width and add 1/2" (1.3cm) (which allows for 1/4" (6.4mm) seam allowances). Therefore, a 1" (2.5cm) wide band starts out 2-1/2" (6.4cm) wide because it is folded in half and stitched with a 1/4" (6mm) seam allowance.

---

**Sew-How:** *For a crew neck, sleeve band, cuff, or ankle band, cut band two-thirds the circumference of the opening. For a V-neck or U-neck, band length is cut three-forths the circumference of the neckline opening.*

---

2. Trim neckline seam allowance to 1/4" (6mm). Pin band into a circle so narrow ends are right sides together. Stitch a 1/4" (6mm) seam using a tiny zigzag stitch (1.5 length, 1 width). Gently steam-press seam open.

3. Fold band in half the long way so the seam is on the inside of band. If ribbing is difficult to handle, speed-baste raw edges together, using the longest 4 width zigzag stitch and a loosened upper tension. Carefully steam-press band.

4. Quarter and mark bands with pins.

**New Sewer's Note:** *You may find it easier to mark band and neckline into eight, rather than four, equal parts. If your shirt has a crew or turtle neck, pin band into neckline, raw edges even, matching quarter marks to center front, center back, and shoulder seams (Fig. 2.17).*

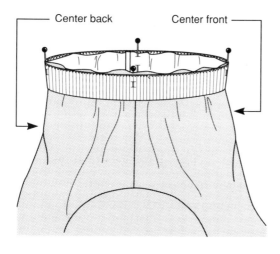

Center back          Center front

**Fig. 2.17**
Pin band into neckline opening at center front, center back, and shoulder seams.

**Sew-How:** *For a V-neck or U-neck, quarter and mark the neckline in the shirt. The quarter marks will fall on center front, center back, and be slightly forward of the shoulder seams.*

5. With the band side up, stitch a 1/4" (6mm) seam, using either method described above. **Note:** If you have a free-arm on your machine, slip the neckline around it and stitch.

**Sew-How:** *To stretch band to fit opening, pull the band with your right hand while guiding the neckline with the left (Fig. 2.18).*

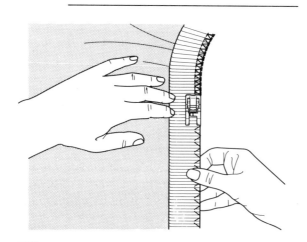

**Fig. 2.18**
Pull band with your right hand while guiding the neckline with the left.

## HEMMING

The fastest, easiest, and most secure way to hem a knit is with twin needles. Two needles, positioned on a crossbar and shank, are threaded on the top. The bobbin thread shares itself between the two top threads, creating a zigzag stitch on the underside (see Fig. 8.9). The shirt found in the color pages was hemmed with a size 3.0/90(14) twin needle. This means the needles are 3mm (1/8") apart, and the needles are a size 90/14.

For a ready-to-wear look to the neckline ribbing, use your twin needle to topstitch under the neckband through the seam allowance 1/8" (3mm) from seamline.

---

**Sew-How:** *Twin-needle hemming is only possible if your machine has a top- or front-loading bobbin. If your bobbin loads from the side, twin needles sit in the machine sideways and will not work.*

---

If your machine has a side-loading bobbin, blind hem knits as shown in Figs. 8.29, 8.30, and 9.12.

*Step Four:*

# PROJECT VARIATIONS

### INSTANT T-SHIRTS

For an "instant" coordinate to your shorts, try purchasing a ready-made T-shirt or sweatshirt and adding custom touches. You can also add embellished pockets like the ones made in Chapter 3, "Sew Embellishments."

Many households have a "button jar" or an odd collection of buttons that can be stitched to a T-shirt or sweatshirt. If you don't have such a collection, find interesting buttons at garage sales, flea markets, or in the bargain bin at your favorite discount or fabric store.

If this project is for a child, use a variety of buttons identifying a special interest— dinosaurs, hearts, or animal shapes, for instance.

### BUTTON SEWING BY MACHINE

The fastest and easiest way to stitch on a lot of buttons is by machine. **Note:** In this project, buttons sewn on the T-shirt or sweatshirt are for decoration only. They will never be buttoned through another layer of fabric. Therefore, it's not necessary to create a shank between the fabric and button. See Figs. 8.16, 9.17, and 9.19 for machine settings.

### ATTACHING RIBBONS AND BOWS

Sandra Betzina, newspaper columnist and author of *Power Sewing*, said her daughter tied and stitched bows all over a ready-made T-shirt and was out the door wearing it in 45 minutes. Use the same principles as attaching a button by machine, but use nylon monofilament thread on top so you don't have to rethread for each color ribbon.

For a boy, add a fabric stripe, fabric paint, custom patches, or woven labels to a ready-made T-shirt or jacket. For adults, remove ribbing and hems from T-shirt. Then add a pocket, knitted collar, and contrasting sleeve, neck, and waistbands.

# TRANSFERABLE LEARNINGS

The information and techniques you have learned by making the woven shorts and knit top have given you the skills necessary to sew many other projects. You have learned how to:

• Read a pattern and pattern envelope and buy the correct type and amount of fabric and appropriate notions.

• Understand pattern layout and cutting.
 ❖ Lengthwise grain is parallel to selvage edge and/or fold.
 ❖ Knits are laid out and cut with the most stretch around the body.
 ❖ Patterns are cut on the black cutting line.
 ❖ Notches are snip-marked using scissor tips for speed and accuracy.

• Mark pattern pieces.
 ❖ Mark light-colored fabrics with vanishing or water-erasable marker.
 ❖ Mark dark fabrics with soap sliver or disappearing dressmaker's chalk (Clo-Chalk—see Sources of Supply).

• Stitch and finish 5/8" (1.5cm) or 1/4" (6mm) seam allowances on knit and woven fabric.

• Topstitch 1/4" (6mm) from a finished edge using center needle position and guiding the edge of the standard zigzag foot by the finished edge of the fabric.

• Permanently bond a fusible interfacing to fashion fabric using heat, moisture, and pressure.

• Stitch elastic in a casing in one step. This technique can be used for elastic insertion at a waistline, wrist, or ankle.

• Blind hem woven fabrics with the blind hem foot and blind hem stitch. Hem knits with twin needles.

• Easestitch "plus" the sleeve before it is stitched into the armhole. Final stitch sleeve into the arm hole with the sleeve side against the feed dogs to ease in the fullness.

---

You have learned a lot in this chapter about sewing woven and knit fabrics. I hope this approach encourages you to think through a project to best utilize your tools, accessories, and your sewing machine.

Next, you will "Sew Embellishments" and decorate a tote bag. The design you see in the tote can also be translated to a pocket on the pair of shorts or T-shirt you just made (see color pages).

# SEW EMBELLISHMENTS— MACHINE APPLIQUÉ AND EMBROIDER

- *Step One: Plan Your Project*

- *Step Two: Compass Tote*

- *Step Three: Project Variations— Pocket and T-shirt Embellishment*

- *Transferable Learnings*

---

ma.chine (me shEn´) *noun*, a structure consisting of a framework and various fixed and moving parts, for doing some kind of work; mechanism [a sewing machine]

ap.pli.qué (ap´le ka´) *noun*, a decoration or trimming made of one material attached by sewing, gluing, etc., to another. *adj.*, applied as such a decoration. *verb* -quéd´, -qué´ing, **1.** to decorate with appliqué **2.** to put on as appliqué

em.broi.der (im broi´der) *verb*, **1.** to ornament (fabric) with a design in needlework **2.** to make (a design, etc.) on fabric with needlework **3.** to embellish (a story, etc.); add fanciful details to

This chapter will investigate machine appliqué and machine embroidery as ways to embellish a base fabric. We will work the design on a base fabric that can be put in your notebook or turned into a pocket for the Compass Tote Bag. Once you have mastered the compass design, you will embellish a ready-to-wear T-shirt with it, or a pocket for a pair of shorts (see color pages). If your appetite for machine embellishment has been whetted, see the bibliography for more on machine appliqué and machine embroidery.

**Sew-How:** *If you like the tote bag, you may want to embellish the shorts and T-shirt you made in Chapter 2 to match, using the techniques learned in this chapter.*

*Step One:*

# PLAN YOUR PROJECT

The compass design teaches you how to turn corners, as well as how to use some closed decorative stitches available on your machine. But first you need to know about fabrics, threads, and other embroidery supplies (Fig. 3.1).

**Fig. 3.1**
Threads, fabrics and other embroidery supplies.

## FABRICS AND THREADS

All-natural fabrics are easiest to use for machine appliqué and embroidery because they are more forgiving than their synthetic counterparts. If puckering occurs, pressing usually removes the worst of it. Wool felt and woven fabrics are also easier to work with than knits because they don't distort in a hoop. Cut wool felt, all-cotton duck or kettle cloth, and organza into 9" (23cm) practice squares. Use them as "doodle cloths" and for stitch testing, then put them in your notebook for future reference.

The best threads for machine appliqué and embroidery are all-cotton or rayon embroidery thread. Both have a nice sheen and cause little or no tension problems. They are also generally finer than thread used for clothing construction. Look for brand names like DMC, J. & P. Coats, Mettler, Sulky, and Zwicky in your local sewing machine dealership or in better fabric stores.

---

**Sew-How:** *If you have old cotton thread that shreds, splits, or breaks when you are using it, put it in the refrigerator overnight. The moisture in the refrigerator is absorbed by the thread so that it regains its original tensile strength. If you don't have time to wait, accomplish the same thing by dribbling a line of Needle-Lube™ on the thread along the length of the spool.*

---

Other threads used for machine embroidery are **cotton darning thread** and **nylon monofilament thread**. Because darning thread is very fine—a size 70 or 120—it does not create bulk, even in heavily stitched areas. This makes it a good bobbin thread for embroidery. Since darning thread is available only in black and white, it is necessary to loosen top thread tension so stitches lock under the fabric. This way, bobbin thread will not pull up to the surface and show. This method saves time because a single bobbin of darning thread can be used with a variety of colors. Also, because darning thread is so fine, a bobbin holds more of it than other threads.

---

**Sew-How:** *Darning thread is too fine to use for clothing construction; however, when it's on the bobbin, it looks like any other white or black thread. To prevent confusion, mark bobbins wound with darning thread with fingernail polish.*

---

Nylon monofilament thread is transparent and has many of the same advantages as cotton darning thread—you can get a lot on a bobbin, and you don't need to wind and thread new bobbins when changing the top thread color. However, some brands are stiff and wiry, and won't hold a knot. The best type I've used is called "Invisible Nylon Thread." It's as fine as hair, breaks like regular sewing thread, and is available through mail-order sources.

## Other Embroidery Supplies

To ensure a smooth finish, you need a way to stabilize the fabric so the embroidery does not pucker while you are stitching. This can be accomplished by using an embroidery hoop; by backing the fabric with a stabilizer such as iron-on freezer wrap, tear-away, or fusible interfacing; or by using a combination of the above.

The easiest type of embroidery hoop to use for machine embroidery is a **spring hoop**. It's narrow enough to fit under the presser foot and needle, and it's easy to move when your work is in the machine. Spring hoops are available in 3" (7.5cm), 5-3/8" (13.7cm) and 7" (18cm) sizes. I use the 5-3/8" (13.7cm) the most. Purchase a spring hoop through your local sewing machine dealer or mail order source.

**Plastic-coated freezer wrap**, used as an iron-on stabilizer, helps prevent skipped stitches and puckering. It is also easily removed after stitching and available at your local grocery store. Iron the shiny side to the underside of your fabric.

**Tear-Away™** or **Stitch-n-Tear™** are fabric stabilizers. These do not iron on and are easily removed after stitching.

**Fusible interfacing** supports a limp fabric and can stabilize a knit fabric when the interfacing is fused to the back. This makes pucker-free embroidering on a knit possible.

Other supplies you will see listed in this chapter are:

- **Wonder-Under™** Transfer Web—fusible web on one side, paper on the other; makes any fabric fusible without "gunking up" the iron (see instructions below).

- **Water-erasable** or **vanishing markers**—the mark is removed with clear water or disappears after 24–48 hours.

- **Liquid seam sealant**—put a drop on thread ends so they don't have to be tied off or to prevent a knot from coming untied. A common brand is Dritz Fray Check.

*Step Two:*

# COMPASS TOTE

We tote our possessions to school, to the beach, to class, and back. We tote things on vacation and tote notes to a lecture. We tote things home from the mall, so we can tote the same things elsewhere. So why not make something large and attractive to do the toting? The finished dimensions of the Compass Tote are 14" X 17-1/2" X 5" (35cm X 44cm X 12.5cm), and it has a 7" (18cm) embroidered pocket on the front.

The embroidery on the pocket will be done with the feed dogs up. This means that the machine will move the fabric under the presser foot while the needle moves from side to side creating a decorative stitch.

After making the pocket, you will freely embroider a label or name tag to stitch to the inside of the tote. This means the feed dogs are lowered or covered; the fabric is stretched in a hoop, then moved manually under the needle.

---

**New Sewer's Note:** *It takes practice to perfect your embroidery skills, so you may want to practice the embroidery techniques on squares to go in your notebook. If you find one of your practice squares acceptable, turn it into a pocket to stitch to your tote as instructed. If you aren't happy with your embroidery sample, and if you need more practice, either make a plain pocket, or stitch a purchased crest or woven label on the pocket in lieu of the embroidery.*

---

In addition to the embroidery supplies mentioned above, to make the tote you will need:

- 1/2 yd. (45.5cm) Wonder-Under

- 2/3 yd. (61cm) of 5/8" (1.5cm)-wide white grosgrain ribbon

- 1/4 yd. (23cm) of 1-1/2" (4cm)-wide white grosgrain ribbon

- water-soluble stabilizer, double layer to fit into embroidery hoop

- white canvas cut 24" wide X 16-1/2" long (60cm wide X 41cm long)

- yellow canvas cut 24" wide X 20" long (60cm wide X 50cm long)

- yellow canvas cut 16 " wide X 3-3/4" long (40.5cm X 9.5cm) for stripes

- 9" (23cm) squares: 2 of fusible interfacing, 3 of black woven cotton, 2 of cotton woven for practice squares

- 9" (23cm) tear-away stabilizer

- 48" (120cm) of 1" (2.5cm) webbing cut in half for the handles

- black and yellow fabric paint to match tote fabrics

---

**Sew-How:** *The handles are black on one side and yellow on the other. Rather than buying twice the amount of webbing specified to get the two-toned effect, buy white webbing and paint one side black, the other side yellow to match the canvas.*

---

- rayon embroidery thread in white and yellow to match canvas; white darning thread for bobbin; black, white, and yellow all-purpose thread for bag construction

- white or gray dressmaker's carbon paper and empty ballpoint pen

- vanishing marker

- ruler

- rotary cutter, mat, and see-through cutting ruler to cut everything square

- spring hoop

- heavy cardboard cut to fit the bottom of the bag

- small fusible letters (N, S, E, W)—optional

## TRACE AND TRANSFER THE DESIGN

1. Fuse the square of interfacing to the wrong side of a 9" (23cm) black square. Iron a square of freezer wrap to the wrong side of the interfaced square. The freezer wrap stabilizes the fabric so an embroidery hoop is not necessary for this embroidery.

---

**Sew-How:** *Prepare two squares as described in Step 1. Use one for experimentation to properly adjust the stitch length, width, and tension; use the other as your finished square.*

---

2. Enlarge the design in Fig. 3.2 to twice the size shown here on a photocopier at your local copy center.

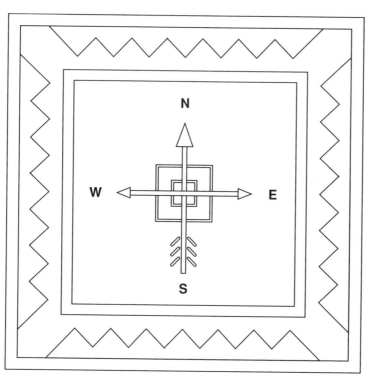

**Fig. 3.2**
Compass embroidery
design.

Tote pocket pattern is 1/2 size.

---

**New Sewer's Note:** *To finger-press a fold, crease or press the fabric by hand without using an iron. In this case the crease temporarily marks the center of the tote to help with the pocket placement.*

---

3. Find the exact center of the black fabric square. To mark the center, fold the square into quarters and finger-press. Stick a straight pin through the back of the fabric square where the pressed lines intersect, so the point of the pin is up. Place the black fabric square on a table, right side up, so the point of the pin is up. Stack the dressmaker's carbon and the pattern over the fabric, pushing the pin through the center of the design. Pin pattern and carbon paper to the fabric so they won't shift. Remove the straight pin from the center.

4. Using the empty ballpoint pen and ruler, trace the compass design and border on the fabric. Remove the pattern. Can you see the lines clearly? If not, fill in the lines using marking chalk.

## EMBROIDER THE POCKET

1. Stitch compass center squares.

**Machine Readiness Checklist**

**Stitch:** zigzag
**Length:** 0.3–0.5; 60 spi
**Width:** 2–2.5
**Foot:** transparent embroidery
**Needle:** 90/14 stretch
**Thread:** top, white rayon embroidery; bobbin, white darning
**Tension:** top, loosened slightly; bobbin, normal or tightened slightly
**Fabric:** 9" (23cm) black interfaced woven cotton backed with ironed-on freezer wrap

**Sew-How:** *Test and practice each technique on your practice square before stitching on the pocket square.*

Starting in the center of the right side of the smaller square, stitch to the corner, stopping with the needle in the left side of the stitch. Lift the presser foot and pivot the fabric slightly. Put the foot down and zigzag so the needle stitches over and back into the pivot hole in the corner (hold the fabric firmly to keep it from feeding). Lift the presser foot, pivot slightly, stitch, and so on, so the stitches fan out from the same point around the corner (Fig. 3.3).

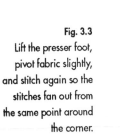

Fig. 3.3
Lift the presser foot, pivot fabric slightly, and stitch again so the stitches fan out from the same point around the corner.

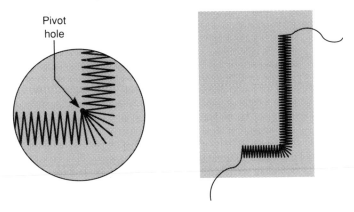

Stitch the rest of the small square, and around the larger square, fanning stitches at each corner as described above.

2. Stitch compass crossbars. Use the same needle, thread, and tension settings as described in Step 1.

**Machine Readiness Checklist**

**Stitch:** zigzag

**Length:** 0.3–0.5; 60 spi

**Width:** 2.5–3

**Foot:** transparent embroidery

Center the line of the vertical crossbar in the center of your embroidery foot. Satin stitch the length of the crossbar. Repeat for the horizontal crossbar. Stitch over crossbars a second time with a slightly longer satin stitch. This gives the embroidery a high, rounded appearance.

3. Stitch the small arrow heads. If you have a decorative stitch available that looks like the small arrowhead pictured at the end of the horizontal crossbar in Fig. 3.2, set your machine as follows. (If you don't have an arrowhead design on your machine, you can create one by manually tapering a satin stitch. Before you proceed to Step 4, do the Warm-Up Exercise below.) Use the same needle, thread, and tension settings as described in Step 1.

**Machine Readiness Checklist**

**Stitch:** closed arrowhead

**Length:** 0.3–0.5; 60 spi

**Width:** widest

**Foot:** transparent embroidery

**Sew-How:** *The easiest way to stitch the arrowhead is to start sewing it at the end of the crossbar and stitch from the widest part of the arrowhead to the point. If the arrowhead on your machine starts stitching at the point end, see if you have an end-to-end mirror image feature on your machine, so you can flip the pattern over.*

If you can't start the arrowhead at the wide end, stitch a few individual arrowheads on your test square and measure them. On your pocket square, mark where to start the arrowhead so the wide part meets the end of the crossbar. Then stitch.

## WARM-UP EXERCISE: TAPERED SATIN STITCH

The needle, thread, and tension settings are the same as described in Step 1.

### Machine Readiness Checklist

**Stitch:** zigzag
**Length:** 0.3–0.5; 60 spi
**Width:** widest tapering to 0
**Foot:** transparent embroidery
**Needle position:** center

On your practice square, satin stitch while you slowly move the width control from wide to narrow. Once you gain some confidence, run the machine at the fastest speed. You should find that tapered satin stitch shapes are smoother and more uniform when you run the machine quickly and the width control slowly.

Now practice the arrowhead shape. When you have perfected it, stitch an arrowhead on each end of the horizontal crossbar.

4. Stitch the large arrowhead. Use the same needle, thread, and tension settings as described in Step 1.

### Machine Readiness Checklist

**Stitch:** half-arrow or tapered satin stitch
**Length:** 0.3–0.5; 60 spi
**Width:** 0–widest
**Foot:** transparent embroidery
**Needle position:** left; right

To create the large arrowhead, use two closed decorative half-arrow designs. One should taper out from the left; the other should taper out from the right (Fig. 3.4).

Fig. 3.4.
Create the large arrow by using two closed decorative half-arrow designs. One should taper out from the left, one should taper out from the right.

On your practice square, make an arrowhead, stitching one side; then turn the fabric around and make the other side. The straight side of the stitch should meet in the middle of the arrowhead. Each machine varies, so you may have to experiment with some of the stitches on your machine to get the arrowhead effect you want.

If you don't have an arrowhead design, create the same effect by tapering a satin stitch. See the Warm-up Exercise in Step 3 above, and set your machine in left needle position as described. Notice that the straight side of the stitch is on the left, while the stitch tapers out to the right.

Next, decenter the needle to the right and satin stitch. Now the straight part of the pattern is on the right while the stitch tapers out to the left. Practice satin stitching in right and left needle positions until you get a smooth, even taper. Practice until you perfect your arrowhead, tapering from left and right needle positions. Stitch the large arrowhead at the top of the vertical crossbar.

5. Stitch the bartack feathers at the bottom of the vertical crossbar. Use the same needle, thread, and tension settings as described in Step 1.

**Machine Readiness Checklist**

| | |
|---:|---|
| **Stitch:** | zigzag |
| **Length:** | 0 or drop feed dogs |
| **Width:** | widest; 0 |
| **Foot:** | transparent embroidery |
| **Needle position:** | left |

Place the embroidery foot over the mark for feather placement, and stitch five or six stitches in place. Move the width to 0 and take a few stitches in place. Remove the work. Cut the threads, leaving them long enough to tie off, and stitch another bartack feather. Repeat until all feathers are stitched. Pull threads to the back and tie them off. Remember to raise the feed dogs for normal sewing.

6. Stitch the yellow border.

**Machine Readiness Checklist**

| | |
|---:|---|
| **Stitch:** | zigzag |
| **Length:** | 0.3–0.5; 60 spi |
| **Width:** | widest |
| **Foot:** | transparent embroidery |

Start sewing in the middle of one of the borders and stitch to the end. To turn the corner, remove the fabric. Cut the threads, leaving them long enough to tie off, and turn the fabric 90 degrees. Start the next row of stitching at the edge of the first row; then stitch to the end of the next border (see color pages). Repeat for the other sides.

7. If your machine can embroider the alphabet, stitch the letters N, E, S, W as shown. Do this by stitching a test swatch for proper positioning. If you don't have the lettering option on your machine, purchase small white fusible letters at the fabric store and fuse them in place.

## Stitch the Ribbon Work

This tote pocket features a sawtooth ribbon point border using white grosgrain ribbon appliquéd to the pocket.

1. Cut four 6" (15cm) lengths of 5/8" (1.5cm)-wide white grosgrain ribbon. Place the strip of ribbon over your enlarged pocket pattern copied from Fig. 3.2, and mark the points of each sawtooth with a vanishing marker.

2. Using a sharp pair of embroidery scissors, clip ribbon from the bottom edge to the dot close to the top edge of ribbon as shown (Fig. 3.5).

3. Pin top edge of ribbon to the ironing board. Fold under the edges of the cut ribbon to create the sawtooth design and press (Fig. 3.5).

**Fig. 3.5**
Clip ribbon from the bottom edge to the dot close to the top edge of the ribbon. Fold under ribbon edges to create the sawtooth design, and press.

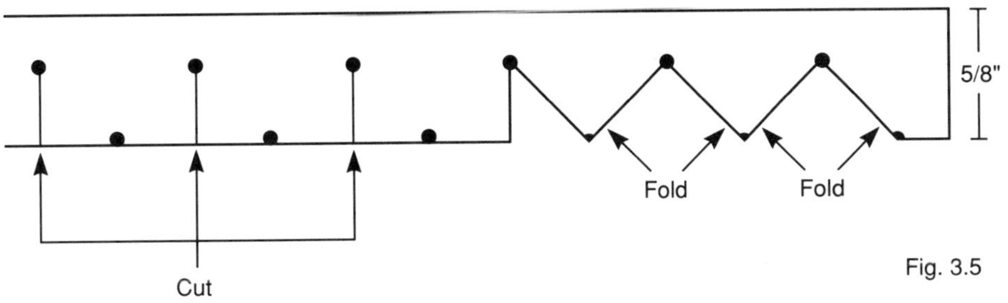

5/8"

Fold    Fold

Fig. 3.5

Cut

4. Pin and stitch sawtooth ribbon points around the pocket square, guiding as close to the edge as possible.

### Machine Readiness Checklist

| | |
|---|---|
| **Stitch:** | straight |
| **Length:** | 2.5; 10–12 spi |
| **Width:** | 0 |
| **Foot:** | transparent embroidery or standard metal zigzag |
| **Needle:** | 80/12 universal |
| **Thread:** | white all-purpose |
| **Tension:** | normal |

## Finish the Pocket

1. Pull off freezer wrap from the wrong side of embroidered pocket. Press the embroidery from the wrong side.

**Sew-How:** *With the right side down, press embroidery over a soft terrycloth towel. The embroidery embeds itself into the terrycloth while the rest of the fabric can be pressed smoothly around the stitches.*

2. Pin a plain black square to the embroidered pocket square, right sides together.

**Machine Readiness Checklist**

|  |  |
|---|---|
| **Stitch:** | straight |
| **Length:** | 2.5; 10–12 spi |
| **Foot:** | standard metal zigzag |
| **Needle:** | 80/12 universal |
| **Thread:** | black all-purpose |
| **Tension:** | normal |

To finish the pocket, use a 1/2" (1.3cm) seam allowance. Starting at the bottom of the pocket, sew all the way around, leaving 2" (5cm) open at the bottom to turn the pocket through.

3. Clip each corner as shown (Fig. 3.6), and turn pocket through the opening at the bottom. To square a corner, push it out with a point turner or the point of a pair of curved-blade scissors. Top-press pocket with steam and a press cloth.

**Fig. 3.6**
Clip pocket corners and turn it, right side out, through the opening at the bottom.

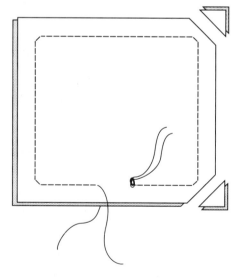

**New Sewer's Note:** *To top-press, place pocket on the ironing board with the right side up. Cover pocket with a press cloth and press pocket with steam.*

Press the opening closed at the bottom of pocket. Set pocket aside and admire your work. This will become the focal point of the tote bag. **Note:** The opening will be stitched closed when you topstitch the pocket on the tote bag.

### Embroider the Label

Another way to embroider is freely by machine, which means moving the fabric freely under the moving needle as if you were moving a piece of paper under a stationary pen or pencil. If you have never tried this technique, stitch the following Warm-Up Exercise.

## WARM-UP EXERCISE: SEWING MACHINE SPAGHETTI

Before stitching your label, try this warm-up exercise on a 9" (23cm) practice square.

**Machine Readiness Checklist**

|  |  |
|---|---|
| **Stitch:** | straight; zigzag |
| **Length:** | 0 |
| **Width:** | 0, 2, 3, 4—widest |
| **Foot:** | darning foot/spring or none |
| **Needle:** | 90/14 stretch |
| **Thread:** | top, dark-colored rayon embroidery; bobbin, darning |
| **Feed dogs:** | down or covered |
| **Pressure:** | released to 0 |
| **Tension:** | top, loosened slightly; bobbin, normal or tightened |
| **Fabric:** | 9" (23cm) square of light-colored woven cotton |
| **Accessories:** | tear-away stabilizer, spring hoop, vanishing marker |

1. Place the fabric in the spring hoop, and pull it taut. Then place the piece of tear-away stabilizer under the fabric. The tear-away prevents the fabric from puckering.

---

**Sew-How:** *When stretching fabric in a hoop for free-machine embroidery, it looks upside-down from hand embroidery because the flat side must be against the bed of the machine. The fabric should also be taut enough that, when you tap it with your finger, it sounds like a drum beat.*

---

2. Put your practice "doodle cloth" under the sewing machine needle. (You may want to try this technique with and without the darning foot/spring to find out what is most comfortable (see Fig. 9.28)). Although you may prefer not using a foot on the machine, you must lower the presser foot (presser bar lever) before sewing. This engages the upper tension—important for proper stitch formation. If you forget this step, your machine usually tells you by making a lot of noise or tangling the thread so you have to start over.

3. Lower the needle into the fabric and pull bobbin thread to the surface of the fabric. With stitch width at 0, take a couple of stitches in one place to lock off the threads. Trim thread tails off at the surface of the fabric, being careful not to cut the thread from the spool.

4. With the needle up, set stitch width to 2. Running the machine at a moderate to fast speed, begin moving the fabric smoothly to the left, then to the right. The faster you run the machine and the slower you move your work, the closer together the zigzag stitches become. Practice moving the fabric smoothly from side to side, creating a spaghetti-like row of stitching (Fig. 3.7).

**Fig. 3.7**
Practice moving the fabric smoothly from side to side, creating a spaghetti-like row of stitching.

Do not pivot the hoop at a curve. This way, the stitches taper as you change direction. (The resulting stitches look as if the line was created by a calligrapher's pen.) Try this exercise with varying zigzag widths so you are comfortable. Then practice writing your name or initials. Remove tear-away stabilizer after stitching. When you have perfected your name or initials, you are ready to embroider your label.

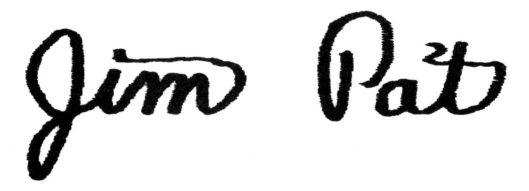

**Fig. 3.8**
To cross the letter t, or dot the letter i, extend the stem of the last letter.

---

**Sew-How:** *To cross the letter "t" or dot the letter "i", extend the stem of the last letter and bring it around as shown in Fig. 3.8. If you are having difficulty perfecting your lettering, you may choose to embroider a design instead. To do this, practice filling in a design on your doodle cloth as follows.*

---

5. Draw a sailboat on your doodle cloth with the vanishing marker as shown in Fig. 3.9. Place the bottom sail under the needle so it is sideways under the needle. With stitch width at 0 and starting at the left side, bring the bobbin thread up, take a few stitches in one place, and then cut off thread tails at the fabric. With a stitch width of 2 or 3, begin filling in the sail by moving your work to the left and right, in a long, side-to-side motion.

When you get to the straight edge of a sail, change direction, filling in the shape of the sail and moving your work smoothly, side to side to the right. This is called a fill-in stitch.

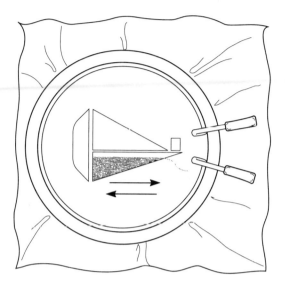

**Fig. 3.9**
Draw sailboat design on your doodle cloth with a vanishing marker.

Repeat this for the other sail and the boat. **Note:** Use the fill-in stitch and move the fabric side to side the length of the boat. For smaller areas, reduce the width of your zigzag.

---

**Sew-How:** *If you don't know which direction to move the fabric to fill in a design, test it on a scrap. If you are stitching an animal, follow the way the fur grows. If you are stitching a flower petal or leaf, stitches generally fan out from the center by moving the fabric side to side the length of the leaf or petal, in the same way as you stitched the length of the sail. For a totally different texture, move the fabric up and down to create a "corn-row" effect.*

---

6. To make the label, set your machine as follows:

| Machine Readiness Checklist | |
| --- | --- |
| **Stitch:** | zigzag |
| **Length:** | 0 |
| **Foot:** | darning foot/spring or none |
| **Width:** | 2–4 |
| **Needle:** | 90/14 stretch |
| **Thread:** | top, black rayon embroidery; bobbin, black darning |
| **Feed dogs:** | down or covered |
| **Pressure:** | 0 |
| **Tension:** | top, loosened slightly; bobbin, normal or tightened slightly |
| **Fabric:** | 1/4 yard (23 cm) of 1-1/2" (4cm)-wide white grosgrain ribbon |
| **Accessories:** | vanishing marker, water-soluble stabilizer, spring hoop |

Stretch ribbon and a double layer of water-soluble stabilizer in the spring hoop so stabilizer is underneath. Draw your initials, name, or design on the ribbon, and freely embroider as you did on your doodle cloth. Remove the ribbon and wash away the stabilizer. Cut label beyond the lettering or design so you can fold 1/4" (6mm) hems at the raw edges. The label will be stitched into the tote at the center back.

## CONSTRUCT THE COMPASS TOTE

1. Cut the white and yellow canvas as described above using the rotary cutter, mat and see-through cutting ruler.

2. Fuse Wonder-Under on the wrong side of the yellow canvas scraps. From these scraps, cut 5 stripes, 3/4" wide X 16" long (2cm X 40.5cm). Then cut each stripe in half so you have ten 8" (20.5cm) stripes. The stripes will be appliquéd to the front of the bag on either side of the pocket.

3. Finger-press a crease down the center of the white canvas by folding it in half on the lengthwise grain.

4. Position the pocket 5-1/2" (14cm) down from the cut edge of the white canvas, centering pocket over finger-pressed crease. Using a vanishing marker, put a dot on the canvas at each corner of the pocket to mark pocket placement. Remove pocket.

5. Remove the paper backing from the stripes.

---

**Sew-How:** *After the Wonder-Under paper backing has been peeled away from larger pieces of fabric, use it as a "paper press cloth" on top of and underneath other appliqués so the adhesive won't "gunk up" your iron or ironing board.*

---

Place top stripes so the top of each stripe is even with the top of the pocket. Place the bottom stripes so the bottom of each stripe is even with the bottom of the pocket (Fig. 3.10). Position the other stripes equidistant from each other. Once stripes are positioned, fuse them in place, following the manufacturer's instructions.

**Fig. 3.10**
Place top stripes and bottom stripes so they are even with the top and bottom of the pocket. Position the rest of the stripes equidistantly in between.

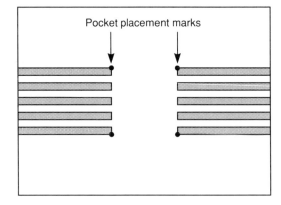

Pocket placement marks

**Sew-How:** *The following are the manufacturer's instructions for the proper use of Pellon's Wonder-Under:*

*Place the rough side of Wonder-Under against wrong side of fabric. Press for 3 seconds with a hot, dry iron. Let fabric cool.   Cut this new fusible fabric into desired shapes (shapes can be traced directly onto paper backing before cutting). When ready to use, gently peel off paper backing.*

*Position fusible fabric, coated side down, on base fabric. Cover with a damp press cloth. With iron on "wool" setting, press for 10 seconds. For a large area, repeat fusing process, overlapping iron until all fabric is fused.*

## Machine Appliqué

Appliqué the yellow stripes to the white canvas by satin stitching along the straight edges of the stripes (see Fig. 8.25).

**Machine Readiness Checklist**

| | |
|---|---|
| **Stitch:** | zigzag (satin stitch) |
| **Length:** | 0.5–0.8; 60 spi |
| **Width:** | 2–3 |
| **Foot:** | transparent embroidery |
| **Needle:** | 80/12 universal or 90/14 stretch |
| **Thread:** | top, yellow rayon embroidery thread; bobbin, white darning thread |
| **Tension:** | top, loosened slightly; bobbin, normal or tightened slightly |

Practice the following technique on a scrap to become comfortable with guiding the appliqué.

1. Starting with the bottom stripe, satin stitch over the cut edge so the needle enters the stripe on the left and swings over the raw edge on the right. Repeat for both edges of each stripe. Pull threads to the back and tie them off.

2. Attach the pocket. Rethread your machine with all-purpose black thread, top and bobbin. Use a straight stitch, length 2.5 (10–12 spi), the standard metal presser foot, and topstitch around the pocket, stitching 1/8" (3mm) from the edge (see Stitch Encyclopedia, Fig. 8.8).

## Finish the Tote

**Machine Readiness Checklist**

| | |
|---|---|
| **Stitch:** | straight |
| **Length:** | 3–3.5; 6–9 spi |
| **Width:** | 0 |
| **Foot:** | standard metal zigzag |
| **Needle:** | 90/14 jeans |
| **Thread:** | white all-purpose |
| **Tension:** | normal |

1. To make the body of the tote, place the narrow end of the yellow canvas to the bottom edge of tote front, right sides together. Stitch a 1/4" (6mm) seam allowance (Fig. 3.11). Press the seam allowance toward the front of the tote and understitch (see Fig. 8.10).

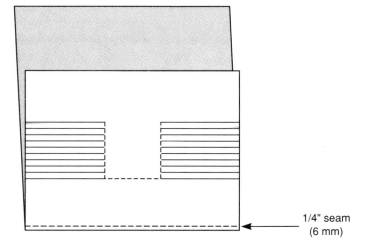

**Fig. 3.11**
Place the narrow end of the yellow canvas on the bottom edge of the tote front, right sides together, and stitch a 1/4" (6mm) seam.

1/4" seam (6 mm)

2. Overcast the long sides of the tote with the three-step zigzag (see Fig. 8.41). To stitch the side seams, fold the bag in half and use a 1/4" (6mm) seam allowance. Press this seam allowance open (Fig. 3.12).

**Fig. 3.12**
Fold bag in half and seam edges together using a 1/4" (6mm) seam allowance. Position webbing handles and stitch around the top of the bag, catching the handles in the stitching.

3. To finish the top of the bag, fold a double hem. To do this, fold down the top edge of the tote 1" (2.5cm) and press. Fold hem down again and press.

4. Draw a line 1-1/2" (4cm) from each end of webbing handle. Make an arch with one length of webbing and position it on the front, centering ends over the pocket. The lines on each end of the webbing should be even with the top of the bag. Pin handle in place. Repeat for the back of the bag (Fig. 3.12).

5. Topstitch around the top of the bag, guiding 1/8" (3mm) from the fold. Stitch the hem again, guiding slightly less than 1" (2.5cm) from the fold, catching the bottom edge of the hem and webbing handles in the stitching.

6. Position your embroidered label between the webbing handles on the back of the bag, and straight stitch it to the bag at the narrow ends.

7. To box the bottom corners of the bag, measure up from the bottom fold 2-1/2" (6.4cm) and mark a dot in the seam allowance with the vanishing marker. Fold one side seam so it lies along the bottom fold in the fabric (Fig. 3.13).

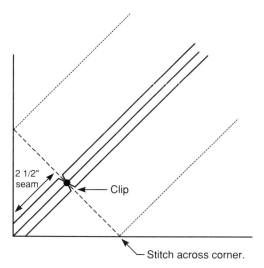

**Fig. 3.13**
Fold one side seam so it lies along the bottom fold in the fabric. This boxes the corner.

Draw a line on either side of the dot in the side seam, perpendicular to the side seam, and stitch along this line. Repeat for the other side. Turn tote inside out and push the triangles against the bottom of the bag.

8. Cut a piece of cardboard to fit snugly into the bottom of the bag to give it shape, and stability at the base.

*Step Three:*

# PROJECT VARIATIONS—
# POCKET AND T-SHIRT EMBELLISHMENT

## POCKET EMBELLISHMENT

Embellish a pocket to stitch to the back of the shorts you made on Chapter 2, or to give an old pair of shorts, pants, or skirt a new look.

1. Using a white piece of woven cotton, cut a pocket 7" (18cm) wide X 6-1/2" (16.5cm) long.

2. Interface the pocket with fusible interfacing. Back pocket with iron-on freezer wrap. Prepare another piece of fabric the same way for practice. Transfer the enlarged compass design from Fig. 3.2. onto the pocket, using dressmaker's carbon and an empty ballpoint pen.

3. Follow the embroidery instructions for the compass embroidery above, using white rayon embroidery thread. (The shininess of the rayon makes this white-on-white embroidery visible—and elegant.)

4. Using black 5/8" (1.5cm)-wide grosgrain ribbon, trace, clip, fold, and press the ribbon points as described above. Place the straight edge of the ribbon points, 5/8" (1.5cm) down from the top edge of pocket, centering ribbon over compass embroidery.

5. Rethread your machine with yellow rayon embroidery thread on the top and white darning thread in the bobbin. Sew a row of 3–4 width satin stitches (see Fig. 8.25), guiding 1/4" (6mm) under ribbon points (see color pages).

6. Remove freezer wrap from the wrong side of embellished pocket. Cut another pocket piece, 7" (18cm) wide X 6-1/2" (16.5 cm) long. Place pocket pieces, right sides together. Stitch, trim, turn, as described above for tote bag pocket using a 1/2" (1.3cm) seam allowance. Topstitch pocket to shorts, pants, or skirt (see Fig. 8.8).

## T-SHIRT EMBELLISHMENT

Embellish a ready-to-wear T-shirt or the T-shirt you made in Chapter 2 with the compass embroidery.

1. Using a water-erasable or vanishing marker, trace the enlarged design in Fig. 3.2 on a piece of tear-away stabilizer.

---

**Sew-How:** *Use a water-erasable or vanishing marker to trace the design on the tear-away stabilizer. If you use a pen or pencil, the mark may show and be difficult to wash out.*

---

2. To stabilize the knit so the embroidery will not distort the fabric, place a 4–5" (10–12cm) square of tear-away stabilizer under where the embroidery will be stitched. Place decorated tear-away on top of where the embroidery will be stitched. Pin through all three layers so the design and fabric will not shift.

**Sew-How:** *Find a similar piece of knit fabric to the T-shirt knit and test stitch before embroidering on your T-shirt.*

3. Using white rayon embroidery thread, stitch the compass design as described above for the tote bag.

4. Remove the tear-away from the right and wrong sides of the shirt.

**Sew-How:** *Because you are embroidering a white design on a white piece of fabric, the color from the marker may show through the thread. Rinse the shirt with clear cold water before pressing.*

5. Place embroidery face side down on a clean white terry-cloth towel and press. The stitches nestle into the soft terry-cloth, while the fabric between the stitches presses flat.

# TRANSFERABLE LEARNINGS

The information and techniques you have learned by embellishing the tote bag pocket and the pocket for the shorts, embellishing the T-shirt, and constructing the tote bag give you the skills necessary to sew many other projects. You have learned how to:

• Loosen the top thread tension when embroidering, so stitches lock on the underside of the fabric. This also applies when satin stitching an edge and free-machine monogramming.

• Use iron-on, tear-away, or water-soluble stabilizer under your work when using closed decorative stitches and when free-machine embroidering to eliminate skipped stitches and puckering.

• Use the decorative stitches on your machine to create a design. Not only can you create a compass, but a crest, flower, and other shapes, utilizing the decorative stitches available.

• Taper a satin stitch from left, center, and right needle position. Use a tapered satin stitch to monogram, create a stem or narrow leaf, or as a way of giving a straight line of stitching some dimension.

• Satin stitch around a corner. This technique is also used when turning a corner on an appliqué.

• Interface and line a pocket. Clip fabric across each corner so corners are sharp. Leave an opening to turn the pocket through before topstitching it.

• Press embroidery right side down on a lofty surface so stitches bury themselves in the loft and the fabric between the stitches can be pressed flat.

• Topstitch a pocket close to the edge. This technique is used to topstitch collars, cuffs, front tabs, yokes, and other parts of a garment.

• Fuse and use Wonder-Under. Besides appliquéing, cut it in into small pieces or strips and use to fuse-tack facings or to press up a hem.

• Move the fabric under the needle like moving a piece of paper under a stationary pen or pencil for free-machine embroidery. Use this technique for freehand monogramming, free-machine quilting, and other free-machine techniques (see bibliography for *Know Your Sewing Machine* book series by Jackie Dodson, Chilton Book Company).

---

Next, we will "Sew for Your Home." Besides the personal gratification, sewing for your home is a great way to stretch your decorating budget, and to give a new look to an old room — in this case, to your kitchen or dining area. We will make placemats and matching "lapkins" while practicing edge finishes, buttonholes, and topstitching at the same time.

# SEW FOR YOUR HOME

- *Step One: Plan Your Project*

- *Step Two: Envelope Placemats*

- *Step Three: Project Variation—Envelope "Lapkins"*

- *Transferable Learnings*

*Step One:*

# PLAN YOUR PROJECT

Although a lot of us sew for the pleasure of it rather than to save money, one of the best places to economize is by sewing for your home. A lot of it is straight sewing, so the challenge is finding fabrics to work effectively with your color scheme.

Unlike a piece of clothing you can hang in the back of your closet if you don't like it, projects you stitch for your home require careful planning, because you may have to live with your decisions until you can afford to change them. For that reason, many people consult an interior designer. However, if you keep some basic principles of color in mind, you can gain the confidence and train your eye well enough to do it yourself.

## COLOR SELECTION

Color has either a blue or yellow base. If you have had your personal colors done, you may know that winter and summer colors are cool, blue-based colors. Spring and autumn colors are warm, yellow-based colors. Color for your home works the same way.

When selecting colors for your home, work with the large surface areas first—the floors and counter tops. Once these colors have been chosen, everything else is planned around them. If you are not going to change the floor covering or counter tops, then take a closer look at what you have.

Is it bright and clear or grayed earth tones? To determine if your colors have a cool or warm base, take carpet swatches with you when you go shopping and compare them with other fabrics and colors in natural light. If you have to, take fabric and carpet swatches outside in the shade for a better look. The shade best duplicates a room in natural light. When you put a fabric next to your carpet, does the fabric look dirty? If so, chances are one of them is a cool blue-base and the other a warm yellow-base—neither one enhancing the other. After some comparison, you should begin to see the difference.

Another principle of color selection is to work with an odd number of colors in one room—three or five colors are more interesting than two or four. For example, if you've chosen three colors, two dominate, the third is an accent and used sparingly in a room. For example, you could have a white carpet, black bedspread, black and white draperies, and use red as an accent color in a pillow or flower arrangement. If a bathroom or sitting room adjoins, the accent color (in this case red) can dominate with black or white. The third color becomes the accent.

Once you have trained your eye, you'll begin to notice what works well together, and what doesn't. If you have to study something a while or aren't sure your choices compliment each other, they probably don't.

Now, let's start with something small and spruce up your dining area with a new table setting. In this chapter we'll make four placemats and matching "lapkins"—a napkin that has slots to hold the silverware, then unrolls to be used on your lap.

## FABRICS, THREADS, AND OTHER SUPPLIES

Once you have decided on the color scheme, let's select the fabric. A woven cotton or cotton blend is your best bet for easy care and trouble-free sewing—poplin, kettle cloth, and lightweight duck are good choices. If you choose to make a contrasting appliqué, as we did here (see color pages), be sure the fiber contents of both fabrics are similar. As always, preshrink the fabric before cutting (see page 41 for preshrinking instructions).

Threads used in this project are:

- cotton or rayon embroidery thread in the appliqué color

- white or black darning thread wound on a bobbin

- nylon monofilament thread wound on a bobbin

- #5 pearl cotton in the contrasting appliqué color

- all-purpose sewing thread in the prominent color of the placemat

You also need some Wonder-Under for the appliqués, a straight edge (preferably a see-through cutting ruler), a vanishing marker, and, for easy cutting, a rotary cutter and mat.

*Step Two:*

# ENVELOPE PLACEMATS

The placemat looks like the back of an envelope with a button closure (see color pages). Each mat has a contrasting appliqué and a topstitched flap with a buttonhole that buttons over a machine-stitched button. The corners of each mat are mitered, then satin stitched with a narrow border.

The techniques used in this project apply to many aspects of sewing, and, because you will stitch each technique four times (by making four placemats and four lapkins), you will master each one. Here's what you'll need:

- 1-1/2 yds. Wonder-Under

- 3 yds. of 45" (1.14m)-wide white poplin, weaver's (kettle) cloth, or lightweight duck

- 3/4 yd. (23cm) contrasting fabric to poplin

- four 1/2"–5/8" buttons (two- or four-hole)

- black cotton or rayon embroidery thread

- transparent tape (optional)

---

**Sew-How:** *Yardage requirements are for four placemats and four lapkins. Instructions below are written for one placemat and one lapkin.*

---

## CUT

1. Cut one piece of white poplin 16" wide X 12" long (41 cm X 30.5 cm). This we'll call the "base mat." Cut another piece of white poplin 18" (46cm) wide X 14" (35.5cm) long. This we'll call the "back mat." Note that the lengthwise grain is parallel to the short sides of each mat piece.

2. Cut two pieces of white poplin 10" (25cm) wide X 12" (30.5cm) long. In the upper left corner, mark the lengthwise grain on all poplin pieces using the vanishing or water-soluble marker.

3. Cut one piece of the contrasting appliqué fabric 10" (25cm) wide X 12" (30.5cm) long. Mark lengthwise grain in upper right corner with a marker.

---

**Sew-How:** *If contrasting fabric is dark, mark grainline on a piece of transparent tape and stick tape in the upper right corner.*

---

4. Cut one piece of Wonder-Under 10" (25cm) wide X 12" (30.5cm) long and fuse it to the back of the contrasting 10" (25cm) X 12" (30.5cm) fabric.

**Sew-How:** *See instructions for use of Wonder-Under in Chapter 3, page 77.*

5. Mark a dot 6" (15 cm) in from the edge of longer side on all three 10" (25cm) X 12" (30.5cm) fabric pieces. Cut a triangle from each piece as shown (Fig. 4.1). On the contrasting triangle, trim angled edges 1/4" (6mm).

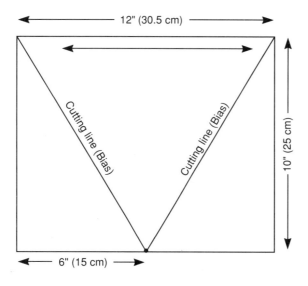

**Fig. 4.1**
Mark a dot, 6" (15cm) in from the side and cut a triangle. On the contrasting fabric, trim bias-cut edges 1/4" (6mm).

**Sew-How:** *This triangle has two bias-cut edges and one edge cut on the lengthwise grain. Notice the bias-cut edge hardly ravels compared to the edge cut on the lengthwise grain. Because of this, the bias-cut edge of the appliqué is finished differently than other raw edges are finished.*

## APPLIQUÉ

1. Remove the paper backing. Center contrasting triangle on the 16" (41cm) X 12" (30.5cm) poplin so the lengthwise grain of the appliqué and the lengthwise grain of the base mat are in the same direction (Fig. 4.2). Fuse contrasting triangle to the base mat.

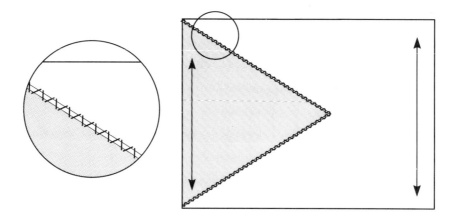

**Fig. 4.2**
Center triangle so the lengthwise grain of the appliqué is positioned on the lengthwise grain of the base mat.

2. Appliqué the contrasting triangle to base mat.

**Machine Readiness Checklist**

| | |
|---|---|
| **Stitch:** | zigzag |
| **Length:** | 2; 13 spi |
| **Width:** | 2.5 |
| **Foot:** | transparent embroidery or narrow braiding |
| **Needle:** | 90/14 stretch |
| **Thread:** | top, rayon embroidery to match contrasting fabric; bobbin, darning thread |
| **Tension:** | top, loosened slightly; bobbin, normal |
| **Accessories:** | double strand of #5 pearl cotton |

Place a double strand of pearl cotton under the embroidery foot or in the clip of the narrow braiding foot. Place bias-cut edge of triangle appliqué under the foot so the pearl cotton is stitched on the edge of it. Sew. The needle will stitch over the cord, attaching it to the fabric. This technique is called couching (see Figs. 8.31, 9.21, 9.22, 9.23, 9.24).

At the corner, stop with the needle on the inside of the corner, lift the presser foot, pivot the work, and pull the pearl cotton under the foot so it will follow the other edge of the appliqué. Lower presser foot, and couch over the pearl cotton along the other edge of the appliqué.

## MAKE THE FLAP

1. Place two poplin triangles right sides together, and straight stitch (length 2.5–3; 12 spi) a 1/4" (6mm) seam on the two bias cut edges. Shorten the stitch length, and take one or two stitches across the corner (Fig. 4.3). This insures a sharp corner when the flap is turned and pressed.

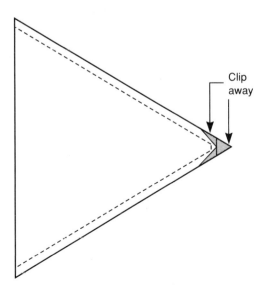

Clip
away

**Fig. 4.3**
Shorten the stitch length and take one or two stitches across the corner.

---

**Sew-How:** *Use this technique on collar point, cuffs, or when lining a square-cornered pocket.*

---

2. Clip away the fabric at the corner as shown (Fig. 4.3), and turn the flap right side out. Using a point turner or the rounded end of a pair of scissors, gently push the corner out to a nice point without pushing the points through the fabric.

3. For a straight crisp edge, pin flap around the edge so the seamline is on the edge of the flap. Press flap *without* pressing over the pins.

4. Using a straight edge and vanishing marker, draw a line to mark the center of the flap. Measure 5/8" (1.5cm) in from the point and draw a line perpendicular to the center line. The buttonhole starts where the lines intersect (Fig. 4.4).

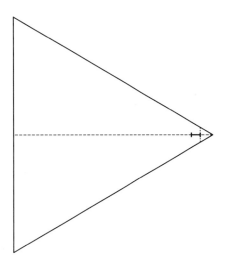

**Fig. 4.4**
Start the buttonhole where the lines intersect.

5. Set your machine for a buttonhole, and stitch a sample buttonhole on a double layer of scrap poplin to determine what size is needed for your button.

---

**Sew-How:** *To determine what size buttonhole you need for a particular button, cut a narrow strip of paper about 2-1/2 times longer than your button is in diameter. Fold the paper strip in half, and slip the button into it as shown, snugging one edge of the button in the fold of the strip (Fig. 4.5A). Hold the paper firmly and crease it at the opposite edge of the fold with your fingernail. Remove the button and flatten the paper strip. The length of the buttonhole needed is the distance from the fold to the fingernail crease in the strip of paper (Fig. 4.5B).*

---

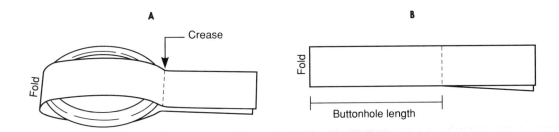

**A**

Crease

Fold

**B**

Fold

Buttonhole length

6. Make the buttonhole starting at the mark 5/8" (1.5cm) from the point of the flap. Cut the buttonhole open (see Figs. 8.14, 8.15).

7. Pin triangle flap on base mat and mark the button placement. To do this, find the middle of the buttonhole, and push a pin straight through the buttonhole and base mat. Using a fabric marker, put a dot on the base mat where the pin enters the fabric. Remove the pin.

8. Remove the flap and machine stitch the button in place (see Figs. 8.16, 8.17).

9. Button flap over button and pin flap on base mat for topstitching. Topstitch flap in place.

## Machine Readiness Checklist

| | |
|---|---|
| **Stitch:** | straight |
| **Length:** | 3.5–4; 6–9 spi |
| **Width:** | 0 |
| **Foot:** | standard zigzag or teflon |
| **Needle:** | 90/14 stretch |
| **Thread:** | 2 threads through the same needle in a thread color to match appliqué |
| **Tension:** | normal |
| **Needle Position:** | left |

Topstitch around flap, guiding 1/4" (6mm) from the edge. Note that sewing in left needle position allows you to avoid hitting the button. Two threads through the same needle gives the topstitch a bolder appearance (see Fig. 8.8).

---

**Sew-How:** *Heavier topstitching threads are available in a rainbow of colors at your local fabric store. Most are 100% polyester and must be used with a heavy needle. Although a size 14/90 needle is usually large enough, there is a special topstitching needle with an elongated eye designed to accommodate the heavier thread. See the Fabric, Needle, Thread, and Presser Foot Guide, Table 1.1 on page 5.*

---

## ATTACH BASE MAT TO BACK MAT

Rather than stitching on a separate border, which is tricky and cumbersome, the back mat is cut larger than the base mat so it can be folded over the base mat to create the border. The corners are mitered, then the border is topstitched all the way around both to finish the border and to frame the placemat.

1. Center the base mat on the back mat, wrong sides together. Fold the edges of the back mat over the base mat to create a 1" (2.5cm) border. Use an iron and steam to crease a border all the way around on the right side. Remove the base mat.

2. To miter a corner, press one border edge toward the right side. Fold a triangle at the corner the depth of the border (Fig. 4.6A).

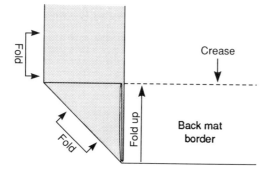

**Fig. 4.6A**
Fold a triangle at the corner the depth of the border.

3. Fold edge perpendicular to the base mat border over the triangle made in Step 2. Crease and press (Fig. 4.6B).

**4.6B**
Fold edge perpendicular to the border over the triangle. Crease and press. Mark the angle of the miter on the border, and along the side of the fold.

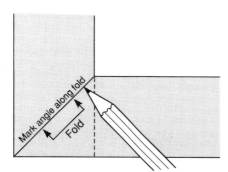

4. With a water-erasable or vanishing marker, mark the angle of the miter on the border, so that the marker touches both fabric edges on the angle.

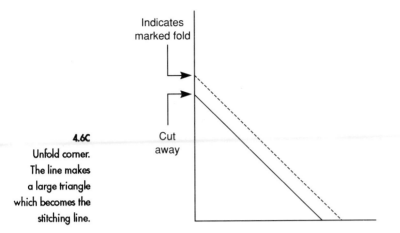

**4.6C**
Unfold corner.
The line makes
a large triangle
which becomes the
stitching line.

5. Unfold the corner. When connected, your lines make a large triangle in the corner which becomes the stitching line (Fig. 4.6.C). Set the base mat aside. You will be stitching just the back mat.

6. Fold triangle in half, placing right sides of back mat together, and straight stitch on the line marked in Step 5. Trim seam allowance to 1/4" (6mm) and finger-press seam open. Turn mitered corner to the right side, and press corner with an iron and steam.

---

**Sew-How:** *For a sharp point at the corner of each miter, clip excess seam allowance at the corner close to the stitching line as you did at the point of the flap.*

---

## FINISH THE ENVELOPE PLACEMAT

1. Slip the base mat into the back mat, snugly fitting corners of base mat into the mitered corners of the back mat. If the base mat ripples a little or does not lie flat, remove from back mat and slightly trim around the outside edge.

2. Using one or two strands of pearl cotton, couch the cord around the edge of the border as you did for the appliqué, guiding 1/8" (3mm) from the raw border edge.

3. Using cotton or rayon embroidery thread on the top and darning thread on the bobbin, stitch over the cord with a 3 width satin stitch to create a narrow border (see Fig. 8.25). The cording gives the stitch a higher, rounded appearance.

4. Steam press the envelope mat with the right side against the ironing board.

*Step Three:*

# PROJECT VARIATION—ENVELOPE "LAPKINS"

The lapkin is also appliquéd like the placemats. The edge is finished with a corded satin stitch, to emulate a serged rolled hem.

1. Cut a 16" (41cm) square out of white poplin.

2. Cut a 9-1/2" (24cm) square out of contrasting fabric and of Wonder-Under.

3. Fuse Wonder-Under on the wrong side of contrasting fabric square. Cut square in half diagonally so you have two triangles.

4. Remove paper backing and fuse contrasting triangles on opposite corners of the poplin square (Fig. 4.7).

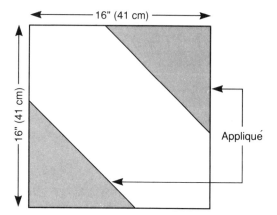

**Fig. 4.7**
Fuse contrasting triangles on opposite corners of the poplin square.

5. Appliqué the triangles as described above for the contrasting appliqué on the placemat, using monofilament thread on the bobbin. This way the bobbin thread will not show when the lapkin is loaded with silverware, and rolled up next to the placemat.

6. Cord the edge of the lapkin.

## Machine Readiness Checklist

| | |
|---|---|
| **Stitch:** | zigzag |
| **Length:** | 2; 13 spi |
| **Width:** | 1.5–2 |
| **Foot:** | transparent embroidery or narrow braiding |
| **Needle:** | 90/14 stretch |
| **Thread:** | top, cotton or rayon embroidery; bobbin, darning |
| **Tension:** | top, loosened slightly; bobbin, normal |
| **Accessories:** | #5 pearl cotton |

Place a strand of pearl cotton under the foot and couch over it, guiding 1/4" (6mm) from the raw edge. When you come to the corner, leave the needle on the inside corner, lift the presser foot, and pivot the work, pulling the cord so it will follow the second edge of the lapkin. Lower foot, then continue sewing. This gives the corner a slight curve.

7. Trim the excess fabric up to the stitching, being careful not to cut the stitches (Fig. 4.8). Satin stitch around the outside edge of the lapkin with a 4 width satin stitch (see Fig. 8.25). Guide the fabric halfway under the foot, so the needle stitches just over the cord on the left, and swings off the raw edge on the right. Satin stitch around the lapkin. Pull threads to the back and tie them off.

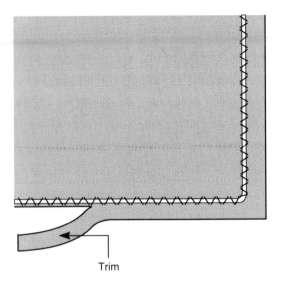

**Fig. 4.8**
Trim excess fabric up to the corded stitching being careful not to cut the stitches.

Trim

---

**Sew-How:** *For a professional-looking satin-stitched corner, stop with the needle on the inside, lift the presser foot, pivot the fabric slightly, lower the foot, take a stitch over the cord and back, stopping with the needle on the inside corner in the same pivot hole as before. Continue so the stitches fan out to form the corner (Fig. 4.9).*

---

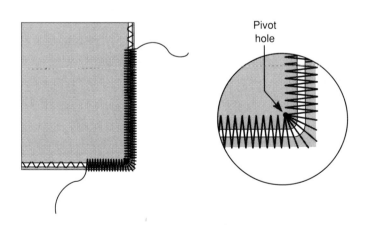

Pivot hole

**Fig. 4.9**
To turn a corner with a satin stitch, stop the needle at inside corner. Lift foot, pivot fabric slightly. Lower foot, stitch and pivot from same pivot hole so stitches fan out around the corner.

8. Stitch the silverware slots. Fold lapkin in half to make a triangle, so the appliquéd corners are at the top and appliqués are on the inside. On the bottom of the triangle, measure 9" (23cm) in from the left corner, and mark a dot. Mark three more dots along the fold to the right, spacing them 1-1/2" (4cm) apart. Fold down top appliquéd corner, creasing it 6" (15cm) above the first fold. Unfold corner, and draw a straight line on the crease, using a vanishing marker.

9. Draw four lines perpendicular to the bottom fold, up to the line drawn on the crease, as shown (Fig. 4.10).

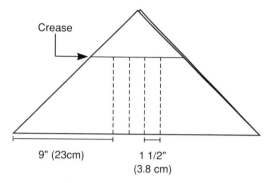

**Fig. 4.10**
Draw four lines perpendicular to the bottom fold, up to the line drawn on the crease. Straight stitch over the lines to create the slots for the silverware to slip into.

Crease

9" (23cm)      1 1/2"
                (3.8 cm)

10. Using all-purpose thread to match the poplin, run four rows of straight stitching from the fold to the line marked in Step 9, backstitching at the top and bottom of each row. Fold the appliquéd corner down and press. Slide a knife, fork, and spoon in each slot. Then roll up the lapkin and put it beside the placemat so the appliquéd corner shows (see color pages).

Lapkins can be made from scratch, or from purchased fabric napkins to match your favorite table setting. For a formal occasion, make them out of linen; for backyard picnics and barbecues, use print bandanas. Play with different color schemes to learn how colors interact.

# TRANSFERABLE LEARNINGS

The information and techniques you have learned by making this table setting have given you skills necessary to sew other projects. You have learned to:

• Stitch, clip, turn, and topstitch a facing to create the flap on the placemat. These techniques are used when sewing a collar, cuff, or lining a pocket.

• Make machine-stitched buttonholes to fit a button. Use this on other projects.

• Miter corners—handy for creating a fabric border on a quilt, mitering a corner with ribbon or trim, or mitering a placket on a sleeve or kick pleat.

• Turn a satin-stitched corner so the stitches fan out from a pivot point. This technique is used around the corner of an appliqué, or any time you turn a corner with a satin stitch.

Next, try some machine quilting techniques by making a small wall hanging. In Chapter 5, you'll try enough to know whether you like machine quilting. If so, you can make a larger lap blanket or a full-sized quilt.

# SEW A QUILT

- *Step One: Plan Your Project*

- *Step Two: Quilted Wall Hanging*

- *Transferable Learnings*

---

What is a quilt? Robbie and Tony Fanning define it in *The Complete Book of Machine Quilting* (Chilton, 1980) as "a sandwich of three distinct layers: a top, some filler (usually called batting, regardless of the material used), and a backing (sometimes called a lining). The top is secured to the backing through the filler with thread to keep the three layers from shifting around."

Some quilts are stitched entirely by hand; others, entirely by machine; still others are a combination of both. As much as I would like to try hand quilting, like many people these days, I don't have the time to perfect it, so let's quilt by machine.

The small quilt wall hanging we'll make in this chapter was designed to help you explore and practice the following machine-quilting techniques:

- free-machine quilting
- piecing and 1/4" seam allowances
- quilt-as-you-go
- stitch-in-the-ditch quilting
- adding borders
- straight-stitch quilting
- machine tying

As you gain experience in each of these techniques, you can decide whether you want to tackle bigger and more complex quilting projects.

*Step One:*

# PLAN YOUR PROJECT

## FABRIC SELECTION

The most exciting part of making a quilt is selecting the fabric. It's also the most confusing. I used primary colors in this, as well as in other projects in this book. They work well together and are a way of preserving scraps from the other projects in my quilt. After all, isn't that what some quilts used to be—a collection of fabric scraps from "Susie's dress," "Johnny's shirt," "Grandma's wedding dress"?

Fabrics best for quilting are light- to medium-weight woven cottons or cotton/polyester blends. Many fabric stores have a special section devoted to quilting fabrics and supplies. Before leaving the store choose a batting, too.

---

**Sew-How:** *For larger, more complex quilts, read* **Speed-Cut Quilts—1200 Speed-Cut Quilt Blocks** *by Donna Poster (Chilton, 1989). In her book, Donna not only presents principles of good color selection, talking about hue, value, and intensity of color; she also illustrates 400 different quilt blocks in three sizes. She has devised an ingenious plan for selecting the yardage for each part of the block, lattice strips, and borders—what a timesaver!*

---

## Batting

Bonded polyester batting is the easiest batting to work with for machine quilting. It keeps its loft, is easy to handle, washes well, holds up well over years of use, and doesn't have to be quilted as closely as cotton batting. It also comes in a variety of sizes and weights. Use lighter weight bat for clothing and table coverings; use medium to heavy for quilts.

## Preshrinking

- Preshrink your fabric the way you intend to care for your quilt after construction.

- Wash light and dark fabrics separately, to prevent dark colors from running on light-colored fabrics. Trim off all selvage edges **after** washing.

- It is not necessary to preshrink the bonded polyester batting.

---

**Sew-How:** *To cut down on raveling and tangling, snip a 1/4" triangle off the four corners of your fabric before washing.*

---

## OTHER MACHINE QUILTING SUPPLIES

Machine quilters find the following items helpful. Each one is described in Chapter 1, Step Two: Assemble Your Tools.

• Rotary cutter and mat—if you become a serious machine quilter, purchase the largest cutter and mat available.

• See-through cutting ruler—for accuracy, use the same ruler throughout a quilting project.

• Glass-head quilting pins—they're extra long and sharp, and pin easily through the quilt sandwich. I love to use them for most other sewing, too.

• Nickel-plated safety pins, 1" (2.5cm) long, to baste your quilt together.

• Water-erasable marking pen or disappearing dressmaker's chalk (for Clo-Chalk, see Sources of Supply).

• 8" screw-type embroidery hoop—necessary for free-machine quilting.

### Needles, Threads, Extra Bobbins and, Presser Feet

**Needles:** As with any new project, your machine must be lint-free and outfitted with a new needle. For piecing, a 70/10 or 80/12 universal needle is recommended. For machine quilting, use a needle with a larger eye so the thread will not shred, wear, or break when you stitch through the quilt sandwich. A 90/14 universal or stretch needle works well. A curved hand needle is also helpful for hand basting the quilt sandwich (optional).

**Threads:** The rule of thumb for almost all sewing projects is to select a thread made of the same fiber or blend of fibers as the fabric. Because it's easier to repair stitches than shredded fabric after the quilt has been washed a few times, use a thread less strong than the fabric. Therefore, if top and backing are 100% cotton, use 100% cotton thread. If fabrics are a cotton/poly blend, a cotton-wrapped polyester (all-purpose) thread works well. If your fabric is lightweight, use a machine-embroidery thread to piece the top, so the fabric won't pucker. When free-machine quilting, if possible, use a lighter-weight cotton machine-embroidery thread. Choose colors to blend with the most predominant colors of the top and backing fabrics.

**Extra Bobbins:** Before starting a quilting project, decide on the colors you'll be using and wind bobbins of each. This saves time and encourages more testing and experimentation because you don't have to take time to wind a bobbin.

**Presser Feet:** The presser feet used the most in machine quilting are:

• The darning foot for free-machine quilting. It provides support around the needle and promotes better stitch formation when you stitch through the quilt sandwich (see Fig. 9.28).

• The standard zigzag foot for precise 1/4" seams (see Fig. 9.5).

• The walking or even-feed foot for straight quilting and quilt-as-you-go techniques. It prevents the quilt sandwich from shifting and minimizes puckering (see Fig. 9.45).

*Step Two:*

# QUILTED WALL HANGING

This wall hanging is constructed from the center out. Let's preview how we'll make it together. First, the center "medallion," or focal point, is free-machine quilted. Look for light- to mid-weight fabric with an allover print of big shapes, or a print panel. I used a child's print for my project. Note that yardage requirements and the size of the pieced border are based on a 10" center medallion square (see color pages).

---

**Sew-How:** *If you can't find a medallion print you like, create your own: find an allover print and cut out shapes to appliqué to a background fabric.*

---

After quilting the center medallion, a pieced border is constructed. The most important principle to practice with machine quilting is accuracy—accuracy in measuring, cutting, and sewing.

Next, the backing is attached. A lattice border and the pieced border are added in separate steps to frame the medallion. Each is attached to the batting and backing to help you learn the quilt-as-you-go and stitch-in-the-ditch quilting techniques.

The last border is created by bringing the backing over the front. Corners are mitered; edges are turned under, then topstitched. This last "frame," created by the backing, is straight-stitch machine-quilted for depth and dimension.

Got the picture? Let's begin. Here's what you'll need:

## Supplies

- 10" light- to mid-weight allover print or print panel for center medallion

- 1/8 yd. each of black, white, and yellow solid-colored, and red mini-print cotton fabric or colors to match your center medallion fabric

- 5/8 yd. blue print

- 5/8 yd. medium-weight bonded batting

- Three 3/4" plastic drapery rings

- Optional: curved hand needle, masking tape

---

**Sew-How:** *Before starting on your finished project, practice each technique on a scrap until you are comfortable with it. Put stitch samples in your notebook.*

---

**Note:** Because precision is important, I have not used any metric approximations in this chapter. I apologize for any inconvenience to our overseas friends.

## FREE-MACHINE QUILT THE MEDALLION

1. Because you're using bonded batting, you don't need a fabric backing to quilt it. Lay batting on a large flat table and cut into a 20" square. Center and pin medallion on batting. Baste in place around four sides using the walking foot (see Fig. 9.45) and a 4–5 length (5–6 spi) straight stitch.

| Machine Readiness Checklist | |
|---|---|
| **Stitch:** | straight |
| **Length:** | 0 |
| **Width:** | 0 |
| **Foot:** | darning |
| **Needle:** | 80/12 universal or 90/14 stretch |
| **Thread:** | cotton embroidery thread in predominant color of print background |
| **Feed dogs:** | dropped or covered |
| **Pressure:** | 0 |
| **Tension:** | top, loosened slightly; bobbin, normal |
| **Fabric:** | center medallion print, batting |
| **Accessories:** | 8" screw-type embroidery hoop, extension table to cover the free-arm |

2. Put outer hoop of embroidery hoop on a flat surface. Loosen the screw. Place medallion, basted to the batting, over the hoop. Press in the inner hoop and tighten the screw, so the fabric is taut. Place project under the needle by tipping the hoop. Put presser bar lever down to engage the upper thread tension. Turn the flywheel one stitch and pull bobbin thread through the surface of the fabric. Take a few up-and-down locking stitches, then cut threads off at the fabric.

---

**Sew-How:** *A small pair of curved-blade scissors come with some Viking and New Home sewing machines. The blades are curved so they won't accidentally snip into the fabric while clipping off threads. If you have a different brand, purchase a pair through your local Viking or New Home dealer.*

---

3. Begin stitching at medium speed while moving the fabric freely under the needle following the outline of the print medallion. Slowly stitch around each shape. If shapes are not connected, stitch around to where you started, take a few locking stitches, lift the presser foot to release the upper tension, and move the fabric to the next shape. Put the presser foot down, take a few locking stitches, then proceed as described above for all shapes (Fig. 5.1). Clip connecting threads and pull them to the wrong side.

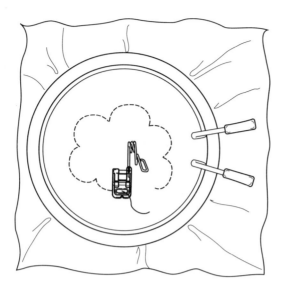

**Fig. 5.1**
With project under needle and darning foot, lower presser bar lever, turn flywheel one stitch, and pull bobbin thread to the surface of the fabric. Lock a few stitches and clip threads off at the fabric. Then free-machine quilt around shapes on your medallion fabric.

## ADD THE BACKING

Cut backing fabric 23" square. Lay backing, wrong side up, on a large, flat surface. Center quilted medallion, right side up, on backing so the lengthwise grain is parallel to the sides. Starting from the center and working out, baste the quilt sandwich together with safety pins, pinning every 3–4" through all layers across the medallion. After each pin, straighten backing by pulling on all four sides to avoid pinning in wrinkles.

**Sew-How:** *For this small project, you may want to hand baste using a long running stitch. To do this, tape the backing, wrong side up, with masking tape to a table top, smoothing out all the wrinkles. Center quilted medallion over the backing. Using a curved needle and a contrasting colored thread, hand baste a row of 1" basting stitches to the backing. Stitch a center row, then successive rows about 1-1/2" apart on either side, working from the center out (Fig. 5.2).*

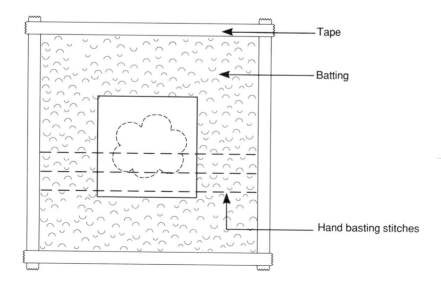

Tape

Batting

Hand basting stitches

**Fig. 5.2**
Hand baste quilted medallion to backing with a curved needle and stitch 1" basting stiches, working from the center, out.

## PIECE A BORDER

1. Using the rotary cutter, mat, and see-through cutting ruler, cut two each 2" x 12" strips of black, white, yellow, red print, and blue print backing so the 12" length is cut across the grain.

2. Cut one each 3" square of black, yellow, red print, and blue print backing.

**Machine Readiness Checklist**

|  |  |
|---|---|
| **Stitch:** | straight |
| **Length:** | 2–2.5; 10–12 spi |
| **Width:** | 0 |
| **Foot:** | standard zigzag |
| **Needle:** | 70/10 or 80/12 universal |
| **Thread:** | all-purpose |
| **Feed dogs:** | up |
| **Pressure:** | normal |
| **Tension:** | normal |
| **Needle position:** | variable |
| **Fabric:** | a couple of strips cut as described in Step 1 above for practice stitching |
| **Accessories:** | sewing gauge, iron, and ironing board |

Using two of your test strips, place right sides together and stitch an exact 1/4" seam. Check it for accuracy against the 1/4" mark on your seam gauge.

---

**Sew-How:** *If there is not a clear-cut guide on your presser foot or needle plate for 1/4" seams, move your needle position slightly to the right or left as needed (see your instruction book to find out how to adjust your needle position). Accuracy is important. If you're off only a 1/16", when it is multiplied by eight cut edges, the difference measures 1/2", which can throw off piecing and overall finished quilt dimensions.*

---

To make a pieced border, pin and stitch strips together in the order shown in Fig. 5.3, piecing with perfect 1/4" seams.

3. From the wrong side, press seam allowances flat and together to set the stitches. Then, using the tip of your iron, press seams open. Cut pieced border into four 3" widths (Fig. 5.3).

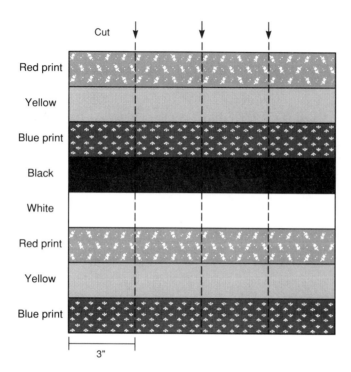

Cut

Red print

Yellow

Blue print

Black

White

Red print

Yellow

Blue print

3"

**Fig. 5.3**
Cut pieced border
into four 3" widths.

4. On one of the pieced border strips, stitch the yellow square so it is above the red print strip using a 1/4" seam allowance. On the other end of that strip, stitch the black square to the blue print strip.

5. On another pieced border strip, stitch the red print square to the blue print strip. On the other end of that strip, stitch the blue print square to the red print strip (Fig. 5.4). Press seams open and set these pieced border strips aside.

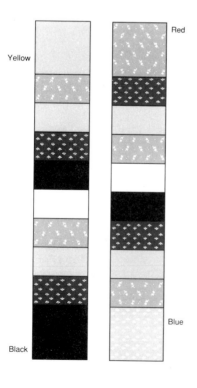

Yellow

Red

Blue

Black

**Fig. 5.4**
Stitch yellow square
next to red print.
Stitch black square
next to blue print.
Stitch red square
next to blue print.
Stitch blue print square
next to red print.

## ADD FRAME BORDER AND QUILT-AS-YOU-SEW

1. Cut two black border strips 1-1/2" x 10". Cut two more black border strips 1-1/2" x 12".

**Machine Readiness Checklist**

| | |
|---|---|
| **Stitch:** | straight |
| **Length:** | 3–3.5; 7–9 spi |
| **Width:** | 0 |
| **Foot:** | walking |
| **Needle:** | 80/12 universal or 14/90 stretch |
| **Thread:** | all-purpose top, to match border strips; bobbin, to match backing fabric |

2. Remove any safety pins that may be in the way and pin short black border pieces, centering them on either side of quilted medallion. Stitch a 1/4" seam allowance starting and stopping at the ends of each border piece. Either lock threads by putting the stitch length to 0 and taking three to four stitches in one place; or pull threads to the front and tie them off. Press side border pieces so the seam allowance is to the inside (Fig. 5.5).

**Fig. 5.5**
Press side border pieces so the seam allowance is to the inside.

**Sew-How:** *To tie a secure knot, give yourself thread tails at least 7" long. Hold threads together in your left hand and form a loop (Fig. 5.6A). Bring the thread end around and through the loop (Fig. 5.6B). Holding the loop in your left hand, work the loop down to the base and hold it in place with your left thumb (Fig. 5.6C). Pull thread taut with your right hand so the loop forms a knot at the base of the fabric.*

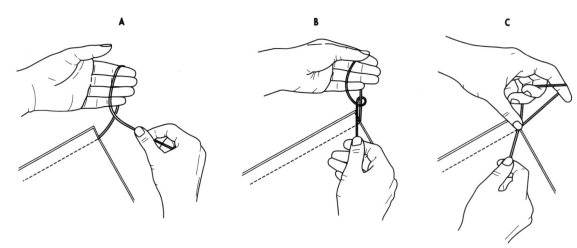

**Fig. 5.6A**
Form a loop.

**Fig. 5.6B**
Bring thread
end around and
through loop.

**Fig. 5.6C**
Work loop down to
the base of the stitch
with your thumb.

3. Place longer border pieces across the top and bottom of quilted medallion, right sides together, so ends are even with side border pieces. Pin and stitch, using 1/4" seams, starting and stopping 1/4" from the end of each strip. Pull threads to the back side and leave them free. Press longer border pieces so seam allowance is to the inside (Fig. 5.7).

**Fig. 5.7**
Press longer border
pieces so seam
allowances are
to the inside.

## ADD PIECED BORDERS AND QUILT-AS-YOU-GO

The pieced border is stitched in the same sequence as the frame border described above—the sides first, then the top and bottom strips. If you have pin-basted, remove safety pins that may get in the way of stitching.

1. Center short pieced borders made in "Piece a Border" above on each side, aligning cut edges, right sides together, against the frame border. Position the red print at the top for the shorter right pieced strip. Position the blue print at the top for the shorter left pieced strip (see color pages). This way contrasting fabric will be on either side of the squares in each corner.

2. Pin and stitch a 1/4" seam. Pull threads to the right side and tie them off as before. Press seam flat, then open. Repeat for the other side.

3. Place longer pieced border strips so the red square is in the upper left corner, the yellow square in the upper right, the black square is in the lower right corner, and the blue square in the lower left (see color pages). Pin top and bottom strips so the square, piecing, and frame border match perfectly in each corner (Fig. 5.8). Stitch a 1/4" seam. Pull threads to the right side of your work and tie them off.

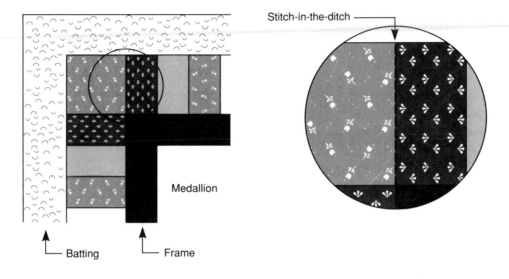

**Fig. 5.8**
Pin top and bottom strips so the square, piecing, and frame border match perfectly in each corner. Stitch-in-the-ditch on one side of the square in each corner.

Stitch-in-the-ditch

Medallion

Batting — Frame

---

**Sew-How:** *To stitch-in-the-ditch means to sew from the right side in the identation between two seamed fabrics. See above or Fig. 8.7.*

---

4. Press pieced border so seam allowance is to the inside. Stitch-in-the-ditch on one side of each corner square so the squares have been quilted around the two inside edges (Fig. 5.8; see also Fig. 8.7).

## FINISH BACKING AND LAST BORDER

Instead of adding another border, the backing is brought over the front, encasing the batting and covering the raw edge of the pieced border.

You have handled your quilt a lot during its construction, so you may have to square up the batting and backing. Measure and trim where necessary so batting and backing are square.

1. Press a 1/2" hem to the wrong side all the way around the backing square.

---

**Sew-How:** *Instead of measuring, pinning, and pressing a narrow hem, take your sewing gauge to the ironing board and move the guide the desired distance required for the hem. Fold the edge over the end of the gauge so the raw edge is even with the guide and press (Fig. 5.9). Continue down the length of the edge, folding and pressing as you go.*

---

# Sew a Quilt

For longer hems, use this same pressing technique with a metal Scovill-Dritz EZY-HEM Gauge, available in sewing stores.

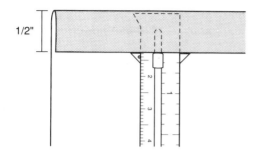

**Fig. 5.9.**
Fold fabric edge over end of gauge so raw edge is even with the guide. Press.

2. Miter each corner as described in Chapter 4 (Fig. 4.6). Note that once the stitching line is established, the miter in your quilt is made by stitching through the 1/2" pressed hem in Step 1 above.

3. Trim a 1/2" square out of each corner of the batting to reduce bulk. Turn batting under 1/2" all the way around. This extra loft gives a fuller look to the outside edge of the border.

4. Turn miter right side out. Pin backing so the hem edge covers raw edges of pieced border. Stitch 1/16" inside the folded edge (Fig. 5.10).

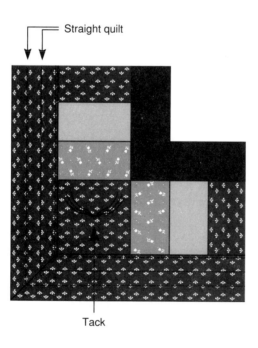

**Fig. 5.10**
Using the walking foot, straight quilt two rows inside backing border, 5/8" apart.

**Sew-How:** *For precise stitching, guide the folded edge by the right inside toe of the presser foot. Then move the needle position so stitching is 1/16" from the fold.*

## STRAIGHT-STITCH QUILTING

1. Using the walking foot, and top and bobbin thread to match backing, straight stitch quilt 5/8" inside the backing border. Quilt another row, 5/8" next to the first (Fig. 5.10). Either guide it by a line on your needle plate or put masking tape on it to use as a guide.

2. Turn your quilt over. You should see a square quilted in each corner and two concentric squares quilted in the middle around the medallion. Look at the threads you have not tied off yet. Are they even with the outside concentric square? If not, loosen a couple of stitches so the rows meet. Then tie off free threads. Three rows of straight quilting should be around the edge to create a border.

3. Hand stitch plastic drapery rings on the top back of wall hanging.

## TIE A QUILT

Another option to quilting-as-you-go or stitch-in-the-ditch quilting, as you did at the squares in each corner, is to tie a quilt together. Use the three-step zigzag and tack a triple strand of 3–4" length of pearl cotton in the center of the strand, through the quilt sandwich (see Fig.5.10 and Fig. 8.43). Lock and tie off the stitches; then tie the pearl cotton into a square knot. Clip ends to 1/2".

# TRANSFERABLE LEARNINGS

The information and techniques you have learned and practiced by constructing the quilted wall hanging have given you skills necessary to sew other projects. You have learned how to:

• Preshrink woven fabrics by snipping a triangle off each corner to cut down on raveling. This is helpful when preshrinking any woven fabric.

• Measure, mark, and cut accurately—necessary for advanced projects like tailoring and more complicated quilting projects.

• Move the fabric freely under a stitching needle. The movement and technique for free-machine quilting is similar to free-machine embroidery.

• Piece using precise 1/4" seams.

• Use a larger-eyed needle when stitching through quilt sandwich or other heavy fabric so thread won't shred or break.

• Quilt using the stitch-in-the-ditch technique. The same technique is used to tack down facings and waistbands.

• Quilt with a straigh stitch to create a textured border. This technique is done with the walking foot to stitch yardage that is cut for jacket or tote bag linings. Using a lighter-weight batting and the quilting guide, then straight-stitch quilt table coverings and other lighter weight-projects.

• Create a border for a quilt or any wall hanging by turning the backing over the front and mitering the corners.

• Adjust your needle position, rather than move the fabric, for precise seam allowances and topstitching.

• Press a narrow hem, using your hem gauge and iron, to save a lot of hand pinning.

• Tie a quilt using the three-step zigzag. This technique is also a way to tack down facings, small appliqués, and embroideries.

---

In the next chapter, Sew Toys, we'll make stuffed fabric blocks and a stuffed hobbyhorse, whimsical projects that help us discover what fun it is to use the fringe foot and weaver's reed.

# SEW TOYS

● *Step One: Plan Your Projects*

● *Step Two: Sew Jumbo Fabric Blocks*

● *Step Three: Make a Hobbyhorse*

● *Transferable Learnings*

---

*Step One:*

# PLAN YOUR PROJECTS

Fabric lends itself beautifully to making toys. It's pliable, washable, and, when stuffed, irresistably cuddly. In this chapter, new sewers start by making fabric blocks. If you don't have a little person in your life, the principles learned here will be helpful in making other stuffed fabric structures. Decorate the blocks and make them smaller for Christmas ornaments. Make them much larger and use canvas or Naugahyde for a hassock or a bean bag chair.

The hobbyhorse is made of both straight and curved shapes—so you'll clip and notch seam allowances to make smooth, continuous curves. You'll also use the fringe foot to make eyelashes and the weaver's reed to make the mane—these accessories add texture and dimension to projects.

## FABRIC AND THREAD

The fabrics and supplies used in both projects are easy to work with—woven cotton/polyester blends, felt, and polyester fiberfill.

Make both projects washable by preshrinking the fabric in the same way you plan to take care of the finished project. Although you may find wool felt, look for washable polyester felt, available in a rainbow of colors at your local fabric or craft store. Make the mane of the hobbyhorse out of a washable nylon or cotton yarn.

Because both the blocks and hobbyhorse are constructed of different colored fabrics, use nylon monofilament thread, top and bobbin, unless directed otherwise. This way, you don't have to rethread with each fabric color change.

*Step Two:*

# SEW JUMBO FABRIC BLOCKS

The following instructions are for making three fabric blocks at a time.

## Supplies

- 1/4 yd. (23cm) each of woven cotton/polyester in a red print and green print; blue, black, white, and yellow solids

- 2 black polyester felt squares

- 1/2 bag of polyester fiberfill (save remainder for hobbyhorse)

- nylon monofilament thread

- red, blue, green, white, and yellow all-purpose, rayon, or 100% cotton embroidery thread

- 5" wide (12.5cm) strip of Wonder-Under (if you are making the game board later in this book, buy a yard [meter])

- rotary cutter, mat and see-through ruler

- tracing paper and vanishing marker

- freezer wrap

- print motif fabric to cut appliqués from (e.g., trucks, airplanes, flowers, etc.)

- woven fusible interfacing

- blunt scissors, point turner, or wooden spoon

## DECORATE THE SQUARES

1. Cut three 6" (15cm) squares each in white, black, blue, and yellow solids; green print and red print.

2. At your local copy center, enlarge letters to twice the size in Fig. 6.1. Using the tracing paper and marker, trace letters from the photocopy to make your pattern.

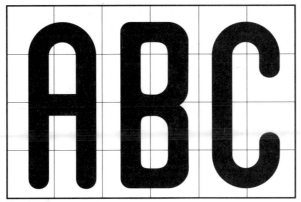

One square = one inch.

Fig. 6.1
Trace letters to make
the pattern for the
fabric blocks. Pattern
is 1/2 size.

3. Fuse Wonder-Under on the wrong side of black felt squares, and the appliqué fabric, following manufacturer's instructions.

4. Cut out three each of the letters from the black felt and remove the paper backing.

- Center and fuse the letter A to two red squares and one yellow square.
- Center and fuse the letter B to two blue squares and one green square.
- Center and fuse the letter C to two green squares and one yellow square.
- Center and fuse the appliqués cut from printed fabric to the three white squares.

5. Stitch black felt letters to the squares.

**Machine Readiness Checklist**

| | |
|---|---|
| **Stitch:** | straight |
| **Length:** | 2; 13 spi |
| **Width:** | 0 |
| **Foot:** | standard zigzag or blind hem |
| **Needle:** | 80/12 universal |
| **Thread:** | nylon monofilament |
| **Tension:** | top, loosened halfway between normal and loose; bobbin, normal |

Straight stitch around each letter, guiding 1/8" (3mm) from cut edge.

**Sew-How:** *If you use the blind hem foot, use the guide in the foot to guide along the edge of the letter. You may have to decenter the needle slightly to stitch 1/8" (3mm) from the edge (see your instruction book) (See Figs. 9.12, 9.13).*

Backstitch or lockstitch at beginning and end of each letter. Press each lettered square with the right side down using a hot iron and steam.

6. Satin stitch around the appliqué (see Fig. 8.25).

7. Iron freezer wrap to the wrong side of each decorated square. Fuse woven interfacing to the wrong side of each undecorated square. Top thread your machine with red thread. Stack the decorated squares and set to one side of your machine. Set the undecorated squares aside. Set your machine for a satin stitch.

### Machine Readiness Checklist

| | |
|---|---|
| **Stitch:** | zigzag (satin stitch) |
| **Length:** | 0.5; 60 spi |
| **Width:** | 2 |
| **Foot:** | transparent embroidery |
| **Thread:** | top, red, blue, yellow, and green rayon, or 100% cotton embroidery; bobbin, darning or nylon monofilament |
| **Tension:** | top, loosened slightly; bobbin, normal |

8. Top thread your machine with red thread. With the right side up, stitch a row of satin stitches, guiding 1/2" (1.3cm) from the raw edge of one side of each square.

9. Using yellow thread on one side, blue thread on one side, and green thread on one side of each square, rethread and satin stitch 1/2" (1.3mm) from the raw edge (Fig. 6.2). On those squares where the thread is the same color as the fabric, rethread the top with white to stitch the last row of satin stitches.

**Fig. 6.2**
With red thread, stitch a row of satin stitches guiding 1/2" (1.3cm) from the raw edge on one side of each specified square. Rethread and repeat for the other three sides using yellow thread on one side, blue thread on one side, and green thread on one side.

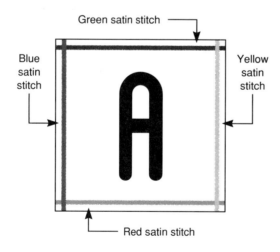

Green satin stitch

Blue satin stitch

Yellow satin stitch

Red satin stitch

---

**Sew-How:** *To satin stitch each square quickly, butt one square up to the next, and satin stitch one side, stitching one color at a time. When stitched, the squares resemble a kite tail. Clip threads between the squares to separate them, then restack for the next satin-stitched color (see Fig. 8.41).*

## ASSEMBLE JUMBO BLOCKS

1. Separate squares so each block is made of one appliqué square, three letter squares (A, B, and C), and two plain squares. Using the vanishing marker, mark dots 1/4" (6mm) from each corner on each square.

2. With right sides together, pin lettered A, B, and C squares next to each other. Then, pin appliquéd square next to the letter A square. Straight stitch squares together, using exact 1/4" (6mm) seam allowances, starting and stopping seams at each dot (Fig. 6.3). Press seams flat and together; then press seams open. Press 1/4" (6mm) seam allowances on the two short ends of the row of stitched squares.

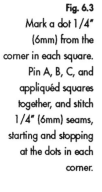

**Fig. 6.3**
Mark a dot 1/4" (6mm) from the corner in each square. Pin A, B, C, and appliquéd squares together, and stitch 1/4" (6mm) seams, starting and stopping at the dots in each corner.

---

**Sew-How:** *To save a lot of time hand tying threads at the beginning and end of each seam, start and stop each seam with the automatic stop or tie-off on your machine. (This feature is not on all machines, so check your instruction book or call your local dealer and ask.)*

---

3. With right sides together, align the bottom of the A square to one side of the plain bottom square, matching dots. Place block under the standard metal or Teflon-coated presser foot so the plain square that makes the bottom of the block is against the feed dogs. Starting at the dot and 1/4" (6mm) from the corner, sew the first side, stopping with your needle in the fabric at the dot in the opposite corner (Fig. 6.4A).

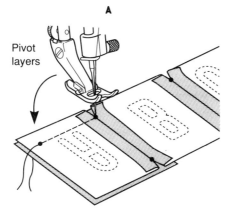

**Fig. 6.4A**
Align the bottom of A square to one side of plain bottom square, and stitch a 1/4" (6mm) seam starting and stopping at the dots in the corner.

Lift the presser foot and pivot work 90 degrees. Align the bottom of the B square with the corresponding side of the bottom square. Lower presser foot and stitch the bottom of the B square to the second side of the plain square, stopping with the needle in the dot at the corner (Fig. 6.4B). Repeat for the other two sides of the bottom square to create the block.

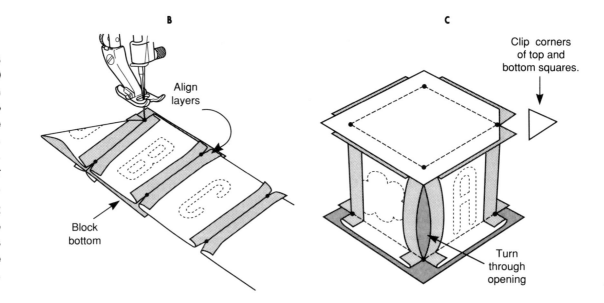

Align
layers

Block
bottom

Clip corners
of top and
bottom squares.

Turn
through
opening

**Fig. 6.4B**
Pivot both layers 90 degrees, and align bottom of B square to corresponding side of bottom square. Stitch to the next dot. Repeat for other two sides.

**Fig. 6.4C**
Stitch the top plain square as shown to create the rest of the block.

4. Repeat Step 3 to stitch the top square to the block (Fig. 6.4C).

5. Turn block right side out, through the opening. Using a pair of blunt-nosed scissors or a point turner, gently push out each corner of the block, so it's sharp and square.

6. Using a handful of fiberfill, begin stuffing the block until it is comfortably full. Use scissor points, wooden spoon handle, or point turner to push fiberfill into each corner.

7. Turn seam allowance of opening toward inside of block, and pin it shut.

8. Decenter your needle to the far left (see your instruction book), and straight stitch the opening closed guiding 1/8" (3mm) from the edge. Tie off thread ends.

Aren't the blocks cute?...and so easy to make. Are you ready for something more challenging? Let's make the hobbyhorse.

*Step Three:*

# MAKE A HOBBYHORSE

### Supplies

- 1/2 yd. (.5m) red cotton print

- 1/8 yd. (12cm) blue and white cotton print

- black polyester felt scrap for eyes and nostrils

- white polyester felt scrap for eyes

- 1 oz. (28g) ball of cotton or nylon yarn for mane

- two 1" (2.5cm) red or blue buttons for the bridle

- nylon monofilament thread
- black thread
- Wonder-Under
- 1/2 bag of polyester fiberfill (remainder used for Jumbo Fabric Blocks)
- graph paper (1" (2.5cm) square preferred), tracing paper, pencil
- French curve (optional)
- 2 yds. (2m) blue 1" (2.5cm)-wide grosgrain ribbon for bridle and reins
- #3 pearl cotton
- hand needle
- 1 broom handle
- weaver's reed
- adding-machine tape
- seam sealant (e.g., Fray-Check)

## MAKE THE PATTERN

1. If you have access to a photocopy machine, enlarge the pattern to twice the size in Fig. 6.5A, B and C. Note that gusset (Fig 6.5B) must be joined at the arrows as shown.

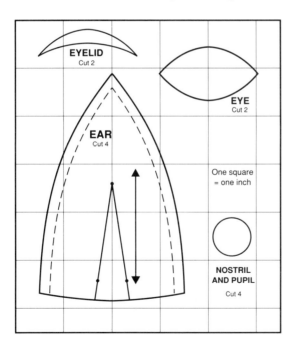

**Fig. 6.5A**
Hobbyhorse pattern
ear and eye pieces.
Pattern is 1/2 size.

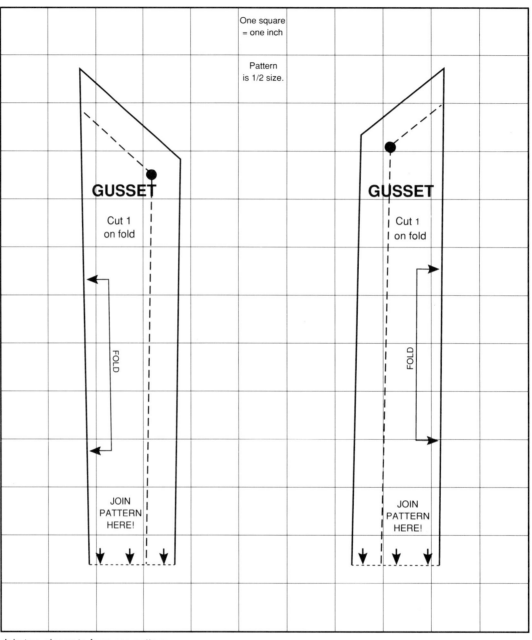

**Fig. 6.5B**
Hobbyhorse pattern
gusset piece.
Pattern is 1/2 size.

Join two pieces to form one pattern.

To enlarge the pattern freehand, each square on the pattern represents a square inch (2.5cm) on your graph paper. Begin counting blocks and plot dots in each square of your graph paper where the direction of the line changes.

2. Use the French curve, moving and pivoting between the dots marked, to approximate the curves. Note that each pattern piece includes the seam allowance. The ear pattern uses 1/4" (6mm) seam allowances; other pattern pieces have 5/8" (1.5cm) seam allowances.

3. On each pattern piece, mark the grainline, dots, and ear and eye placement; then label each piece and mark how many of each one to cut.

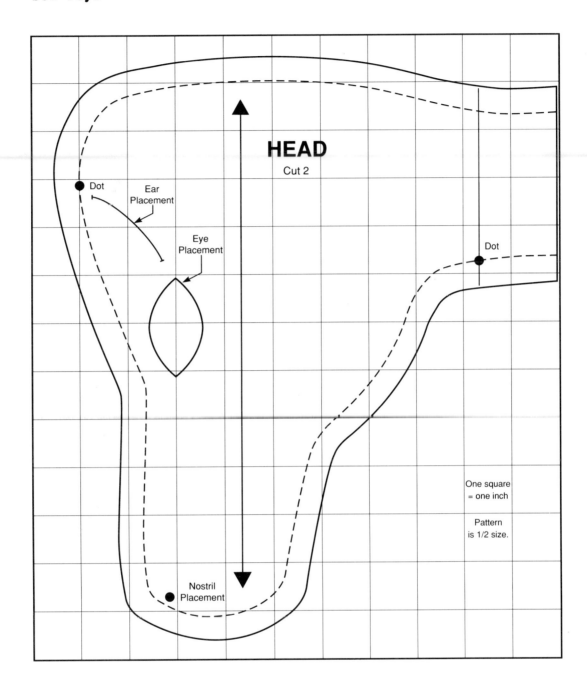

**Fig. 6.5C**
Hobbyhorse pattern
head piece.
Pattern is 1/2 size.

## MAKE THE HORSE

1. Fuse a piece of Wonder-Under to the underside of the black and white felt pieces. Cut out eye pieces and nostrils. Remove paper backing from the black pupils. Center and fuse them to the white eye pieces.

2. Lay out and cut horse pattern pieces, following the grainlines marked on each piece. Cut gusset and ear pieces from blue and white print. Cut head pieces from red print.

3. Mark darts on ear pieces by pushing pins straight through the dots, then mark with chalk (Fig. 6.6).

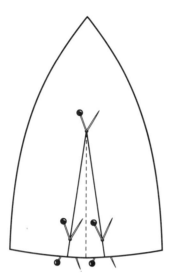

**Fig. 6.6**
Mark darts on ear pieces by pushing pins straight through the dots.

## Ears

**Machine Readiness Checklist**

|  |  |
|---|---|
| **Stitch:** | straight |
| **Length:** | 2–2.5; 10–12 spi |
| **Width:** | 0 |
| **Foot:** | standard zigzag or Teflon-coated |
| **Needle:** | 80/12 universal |
| **Thread:** | all-purpose to match fabric or nylon monofilament |
| **Tension:** | normal |

1. Fold and stitch darts; then press dart to one side.

---

**New Sewer's Note:** *Start stitching a dart at the wide end, stitching to the point. Do not backstitch at the point—you may end up with a pouch that will not press out. Tie off threads at the point of dart.*

---

2. Place two ear pieces, right sides together, and sew a 1/4" (6mm) seam with a 2 length straight stitch, leaving the straight side open. Clip across point at the top, close to the stitching line. Press ear flat. Repeat for other ear (Fig. 6.7).

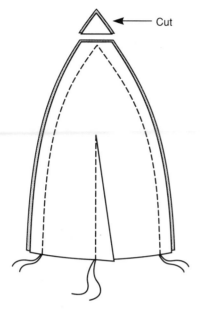

Cut

**Fig. 6.7**
Place two ear pieces right sides together, and sew a 1/4" (6mm) seam with a 2 length (13 spi) straight stitch. Clip across point and press seams flat and together.

3. Trim seam allowance to 1/8" (3mm). Turn ears right side out. Gently push point out with blunt end of scissors or a point turner. Turn under raw edge 1/4" (6mm) at the base of each ear and press.

4. Stuff a little fiberfill in each ear, pushing it to the point with blunt end scissors or point turner. Do not overstuff.

## Head

1. Remove Wonder-Under paper from white eye piece with pupil and fuse to the head as marked.

| Machine Readiness Checklist | |
| --- | --- |
| Stitch: | straight; zigzag |
| Length: | 2–2.5; 10–12 spi |
| Width: | 0; 4 |
| Foot: | transparent embroidery; fringe |
| Thread: | nylon monofilament; black all-purpose |
| Tension: | top, loosened slightly; bobbin, normal |

Using nylon monofilament thread, the transparent embroidery foot, and slightly loosened upper tension, topstitch 1/8" (3mm) from cut edge first on white eye piece, then on pupil.

2. Rethread top and bobbin with black thread. Using the fringe foot, stitch the eyelashes on each eye, guiding the middle of the foot where eyelid and white pieces overlap (see Fig. 9.32).

3. Position and pin ears on each side of the head. Whipstitch ears to head pieces.

**New Sewer's Note:** *A whipstitch is a catching stitch done with a hand needle and thread. Thread needle and tie a knot. Insert needle at right angles and close to the folded edge, picking up a few threads from the ear and head fabrics. Stitches should be close together and slightly angled so ears are stitched securely to the head piece (Fig. 6.8).*

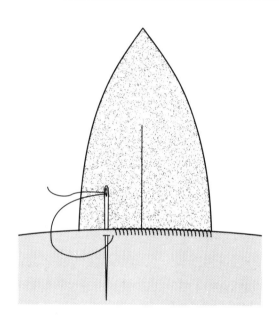

**Fig. 6.8**
Whipstitch ears to head piece by inserting the hand needle at right angles and close to the folded edge, picking up a few threads from the ear and head fabrics. Stitch close together and at a slight angle so ears are stitched securely to the head.

4. Clip each corner of head piece and gusset, cutting into seam allowance 1/2" (1.3cm).

**New Sewer's Note:** *A clip is a short, 1/2" (1.3cm) cut in a seam allowance. When stitching a straight piece to a curved or angled piece of fabric, clipping allows a curve or corner to open and lie flat so the fabric pieces fit together easily. Use your scissor tips to clip, so you don't cut too far into the seam allowance.*

Starting at the dot on the wide end of gusset, place right sides together, pinning one head piece to one side of gusset, following down and around the head piece to the dot at the neck.

**Sew-How:** *Clip 1/2" (1.3cm) into gusset seam allowance when it turns each corner.*

5. Straight stitch on the 5/8" (1.5cm) seam allowance, stitching from the dot at the top of the head, stopping at the dot at the neck. Repeat pinning, clipping, and stitching procedure for the other side of head piece. Seams should come together at the point of each gusset. Clip seam allowance at each curve as shown (Fig. 6.9). Turn right side out.

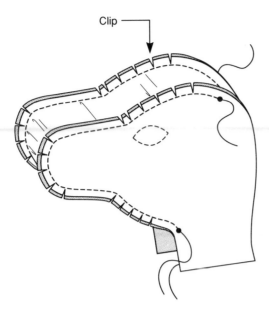

**Fig. 6.9**
Clip 1/2" (1.3cm) into gusset seam allowance each time it turrns a corner. Also clip into the seam allowance at each curve as shown so the fabric smoothly follows the curve of the seam.

6. Place nostrils at the end of the nose and fuse in place. Zigzag tack in the center of each nostril (see Fig. 8.27). It may be easier to stitch this with the head turned inside out.

## Mane and Bangs

1. Cut a piece of adding-machine tape 24" (61cm) long. Wrap weaver's reed with yarn and straight stitch yarn to adding-machine tape to make fringe for the mane (see Fig. 9.46).

2. Cut off about 4-1/2" (11.5cm) of fringe. Pull off the adding-machine tape and pin fringe across the widest part of the gusset (forehead) to make bangs, positioning the long loops toward the nose.

**Sew-How:** *After adding-machine tape has been removed, the fringe grows in length a little bit.*

| Machine Readiness Checklist | |
|---|---|
| **Stitch:** | straight |
| **Length:** | 3; 9 spi |
| **Width:** | 0 |
| **Foot:** | transparent embroidery |
| **Thread:** | all-purpose to match fringe or nylon monofilament |
| **Tension:** | normal |

Stitch fringe to gusset, centering the foot over the original stitching line. Cut another length of fringe, shorter than the first. Pin and straight stitch it above the first row of fringe, overlapping it slightly so the long loops hide the previous row of stitching. Repeat until the crown is covered with fringe, stitching one row of fringe above the next. Cut loops after fringe is secured to the crown.

3. Turn head inside out. Carefully remove adding-machine tape from the unused fringe. Pin back head pieces, right sides together, sandwiching fringe in the seam allowance. Stop fringe 1-1/2" (3.8cm) from the neck opening (Fig. 6.10). Stitch seam.

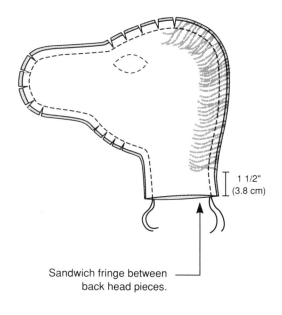

**Fig. 6.10**
Sandwich fringe between the two head pieces. Stop fringe 1-1/2" (3.8cm) from the neck opening and stitch.

1 1/2" (3.8 cm)

Sandwich fringe between back head pieces.

**Sew-How:** *You may have some fringe left. It will be used to thicken the top of the mane.*

4. Turn under raw neck edge 1/2" (1.3cm) and press. Gather over a 10" (25.5cm) length of pearl cotton around neck opening (see Fig. 8.21), guiding 1/8" (3mm) from fold.

**Sew-How:** *The pearl cotton is used to draw up the head once it is attached to the broom handle, so it has to be strong. Therefore, use at least a #3 pearl cotton or fine string so it won't break when pulled.*

5. Turn head right side out. Take remainder of fringe and fold it in half on the stitching line. Starting at the top of the mane, sandwich loose fringe around the fringe stitched in the seam. Straight stitch loose fringe to mane, backstitching at beginning and end. Cut yarn loops. **Note:** If machine stitching is too cumbersome, use a double thread, and hand stitch this extra fringe to the mane.

6. Stuff head with fiberfill. The neck opening should be large enough to reach your hand in to stuff fill into the corners. If it isn't, use a ruler or a wooden spoon to push fill in place.

## Bridle

1. Put ribbon around the end of the nose so it fits snuggly. Cut and seam it into a circle. Put the larger length of ribbon at right angles to create the reins. Seam it into a circle. Pin bridle together where ribbons intersect, long ribbon beneath short ribbon circle, so the seam on the small ribbon is under the chin, and the seam of large ribbon is under the intersection (Fig. 6.11). (You may have to put the bridle on the horse for proper positioning).

**Fig. 6.11**
To make the bridle, put a circle of ribbon around the end of the nose and seam it together. Put a smaller length of ribbon at right angles to the first. Pin where ribbons intersect, so the seam on the first ribbon is under the chin, and the seam of the large ribbon is under the intersect. Machine stitch buttons at each intersect.

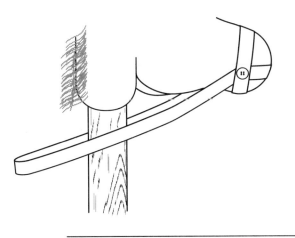

**Sew-How:** *Put a drop of seam sealant on ribbon ends to prevent raveling.*

2. In order to stitch the buttons in place, remove bridle and stitch a button on each side where ribbons intersect (see Fig. 8.16, 8.17, 9.19).

3. Hand tack bridle at each seamline so it won't slip off when hobbyhorse is played with.

4. Put broom handle up in the head. You may have to stuff extra fiberfill around broom handle to secure it.

5. Draw up pearl cotton, gathering the neck around broom handle and tie securely.

# TRANSFERABLE LEARNINGS

The information and techniques you have learned by making the fabric blocks and hobbyhorse have given you the skills necessary to sew many other projects. You have learned to:

• Enlarge and draw a pattern from a reduced version using graph paper and a curve—helpful for enlarging other patterns. Using a curve is also helpful when making some pattern alterations.

• Stitch, turn, stuff, and close three-dimensional shapes. Techniques are the same for stuffed toys, some pillows, a hassock, or a bean bag chair.

• Insert a gusset. Use this technique in garment construction, as well as for slip covers, pillows, and cushions.

• Use Wonder-Under to make any fabric fusible.

• Properly fuse one fabric to the other with heat, moisture, and pressure.

• Appliqué using a straight stitch on a nonraveling fabric. Use this technique with leather, vinyl, or suede.

• Sew a dart. Darts are used in other projects to create shape so that a pattern piece conforms to the shape of the body.

• Use the fringe foot to make eyelashes.

• Make yarn fringe using the weaver's reed. Make fringe trim this way to match any fabric, rather than searching for fringe trim by the yard.

• Gather over a cord for even gathers. This also adds strength to the gathering stitch so thread won't break. This technique is used to gather almost any medium to heavy fabric.

---

I hope that, in addition to your exploring another area in our World of Sewing, your family members will enjoy playing with the blocks and hobbyhorse you made as you stitched your way through in this chapter.

Next you will further your knowledge by sewing gifts. The key rings make great gifts for anyone and take as long to make as it would to shop for something, and each is personalized for the recipient. The fabric game board also makes a welcome gift, for peaceful travel time in a car or plane, or on family vacations.

CHAPTER

7

# SEW GIFTS

- *Step One: Plan Your Projects*
- *Step Two: Sew Three Key Rings*
- *Step Three: Sew a Fabric Game Board and Pouch*
- *Transferable Learnings*

WHEN PEOPLE KNOW YOU SEW, even if it's only once in a while, friends and family sometimes expect a handmade gift. In this chapter, we'll make a few quick gifts using a little ribbon or fabric scraps—you probably have most of the supplies on hand. We will also make a fabric game board and game piece pouch, a welcome gift for family or friends.

*Step One:*

# PLAN YOUR PROJECTS

Everyone needs a set of keys so let's stitch some decorative key rings. I bought a simple metal key ring from the hardware store; the others are kits from a cross-stitch shop (see Sources of Supply). The rest of the supplies are listed under each project.

These small embroideries showcase your stitchery, so use rayon embroidery thread because it has a lot of shine and fills in better than all-purpose thread.

The game board is made of cotton-blend prints and solids, cotton/polyester hem facing (available in 2-1/2 yard [2.3m] packages at your local fabric store), felt, grosgrain ribbon, yarn, and Wonder-Under. The game pouch is made from a red cotton-blend, a black-and-white checked fabric, a zipper, and scraps of turquoise and yellow solids.

---

**Sew-How:** *For a perfect color match to the game board, I had to make this pouch out of knit fabrics. If you, too, have difficulty finding woven fabrics for your pouch, stabilize the knit by fusing a piece of interfacing to the wrong side of each fabric. Then it behaves like a woven fabric.*

---

To make your game board washable, preshrink all the fabrics, except the Wonder-Under and the washable polyester felt. (Washable polyester felt is available at most fabric stores.)

To preshrink hem facing tape without uncreasing the prefolded edges, immerse the tape in very hot tap water leaving it wrapped around the cardboard core; then roll it in a towel to remove most of the moisture. Remove cardboard then line dry or press with a hot iron.

You will also use nylon monofilament thread in both key ring and game board projects. This way, you don't have to rethread the top and bobbin each time you change the fabric color.

*Step Two:*

# SEW THREE KEY RINGS

My machine can stitch letters and numbers—a feature I thought I would use only rarely but which I have come to appreciate. If your machine has the same capacity, make a script monogrammed key ring (Fig. 7.1).

**Fig. 7.1**
Key ring projects

## MAKE THE MONOGRAMMED KEY RING

I subscribe to a lot of needlecraft magazines to see how stitchery of all kinds is stitched and displayed. Although I don't hand cross-stitch, I found many great gift ideas for small stitchery in one of the cross-stitch magazines, which inspired me to seek out a cross-stitch shop in my area. Once there, I found kits of all kinds for bookmarks, paperweights, trivets, and for the key rings described below—an easy way to frame small embroideries stitched on the sewing machine, then to give away as gifts (see Sources of Supply). Take the opportunity to stop into a cross-stitch shop in your area or subscribe to needlecraft magazines for these and other ingenious gift ideas. **Note:** If you can't find key ring kits in your area, skip ahead to the "fob" key ring instructions.

| Machine Readiness Checklist | |
|---|---|
| **Stitch:** | programmed letters |
| **Length:** | varies |
| **Width:** | widest |
| **Foot:** | transparent embroidery |
| **Needle:** | 90/14 stretch |
| **Thread:** | rayon embroidery |
| **Tension:** | top, loosened slightly; bobbin, normal |
| **Fabric:** | 1-1/2 wide x 1-1/2" (3.8 x 3.8cm) long grosgrain ribbon or felt |
| **Accessories:** | key ring kit, freezer wrap, vanishing marker |

1. Iron freezer wrap to the wrong side of ribbon or felt. (Make a test swatch to determine letter spacing.) Mark where to start the lettering and draw a line with the vanishing marker so lettering is straight.

2. Program initials and stitch. Remove the freezer wrap. Press top and bottom up desired amount to fit in acrylic key ring frame. (The key ring kit is similar to a watch. The stitchery fits into a small frame, then a crystal snaps in place over the top.)

## MAKE THE ROUND KEY RING

The round key ring is satin stitched with an off-center plaid design and embroidered initials in one corner.

| **Machine Readiness Checklist** | |
|---|---|
| Stitch: | zigzag (satin stitch) |
| Length: | 0.4–0.6; 60 spi |
| Width: | widest |
| Foot: | transparent embroidery |
| Needle: | 14/90 stretch |
| Thread: | red and blue rayon embroidery |
| Tension: | top, slightly loosened; bobbin, normal |
| Fabric: | closely woven kettle (weaver's) cloth |
| Accessories: | key ring kit, freezer wrap, vanishing marker, seam sealant (optional) |

1. Iron freezer wrap to wrong side of your fabric. Remove crystal from key ring and trace the circle on your fabric. Mark a straight line to follow for the first row of satin stitching.

2. Thread top and bobbin with red thread. Satin stitch one row, starting and stopping just inside the circle. Remove work from the machine and draw another line perpendicular to the first. Satin stitch following that line.

3. Rethread top and bobbin with blue thread. Satin stitch next to the first row of red satin stitches, starting and stopping just inside the circle. Turn your work perpendicular and repeat.

4. Rethread top and bobbin with red thread. Program the appropriate initials. Test for spacing on a scrap. Mark where to start lettering with the vanishing marker. Stitch initials. Remove freezer wrap. Pull threads to the wrong side and tie them off.

---

**Sew-How:** *Put a drop of seam sealant on each knot so they won't pull out.*

---

5. Cut embroidery to fit inside the frame. Snap crystal over the top.

## MAKE THE "FOB" KEY RING

If you can't find a kit like those shown above, buy a simple key ring at the hardware store and embroider a "fob."

**Machine Readiness Checklist**

| | |
|---|---|
| **Stitch:** | closed diamond |
| **Length:** | 0.3–0.5; 60 spi |
| **Width:** | widest |
| **Foot:** | metal embroidery |
| **Needle:** | 90/14 stretch |
| **Thread:** | rayon embroidery; nylon monofilament |
| **Tension:** | top, loosened slightly; bobbin, normal |
| **Fabric:** | Ultrasuede™, Ultraleather™ or felt, fusible interfacing, Wonder-Under |
| **Accessories:** | key ring, tracing paper, vanishing marker |

1. Fuse interfacing to the wrong side of fob fabric. Trace fob pattern in Fig. 7.2.

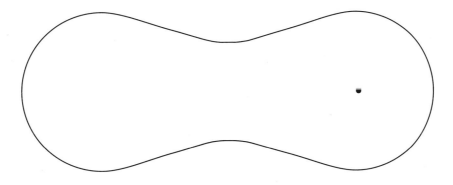

**Fig. 7.2**
Key ring fob pattern.

**New Sewer's Note:** *Set iron on cotton setting. Place interfacing so the rough side is against the wrong side of fob fabric. Dampen a press cloth and fuse interfacing with firm pressure for about 10 seconds. Remove iron, let steam escape, then press again until the fabric and press cloth are dry.*

2. Cut out Ultrasuede, Ultraleather, or felt using the pattern. Cut Wonder-Under slightly smaller than the pattern.

3. On the right side of the fabric, mark the center of one side of fob with a dot, using the vanishing marker (Fig. 7.2).

**Sew-How:** *The design in the center of the fob is a snowflake created by decorative stitches. Before stitching your fob, practice and perfect your technique on a fabric scrap backed with interfacing.*

4. Program your machine for the closed diamond stitch.

---

**Sew-How:** *This diamond flower can be made on many machines because the diamond is a common stitch. However, experiment with other decorative stitches to invent your own motifs.*

---

5. Starting in the center, stitch one diamond and stop. Remove the fabric, cut the threads and turn fob 180 degrees. Stitch another diamond across from the first (Fig. 7.3). Remove fabric, cut threads, and pivot 90 degrees. Starting in the center again, stitch another diamond shape. Repeat for the last diamond. Pull threads to the wrong side and tie them off.

**Fig. 7.3**
Starting in the center, stitch one diamond and stop. Remove the fabric, cut the threads, and turn the fabric 180 degrees. Stitch another diamond across from the first. Remove the fabric, cut the threads, turn the fabric 90 degrees, and stitch another diamond. Repeat for the last diamond.

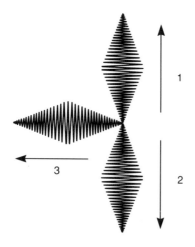

6. Press Wonder-Under to the wrong side of fob, following manufacturer's instructions. After fabric is cool, remove the paper and pull fob through key ring. Line up cut edges and fuse fob together.

7. Rethread top and bobbin with nylon monofilament thread. Put the flat-bottomed Teflon-coated presser foot on the machine (see Fig. 9.5). Decenter the needle to the far left and topstitch 1/8" (3mm) from cut edges. Lock stitches at the end of the stitching.

Wasn't that fun? Let's try something more challenging.

*Step Three:*

# SEW A FABRIC GAME BOARD AND POUCH

The fabric game board is easy to pack, travels well in a car or on a plane, and can stave off back-seat wars during the family vacation. Both backgammon and checker board are combined in one travel game you make yourself.

## Supplies

- 2 packages black wide hem facing (approx. 1-3/4" (4.5cm)) (cotton/polyester blend)

- 2 packages red wide hem facing (approx. 1-3/4" (4.5cm)) (cotton/polyester blend)

- 1 yd. (meter) of 1" (2.5cm) grosgrain ribbon

- 1/2 yd. (45.5cm) Wonder-Under

- 16" (40.5cm) square of cotton/polyester red print fabric

- 1 yellow washable felt square

- 1 blue washable felt square

- 1 white strip and 1 black strip of woven cotton-blend fabric each at least 1-1/2 x 16" (3.8 x 40.5cm)

- nylon monofilament thread

- all-purpose thread in black and white

- 4 yds. (3.6m) black yarn

- tracing paper and water-erasable marker

## MAKE THE BACKGAMMON BOARD

1. Enlarge pattern to twice the size of Fig. 7.4. Trace patterns for triangles and bars.

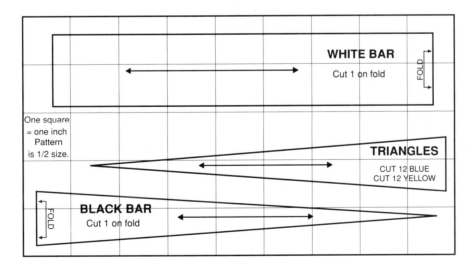

**Fig. 7.4**
Backgammon triangles and bar patterns. Pattern is 1/2 size.

2. Fuse a piece of Wonder-Under on the back of the yellow and the back of the blue felt square, and the wrong side of black and white cotton strips, following manufacturer's instructions.

3. Using the pattern traced in Step 1, cut twelve triangles from yellow felt square and twelve triangles from blue felt square.

**Sew-How:** *To cut both colored triangles at the same time, place yellow and blue felt squares one on top of the other. Use your sharp rotary cutter and see-through ruler to cut through both layers.*

4. Cut out black and white bars.

5. Fold 16" (40.5cm) print square in half and press a crease. Open square. Remove Wonder-Under paper from white strip. Center and fuse white bar over crease on the right side of print square.

| Machine Readiness Checklist | |
|---|---|
| **Stitch:** | zigzag (satin stitch) |
| **Length:** | 0.4–0.6; 60 spi |
| **Width:** | 2 |
| **Foot:** | transparent embroidery |
| **Needle:** | 80/12 universal |
| **Thread:** | white all-purpose or cotton or rayon embroidery |
| **Tension:** | top, loosened slightly; bobbin, normal |

Satin stitch both raw edges of the white bar, centering the raw edge under the foot.

6. Fold square in half again in the other direction, and press a crease. Open square. Remove Wonder-Under paper from the black bar, center and fuse it over crease on the right side of print square. Rethread top and bobbin with black thread and satin stitch both sides of bar.

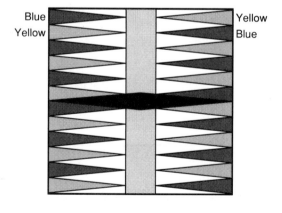

**Fig. 7.5**
Position blue and yellow triangles, alternating colors so the points are exactly opposite one another across the board.

7. Starting on either side of the black bar, remove paper backing and position blue and yellow triangles, alternating colors as shown in Fig. 7.5. Be sure triangle points are exactly opposite one another across the board. Carefully fuse triangles on print square using a damp press cloth and steam.

8. Rethread top and bobbin with nylon monofilament thread.

**Machine Readiness Checklist**

| | |
|---|---|
| **Stitch:** | straight |
| **Length:** | 2; 13 spi |
| **Width:** | 0 |
| **Foot:** | standard zigzag or blind hem |
| **Needle:** | 80/12 universal |
| **Thread:** | nylon monofilament |
| **Tension:** | top, loosened halfway between normal and very loose; bobbin, normal |

Topstitch around each triangle, stitching 1/8" (3mm) from the cut edge. Don't cut threads between triangles. Simply lift the presser foot, turn the fabric around, and continue stitching.

---

**Sew-How:** *When using the blind hem foot, guide the straight edge of appliqué to the inside of the right toe. If necessary, move the needle position slightly to the left so stitching is 1/8" (3mm) from cut edge of felt (see Figs. 9.12, 9.13).*

---

9. With the wrong side up, press backgammon board with steam.

10. Cut a 16" (40.5cm) square of Wonder-Under and fuse it to the wrong side of backgammon board. After cooling, remove the paper backing. This enables you to fuse the checkerboard to the back of the backgammon board.

---

**Sew-How:** *Save Wonder-Under paper to use as a paper press cloth. Put the paper over your work to prevent fusible web from gumming up the sole plate of your iron.*

---

## MAKE THE CHECKERBOARD

1. Cut eight 16" (40.5cm) strips of black hem facing and eight 16" (40.5cm) strips of red hem facing.

2. Starting in the center of the board and working out, pin black hem facing strips next to each other on one side of the board. **Note:** Leave the hems in hem facing strips.

3. Pin red hem facing strips next to each other on a side adjacent to the first, weaving them in and out of black strips as shown (Fig. 7.6).

4. Set iron on the hottest setting. Thoroughly dampen a press cloth and place it over the checkerboard.

**Fig. 7.6**
Pin black strips next to each other on one side of the board. Pin red strips next to each other on a side adjacent to the first, weaving them in and out of black strips.

5. Fuse checkerboard to the back of backgammon board. For a permanent bond, apply a lot of pressure, and press work until it is dry.

## FINISH THE EDGE

1. Straighten the edges of your board using the rotary cutter, mat, and cutting ruler.

2. Starting in the middle of a straight edge, couch over yarn or double strand of pearl cotton.

| Machine Readiness Checklist | |
| --- | --- |
| **Stitch:** | zigzag |
| **Length:** | 2; 13 spi |
| **Width:** | 4 |
| **Foot:** | narrow braiding or transparent embroidery |
| **Needle:** | 80/12 universal |
| **Thread:** | all-purpose black |
| **Tension:** | normal |
| **Accessories:** | black yarn or pearl cotton |

Guide the yarn so the needle stitches into the fabric on the left and swings off the edge at the right (see Figs. 8.19, 9.20, 9.21). Stitch a gentle curve at the corners (with the needle on the inside corner, pivot fabric around it). At the join, cut yarn off, overlap the ends, and zigzag couch over them.

3. Satin stitch over couched yarn or pearl cotton using a 0.6 length (60 spi), 4–6 width zigzag stitch, and slightly loosened upper tension (see Fig. 8.25). Flair stitches out at the corners, using the inside of the corner as a pivot point (see Chapter 3, Fig. 3.3).

4. Satin stitch around the edge again, using a slightly longer stitch length and the widest stitch width. This second row of satin stitches over the first helps to firm up and finish the edge of the board.

5. To smooth out the satin-stitched edge, couch over another piece of yarn around the outside edge of game board.

### Machine Readiness Checklist

|  |  |
|---|---|
| **Stitch:** | zigzag |
| **Length:** | 1.5–2; 13–20 spi |
| **Width:** | 3 |
| **Foot:** | narrow braiding |
| **Thread:** | all-purpose black, top and bobbin |
| **Tension:** | normal |

Guide so the needle stitches just into the satin stitches on the left and swings over the yarn and off the edge on the right. As before, overlap yarn ends and couch over them.

6. Cut a length of grosgrain ribbon, 27" (68.5cm) long, and stitch it onto one end of the board by stitching-in-the-ditch along the satin stitched edge. Roll the board up and tie the ribbon into a bow.

## MAKE THE GAME PIECE POUCH

### Supplies

- Wonder-Under scraps

- two 9" (23cm) squares of red cotton or cotton-blend fabric

- 3 x 9" (7.5 X 22.9cm) strip of black-and-white checked fabric

- 2-1/4" (5.7cm) square of yellow fabric

- 1-5/8" (4cm) square of turquoise fabric (Lycra® spandex swim wear fabric works well)

- fusible interfacing (optional)

- 10–12" (25.5–30.5cm) zipper

- red all-purpose thread; yellow and turquoise rayon embroidery thread

1. Fuse Wonder-Under to the back of the yellow and turquoise fabrics before cutting them out. If the red and checked fabrics are knits, fuse interfacing to the wrong side of each piece.

2. Center and fuse yellow square on checked fabric as shown (Fig. 7.7). Satin stitch around it with a 2.5–3 width zigzag (see Fig. 8.25).

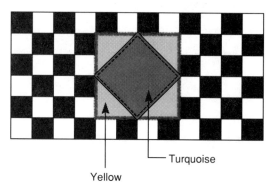

Turquoise

Yellow

3. Turn turquoise square on end, position and fuse over yellow square as shown (Fig. 7.7). If this fabric is a knit, straight stitch around it guiding 1/8" (3mm) from the raw edge. If it is a woven fabric, satin stitch around it, as you did for the yellow square.

4. Fold back a 1/2" (1.3cm) seam allowance on the two long edges of the checked fabric and press toward the wrong side. Center the checked strip on the right side of a red square, and position it so it goes across the grain. Topstitch along the two folded edges with a 3 length (9 spi) straight stitch and red thread (Fig. 7.8).

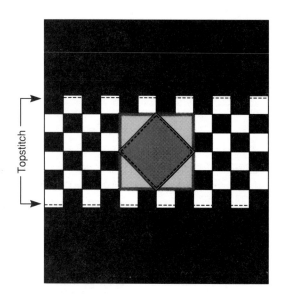

Topstitch

## INSERT THE ZIPPER

1. Place zipped zipper along one 9" (23cm) edge of decorated square, right sides together, so the zipper is parallel to the checkered strip, and aligning the edge of zipper tape with the cut edge. Note that the pull should be at one end of zipper, out of the way (Fig. 7.9A).

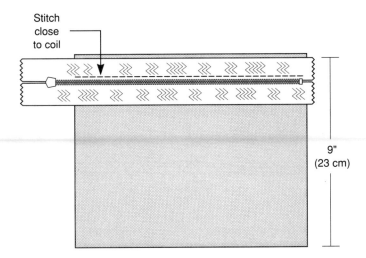

Stitch
close
to coil

9"
(23 cm)

**Fig. 7.9A**
Place decorated pouch
piece and zipper, right
sides together, aligning
edge of zipper and
fabric edge. Pull
should be to one end,
zipper stop at the
other end. Stitch close
to coil.

2. Using your zipper foot (Fig. 9.14) and a 3 length (9 spi) straight stitch, stitch zipper to fabric, sewing next to the zipper coil. Press seam away from the coil (Fig. 7.9B).

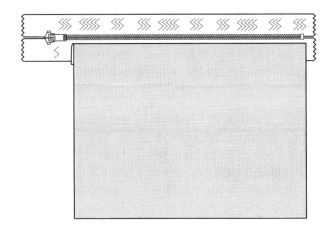

**Fig. 7.9B**
Press seam away
from coil.

3. Repeat for the other edge of zipper on plain fabric square, being sure the cut edge is aligned with the edge of zipper tape and is across the grain and even with the first red square (Fig. 7.9C). This is called an exposed zipper application because the zipper coil is exposed.

**Fig. 7.9C**
Repeat to stitch the
other side of zipper
to other side of
pouch piece.

4. Unzip zipper slightly. Tack top of zipper so the two sides of the coil are together 1/2" (1.3mm) inside the cut edge of pouch (Figs. 7.9D, 8.27). Cut excess zipper tape off, even with the edge of the fabric.

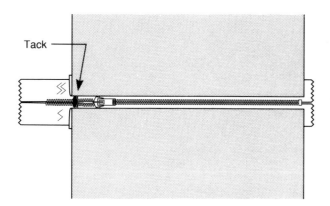

**Fig. 7.9D**
Tack top of zipper coil
so the pull will not
come off track.

**Sew-How:** *If you should accidentally slide the pull off the coil before tacking over it, remove the metal stop at the bottom of zipper. Then slide the pull back on track from the bottom up. Remember to replace the metal stop or tack across the bottom of the zipper.*

5. With the zipper still unzipped about 3" (7.5cm), place pouch, right sides together, and straight stitch around the remaining three sides of the pouch using a 1/2" (1.3mm) seam allowance. Backstitch over zipper coil a few times to secure both ends of the seam. Open zipper all the way, then turn the pouch right side out and press.

**Sew-How:** *To make the zipper easier to work, loop a couple of strands of #3 pearl cotton through the hole in the pull (see color pages).*

## MAKE GAME PIECES

If you don't have an extra set of game pieces, make your own out of red and black felt. Each player needs fifteen game pieces for backgammon (only twelve for checkers), so make thirty pieces.

**Machine Readiness Checklist**

| | |
|---|---|
| **Stitch:** | scallop; satin stitch |
| **Length:** | 0.5; 60 spi |
| **Width:** | widest for scallop; 2 for satin stitch |
| **Foot:** | transparent embroidery |
| **Needle:** | 80/12 universal |
| **Thread:** | yellow and white cotton embroidery |
| **Tension:** | top, loosened slightly; bobbin, normal |
| **Fabric:** | 2 squares each of black and red felt |
| **Accessories:** | Wonder-Under, diappearing dressmaker's chalk, or soap sliver |

1. Fuse a piece of Wonder-Under on one black felt square and one red felt square.

2. Mark fifteen 1-1/4" (3.2cm) squares on remaining black and remaining red felt squares using a soap sliver or disappearing dressmaker's chalk.

3. On twelve squares of each color, sew a decorative stitch to create the crowns for the checkers (optional). I used a partial scallop stitch for the top and a 2 width satin stitch for the bottom of each crown.

---

**Sew-How:** *To center the crown in each square, use the quilting guide along the edge of each square (Fig. 7.10).*

---

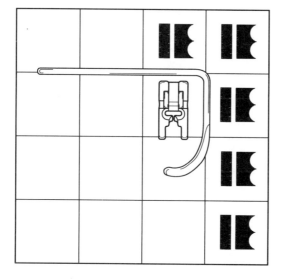

**Fig. 7.10**
Center crown on each square using the quilting guide along the edge of each square.

4. Remove Wonder-Under paper, then fuse a plain black piece of felt on the back of black decorated pieces. Repeat stitching and fusing procedure for red felt piece. Cut 1-1/4" (3.2cm) squares apart. Trim each square into a circle to finish each game piece.

Put game pieces in the pouch, roll pouch in the game board, and tie ribbons into a bow.

.......

# TRANSFERABLE LEARNINGS

The information and techniques you have learned and practiced in making the gifts in this chapter have given you skills necessary to sew other projects. You have learned how to:

• Stitch and center lettering on a project.

• Use nylon monofilament thread top and bobbin so you don't have to rethread for different color fabrics in the same project.

• Appliqué using a straight stitch on fabrics that don't ravel, such as felt, leather, knits, suede, or synthetic leather or suede. Appliqué using a satin stitch on fabrics that ravel.

• Use Wonder-Under to make any fabric fusible.

• Use the blind hem foot to topstitch evenly from a cut or finished edge—helpful when topstitching a pocket, lapel, front tab, belt loop, waistband, tote bag strap—the list goes on.

• Move needle position rather than the fabric to stitch precisely where you want to.

• Couch over a piece of yarn or pearl cotton as a way to add dimension under a satin stitch.

• Satin stitch an edge twice, with a progressively wider and longer zigzag stitch to create a better finish to an edge.

• Couch over a piece of yarn or pearl cotton on the outer edge of satin stitching to clean-finish an uneven edge. This technique is often used on European table linens, napkin edges, and cut work. It's also a way to finish an edge on a fabric too thick to seam and turn to the right side in the conventional way such as denim, leather, canvas, heavy duck cloth.

• Use an exposed zipper in a pocket or a seam.

• Use the quilting guide to guide fabric evenly when you can't guide using the lines on the needle plate. This is helpful when stitching even rows of straight and decorative stitching.

———————————

Now that you've stitched your way through the projects in Part II, I hope you have learned to sew...better. Are you motivated to use the many stitches, presser feet, and accessories available to you? I also hope that you've had fun stitching along with me, that you have a bunch of completed projects to give away or to keep, and that you're inspired to learn more about "The World of Sewing."

In Part III, you'll learn even more about specific presser feet and stitches. Then I share some useful mail-order resources and good books.

Besides collecting fabric and other sewing paraphernalia, I also collect sewing and needlecraft books. In listing them in the bibliography, I feel as if I'm introducing you to dear friends. I encourage you to get to know them better as you further refine your skills. They're not only a helpful reference, but a continuous source of inspiration.

Good-bye for now, and happy sewing.

# STITCH AND PRESSER FOOT ENCYCLOPEDIA

- *Chapter Eight:*
  *Encyclopedia of Stitches*

- *Chapter Nine:*
  *Encyclopedia of Presser Feet*

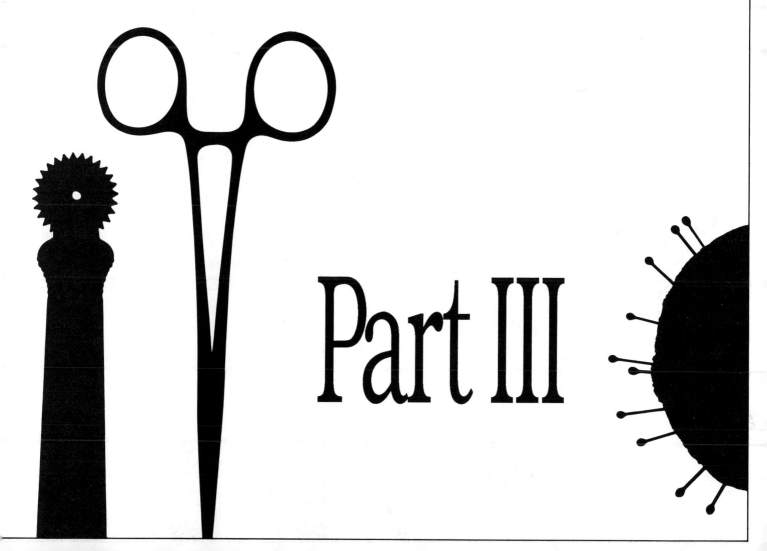

# Part III

PART III

# STITCH AND PRESSER FOOT ENCYCLOPEDIA

## Chapter 8: Encyclopedia of Stitches..............145

Straight Stitch.................................................146
Zigzag Stitch .................................................153
Automatic Stitches ..........................................163
Forward and Reverse Stitches .............................174
Decorative Stitchess ........................................179

## Chapter 9: Encyclopedia of Presser Feet ..180

The Five Best Feet ...........................................181
Extra Presser Feet and Accessories.......................185

Do you know how many stitches are built in to your machine or are available extra and how to use them? Do you know what feet and accessories came with your machine and what they are for?

Part III answers these questions with an encyclopedia of stitches and presser feet. We will explore the most common stitches and presser feet, what they look like, what they are designed to do, and their practical and decorative uses.

When I first learned about machine stitches and presser feet, I started keeping a notebook of samples in a large three-ring binder. I kept my stitch samples and notes in clear, pocket-type pages from an office supply store. My notebook is organized by stitches and feet, similar to this encyclopedia. I continue to maintain this notebook, so I have lots of ideas to choose from for future projects. It's one of the most valuable parts of my sewing room.

As you read through this encyclopedia, why not keep your own notebook, too? Cut light-colored fabric scraps into 6–9" (15–23cm) squares, ready for experiments. Or else use demo cloth, available through your local sewing machine dealer. The fabric is on a roll, firmly woven, and starched so the stitches show up well, plus it's easy to write on. This way you aren't hunting for fabric and you can write machine settings on the sample before it goes into your notebook.

As you experiment and get to know your machine better, keep everything—your successes, failures, and your new discoveries. Then refer to your notebook of ideas for your next project.

Now, find some fabric, your box of accessories, and your machine manual. Then sit down in front of your machine with me and discover the world of stitches and presser feet.

# ENCYCLOPEDIA OF STITCHES

- *Straight Stitch*

- *Zigzag Stitch*

- *Automatic Stitches*

- *Forward and Reverse Stitches*

- *Decorative Stitches*

MOST ENCYCLOPEDIAS ARE ORGANIZED ALPHABETICALLY. This one is not. The reason? I wanted to start with the most common stitches first—those found on machines dating back to the straight stitch and manual zigzag models of the 1940s and 1950s, and then progress through those stitches found on the computerized machines of today.

Most sewing machines made in the last 15 years have three to five utility stitches built in, and from two to an unlimited number of decorative stitches available extra. Others are designed with utility stitches on one panel and decorative stitches on another, sometimes interchangeable, cassette. This encyclopedia focuses primarily on the utility stitches. The decorative stitch applications are covered in the projects section of the book.

Utility stitches are those used most often for basic sewing and mending—straight stitch, zigzag, blind hem, stretch blind hem, three-step zigzag, overlock, double overlock, and a few others (Fig. 8.1). These utility stitches are common to most brands and to most models, from the basic to the sophisticated, computerized versions.

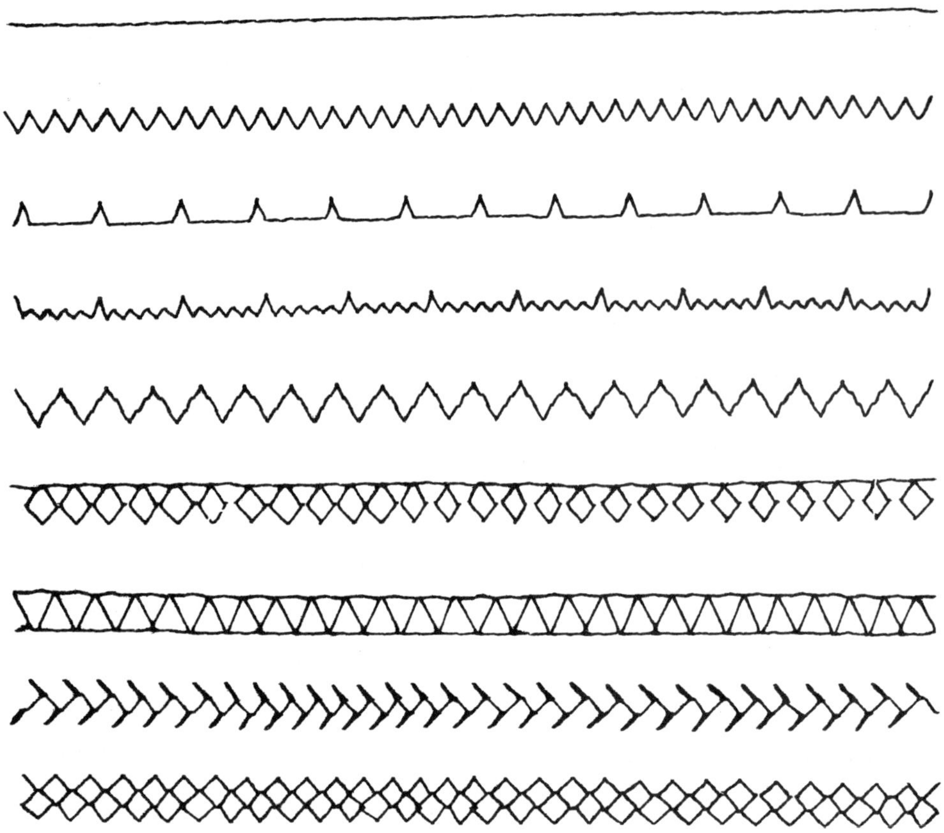

Fig. 8.1

**Fig. 8.1**
Automatic stitches,
from top to bottom:
straight stitch, zigzag,
blind hem, stretch
blind hem, three-step
zigzag. Forward and
reverse feeding
stitches: overlock,
double overlock,
feather, and
smocking stitches.

Stitches are formed in two ways: (1) automatic and (2) forward and reverse. "Automatic" means the stitches feed through the machine in one direction, and the needle may zigzag from side to side; the straight stitch, zigzag, blind hem, and three-step zigzag stitch are examples. "Forward and reverse" means the needle zigzags while the feed dogs move the fabric forward and backward. Examples are the feather stitch or smocking stitch.

Although the straight stitch and zigzag stitch are technically automatic stitches, they are also the most widely used and recognized utility stitches, so they are discussed separately here. Later in this chapter we'll look at other automatic and forward and reverse feeding stitches and their applications. Before we do, however, let's take a closer look at the most common utility stitch—the straight stitch.

## STRAIGHT STITCH

- Basting
- Easestitching
- Edgestitching
- Staystitching
- Stitch-in-the-Ditch

- Straight Seams
- Topstitching
- Twin Needle Hem
- Twin Needle Tucks
- Understitching

The straight stitch is used primarily to sew straight seams on woven fabrics. The stitch length is changed depending on the weight of the fabric. Generally, for a finer fabric, a shorter stitch length is used. For heavier fabrics, a longer stitch length is used. Make a stitch sample for your notebook with each stitch length sewn on the same piece of fabric, so you can see the different effect of various stitch lengths. Label each length. Try different weights of fabric (Fig. 8.2).

**Fig. 8.2**
Try various stitch lengths on a piece of fabric, label each, and put in your notebook.

**Fig. 8.2**

**Sew-How:** *To keep your stitches straight and to count the number of stitches per inch (cm), stitch various lengths on 1" (2.5cm) gingham. If the gingham puckers, iron a piece of plastic-coated freezer wrap to the wrong side of the gingham.*

**Sew-How:** *If your fabric puckers, shorten the stitch length. If the fabric waves out of shape, lengthen the stitch.*

The following section identifies common terms found in pattern instructions using the straight stitch in various techniques..

Fig. 8.3
Pin fabric together and
pull bobbin thread to
adjust ease.

## BASTING

Basting is a line of temporary stitching used to join pattern pieces to check fit and appearance before final stitching a project. For easy removal of basting stitches, set your machine as follows:

### Machine Readiness Checklist

**Stitch:** straight

**Length:** longest

**Width:** 0

**Foot:** standard zigzag

**Needle:** 70/10 or 80/12 universal

**Thread:** top and bobbin contrasting all-purpose

**Tension:** top, loosened slightly

Pull bobbin thread to remove stitches (it's easy to find because you used a different color for the bobbin). After basting, remember to reset your top tension to normal and to change your bobbin thread to match the top.

## EASESTITCHING

Many projects require flat pieces of fabric to fit curved areas. Therefore, the flat fabric must be manipulated to fit by easestitching.

When easestitching, a longer fabric edge is joined to a shorter one, with no folds or gathers visible from the right side of the project.

Easestitching is used for setting in sleeves. It's used in a two-piece sleeve at the elbow, for easing a skirt or pant waistline into a waistband and in other areas as directed in the pattern.

### Machine Readiness Checklist

**Stitch:** straight

**Length:** 2.5 (fine fabrics) –3.5 (heavy fabrics); 12–15 spi

**Width:** 0

**Foot:** standard zigzag

**Needle:** 80/12 universal

**Thread:** all-purpose

**Feed dogs:** up

**Needle position:** far right

**Tension:** normal; for more ease, tighten upper tension

1. On a single layer of the fabric to be eased, stitch between notches, guiding the raw edge at the 5/8" (1.5cm) seamline marked on your needle plate.

2. Pin fabric pieces together matching notches. Pull bobbin thread to adjust ease as needed (Fig. 8.3).

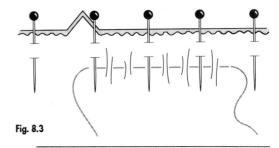

Fig. 8.3

**Sew-How:** *For even more ease, try the easestitch "plus" method. Set your machine as described above. As you sew, hold your index finger behind the foot so the fabric bunches up (Fig. 8.4). Hold fabric until you can't hold it firmly any longer, release, and repeat. The fabric eases automatically without tucks or gathers. This is great for casing a set in sleeve or the edge of a circular or curved hemline.*

**Fig. 8.4**
Hold your index finger behind the foot so fabric bunches up to easestitch "plus."

**Fig. 8.5**
Place edge of fold against the toe or guide in the foot and stitch.

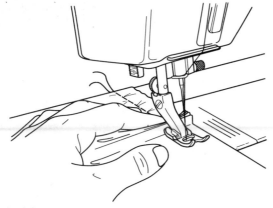

Fig. 8.4

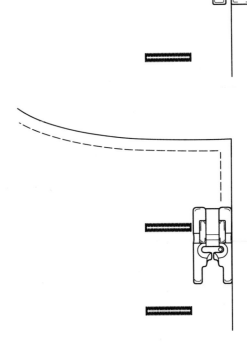

## EDGESTITCHING

Edgestitching is a line of stitching 1/8" (3mm) or less from the finished edge and is generally stitched with thread matching the fabric. Edgestitch a collar, cuff, top of a waistband, hem edge, belt edges, the edge of a pleat, or tuck.

| Machine Readiness Checklist | |
|---|---|
| **Stitch:** | straight stitch |
| **Length:** | normal for the fabric |
| **Width:** | 0 |
| **Foot:** | blind hem or standard buttonhole |
| **Needle:** | appropriate for fabric |
| **Thread:** | all-purpose |
| **Needle position:** | variable |

1. Press edge to be edgestitched. Place edge of fold so it guides against the inside right toe of the blind hem or buttonhole foot (Fig. 8.5).

2. Set your needle position so the needle is the desired distance from the edge and edgestitch. The blind hem foot enables you to edgestitch uniformly from the edge (see Figs. 9.12 and 9.13).

Fig. 8.5

## STAYSTITCHING

Staystitching is a line of stitching just inside the seam allowance which keeps curved and bias cut edges from stretching out of shape as the fabric is handled during construction. Areas commonly staystitched are necklines, armholes, shoulders, and waistlines.

To staystitch, use a normal length straight stitch for your fabric and stitch 1/2" (1.3cm) from the raw edge on a single layer of fabric (Fig. 8.6). To prevent the fabric from distorting, staystitch in the direction of the arrows as shown.

**Fig. 8.6**
To prevent fabric from stretching out of shape, staystitch curved and bias cut edges 1/2" (1.3cm) from raw edge.

**Fig. 8.7**
Stitch-in-the-ditch to tack down facings or finish waistbands.

**Fig. 8.8**
Topstitching on a pocket.

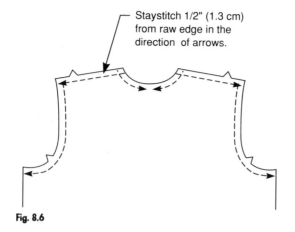

Staystitch 1/2" (1.3 cm) from raw edge in the direction of arrows.

**Fig. 8.6**

## STITCH-IN-THE-DITCH

Tack facings or finish waistbands by stitching-in-the ditch. To do this:

1. Use the blind hem or standard buttonhole foot and a 3 length (9 spi) straight stitch (see Figs. 9.11, 9.12, and 9.13).

2. With the right side up, place the crack of the seam under the foot, centering it under the needle (Fig. 8.7) and stitch.

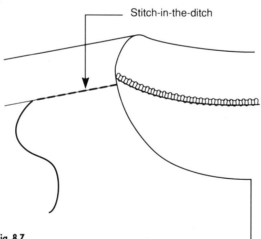

Stitch-in-the-ditch

**Fig. 8.7**

3. Pull threads to the wrong side and tie them off.

## STRAIGHT SEAMS

The straight stitch is used to sew a seam that will be pressed open on a woven fabric.

| **Machine Readiness Checklist** | |
|---|---|
| **Stitch:** | straight |
| **Length:** | 2.5–3.5; 12–15 spi |
| **Width:** | 0 |
| **Foot:** | standard zigzag or Teflon-coated™ zigzag |
| **Needle:** | appropriate for the fabric |
| **Thread:** | all-purpose |
| **Tension:** | normal, top and bobbin |
| **Fabric:** | varies |

With right sides together, sew a seam, stitching 5/8" (1.5cm) from the raw edge. To set the stitches, press over them so seam is flat and together. Then press seam open.

**Sew-How:** *If your seamline puckers, you're probably using a thread too large for the fabric. Try machine-embroidery thread with a 70/10 needle.*

## TOPSTITCHING

Topstitching is a line of stitches sewn on the top side of a project parallel to a

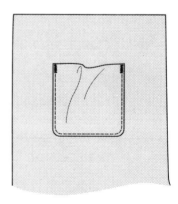

**Fig. 8.8**

finished edge or to a seamline. Topstitching differs from edgestitching because it's not sewn as close to the finished edge as edgestitching, and a longer stitch length is usually used. Topstitching can also be done with a variety of decorative top threads such as silk twist, polyester topstitching thread, or by using two threads through the same needle. Generally topstitching is used to embellish and is not necessary for the construction of a project (Fig. 8.8).

**Machine Readiness Checklist**

**Stitch:** straight
**Length:** 3–4; 6–9 spi
**Width:** 0
**Foot:** standard zigzag or transparent embroidery
**Thread:** two threads through the same needle; or silk twist or topstitching
**Needle:** 80/12 universal, 90/14 topstitching for heavy threads
**Tension:** normal for two threads through same needle; tighten top slightly for heavier threads

---

**Sew-How:** *Be consistent. Use the same stitch length to topstitch all parts of a project. If you have a mechanical machine, stop at a corner so the needle has hit its dead lowest point, and is on its way out of the fabric. This way, the stitch cycle is complete so you don't run the risk of skipping a stitch. Most electronic and computerized machines that can stop sewing with the needle in the fabric do this automatically.*

---

Interface three weights of fabric. Fold each in half and topstitch each using different stitch lengths. Make a note of the best stitch length for topstitching each fabric. Put these samples in your notebook.

## TWIN NEEDLE HEM

This is a fast, professional way to hem a knit that looks as if the hem has been knitted into the fabric (Fig. 8.9). For stretchy knits such as sweater knits, stretch terry, and velour, lengthen stitch to 4–4.5 (4–5 spi).

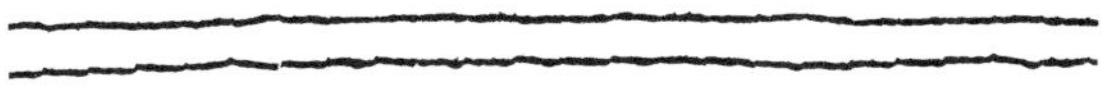

Fig. 8.9

Fig. 8.9 Twin needle hem on a knit fabric looks as if it has been knitted into the fabric.

**Machine Readiness Checklist**

**Stitch:** straight
**Length:** 2.5–3; 10–12 spi
**Width:** 0
**Foot:** transparent embroidery or standard zigzag
**Needle:** twin, size 2.0/80(12)
**Thread:** all-purpose to match fabric
**Tension:** normal
**Fabric:** woven or knit

---

**Sew-How:** *To prevent threads from tangling through the upper tension, place one spool so thread pulls from the front of the spool; place the other spool so the thread pulls from the back of the spool.*

---

If you have only one spool pin on your machine, extend it by putting a drinking straw over it. Now it will accommodate two spools of thread.

1. Fold hem up desired amount and press.

2. With the right side up, place fabric under the foot the width of the hem, so foot is resting on a double layer of fabric. Stitch (Fig. 8.9).

3. Trim excess fabric away from the underside.

---

**Sew-How:** *To prevent cutting a hole where it doesn't belong when trimming away the fabric close to the stitch, use a pair of scissors with one rounded blade or one with a pelican-shaped blade. Position the scissors so the rounded or pelican-shaped blade is between the hem allowance and the wrong side of the project.*

---

## TWIN NEEDLE TUCKS (PINTUCKS)

Twin needles are used on top- and front-loading bobbin machines only. If your bobbin goes in the side of your machine, the needles sit in the machine incorrectly and will not work. Using your transparent embroidery or pintucking foot (see Fig. 9.39) and with the right side up, sew on a single layer of fabric. The bobbin thread shares itself between the two top threads, creating a zigzag stitch on the underside and a tuck on the right side of the fabric.

Applications: Stitch with thread matching the fabric to create texture down the front of a knit sweatshirt, top, or dress. Pintuck the front of an heirloom blouse or christening gown. Run multiple rows around the hem of a skirt for more body.

## UNDERSTITCHING

Understitching prevents the inside layer of fabric from rolling to the outside and is generally done on a facing edge.

After stitching and trimming the seam, press seam allowance toward the facing. With the right side up, stitch 1/8" (3mm) from the seamline using a straight stitch appropriate for the fabric (Fig. 8.10).

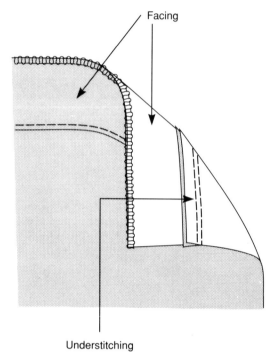

Facing

Understitching

**Fig. 8.10**

Understitching a facing first makes it easier to topstitch later. However, you may not always want to topstitch so try the following Sew-How method.

---

**Sew-How:** *Instead of using a straight stitch to understitch a facing, use a three-step zigzag on a 1.5 length (15 spi) and a 4–5 width (Fig. 8.46). This stitch flattens the bulk and makes the seam allowance lie flat so it may not be necessary to topstitch.*

---

# ZIGZAG STITCH

- Buttonholes
- Button Sewing
- Button and Belt Loops
- Couching with the Zigzag Stitch
- Gathering over a Cord
- 5/8" (1.5cm) Knit Seam
- Lettuce or Rolled Edge
- Overcast a Raw Edge
- Satin Stitch
- Speed Basting
- Thread Tacks

Add stitch width to a straight stitch and you have a zigzag stitch. It's used to make buttonholes, sew buttons, embroider, make belt loops, gather over a cord, stitch a knit seam, overcast a raw edge, satin stitch, tack down a facing, plus much more.

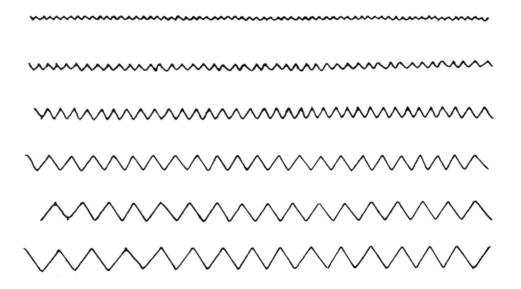

**Fig. 8.11**
Zigzag stitch on varying widths and lengths.

To acquaint yourself with the stitch, sew row after row of zigzag stitches, experimenting with the stitch width and length (Fig. 8.11). Record settings and keep your experiments in your notebook. Once you have a basic familiarity with the zigzag, you will master the following techniques.

## BUTTONHOLES

Making buttonholes may sound difficult, but it doesn't have to be. Today's sewing machines and buttonhole feet make it easier than ever.

In this section, we will discuss the manual buttonhole, in which the fabric must be turned around manually, and the automatic buttonhole, for which your sewing machine does all the work. Then you'll see how to cord buttonholes for strength.

### Manual Buttonholes

If you have a sewing machine without a buttonhole pictured anywhere and it only straight stitches forward and backward and zigzags, chances are it's a manual zigzag machine. Check your instruction book to be sure. To make a buttonhole on this type of machine you must turn the fabric around.

Fig. 8.12
Manual buttonhole
made in four steps.

## Machine Readiness Checklist

**Stitch:** zigzag

**Length:** 0.5–0.8; 60 spi

**Width:** 2; 4; 2; 4; 0

**Foot:** sliding buttonhole

**Feed dogs:** up

**Needle position:** left

**Thread:** all-purpose

**Fabric:** interfaced medium-weight woven cotton or cotton blend

**Accessories:** Fray-Check

---

**Sew-How:** *Check the bobbin thread supply before making your buttonholes. It's difficult to make a good-looking buttonhole if you run out of thread in the middle.*

---

1. Start with the foot shank end of the foot to the back of the slide, stitch width 2. Sew left side of buttonhole, stopping with the needle in the right side of the stitch (Fig. 8.12).

2. Lift presser foot and pivot fabric 180 degrees. Slide foot so shank end is to the back of the slide again, and put it down. Remove needle from the fabric and move the width to 4. Bartack the end of the buttonhole three or four stitches.

---

**Sew-How:** *Hold the fabric firmly so it will not move forward while bartacking the end of buttonhole.*

---

3. Return stitch width to 2 and sew the second side of the buttonhole.

4. Stop with the needle out of the work and move the width to 4. Bartack a few stitches as before. Move width to 0 and take a few stitches in place. Pull threads to the back and either tie or clip them off close to the fabric. Dab Fray-Check on thread ends so they won't pull out.

## Automatic Buttonholes

Most sewing machines built in the last 15 years make an automatic buttonhole—made in one, two, or four steps, without your having to turn the fabric. Each brand and model has its patented process, so you'll have to look in your instruction book for specific information.

## Corded Buttonholes

Corded buttonholes look better and wear longer than ordinary buttonholes. Use them on coats, suits, and areas that receive a lot of stress and wear.

1. Set your machine to make buttonholes.

2. Place a strand of pearl cotton, embroidery floss, or multiple strands of thread matching the fabric under the foot so the loop is at the stress point of the

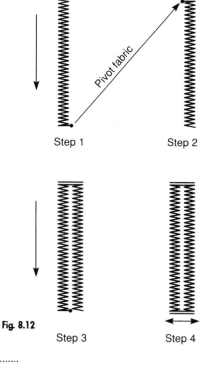

Step 1    Step 2

**Fig. 8.12**

Step 3    Step 4

**Fig. 8.13**
Corded buttonhole.

**Fig. 8.14**
Use the back of your ripper to score the cutting space and separate the two sides of the buttonhole.

**Fig. 8.15**
Use a ripper to cut the buttonhole open.

buttonhole (Fig. 8.13). **Note:** Some buttonhole feet have a prong to anchor or grooves to guide the cord in place while sewing.

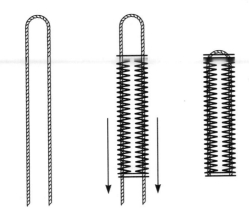

Fig. 8.13

3. Stitch the buttonhole making sure the zigzag stitches cover the cord but don't pierce it.

4. Pull the loop to the bartack. Use a needle threader or a large-eyed needle to pull free ends to the back or between the facing and fashion fabric, then tie them off.

---

**Sew-How:** *To cut buttonholes open, use the back of your ripper to score the fabric between the two rows of stitching (Fig. 8.14). This opens the cutting space. Then use a buttonhole cutter and block to cut the buttonhole open.*

---

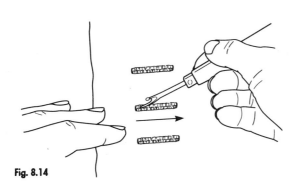

Fig. 8.14

If you don't have a buttonhole cutter, use the ripper, sometimes called a buttonhole knife, to cut the buttonhole open. Put the point of the ripper in the middle of the buttonhole, then bring it up through the fabric in front of the bartack as if it were a pin (Fig. 8.15). Cut. Repeat for the other end of the buttonhole, cutting from the center out. This way you don't inadvertently cut through the bartack. Trim out any fraying threads; then put a little Fray-Check on the inside of the buttonhole.

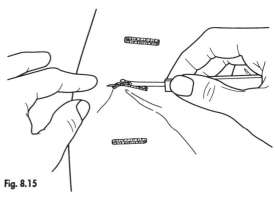

Fig. 8.15

## BUTTON SEWING

Use the zigzag stitch to sew a button on by machine (also see Button Reed and Button Sewing Foot, Figs. 9.17 and 9.19). Unlike commercial machines that use a one-thread chain stitch to attach buttons, the conventional sewing machine has a top and bobbin thread, so buttons are stitched securely. It's also faster than sewing them on by hand.

| Machine Readiness Checklist | |
|---|---|
| **Stitch:** | zigzag |
| **Length:** | 0 |
| **Width:** | 3–4 (test on your button) |
| **Foot:** | transparent embroidery or button sewing (**Note:** If your feet snap on, remove the foot and use the foot shank to anchor the button while sewing.) |
| **Feed dogs:** | down (if possible) |
| **Needle Position:** | left |
| **Accessories:** | removable transparent tape or glue stick, Fray-Check, tapestry hand needle |

**Fig. 8.16**
Button taped to fabric
with tapestry needle
between the holes.

**Fig. 8.17**
Wrap a thread shank
between the
button and fabric.

1. Mark button placement. Place button by taping it on or by dabbing the back with the glue stick.

---

**SEW HOW:** *A thread shank between the button and the fabric allows room for the buttoned fabric. To make a thread shank, place a tapestry needle between the holes before taping over button (Fig. 8.16).*

---

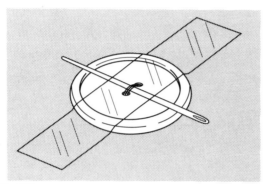

Fig. 8.16

2. Hand turn the machine needle into the left hole of the button and lower the presser bar lever. If sewing on a four-hole button, start with the holes closest to you.

3. Move the flywheel by hand to check the needle clearance; adjust your zigzag width if necessary. Then stitch four to five zigzag stitches. **Note:** By sewing in left needle position, the needle always stitches in the left hole of the button, even when adjusting the stitch width.

4. Move width to 0 and take a few stitches in place to anchor threads. Remove fabric

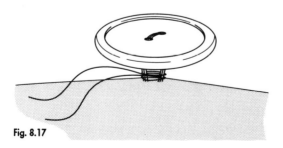

Fig. 8.17

and pull off enough thread to wrap the shank between the button and fabric (Fig. 8.17).

5. After wrapping the shank, thread a hand-sewing needle, pull threads to the back, and clip them off at fabric. Dab Fray-Check on threads to secure them.

## BUTTON AND BELT LOOPS

Rather than hand crocheting button or belt loops, zigzag over pearl cotton or multiple strands of thread.

| Machine Readiness Checklist | |
|---|---|
| **Stitch:** | zigzag |
| **Length:** | 0.5–0.8; 60 spi |
| **Width:** | widest |
| **Foot:** | transparent or metal embroidery, or standard buttonhole |
| **Feed dogs:** | up |
| **Needle position:** | center |
| **Thread:** | all-purpose |
| **Accessories:** | pearl cotton to match thread, large-eyed tapestry needle |

1. Place a double strand of pearl cotton or multiple strand of thread under the foot so 2–3" (5–7.5cm) are behind the foot.

2. Hold top and bobbin thread tails behind the foot and zigzag over pearl cotton or thread so the stitches cover the cord (Fig. 8.18).

3. Thread stitched cord through tapestry needle to insert in seam where desired. Knot both ends together so loop will not pull out.

**Fig. 8.18**
Zigzag over pearl cotton to make belt and button loops.

**Fig. 8.19**
Yarn couched down with a zigzag stitch.

**Fig. 8.20**
Two rows of straight stitches pulled into gathers.

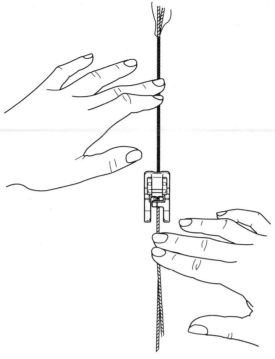

Fig. 8.18

Place cord, floss, yarn, or ribbon on the right side of a single layer of fabric. Zigzag over cord to attach to the fabric (Fig. 8.19; also see Figs. 9.11 and 9.20). If the fabric puckers, back with iron-on freezer wrap or tear-away stabilizer.

Fig. 8.19

## COUCHING WITH THE ZIGZAG STITCH

Couching is a way to attach cord, floss, yarn, or ribbon to the surface of a fabric for an edge finish or decorative treatment.

| Machine Readiness Checklist | |
| --- | --- |
| **Stitch:** | zigzag |
| **Length:** | 1–2; 13–24 spi |
| **Width:** | wide enough to clear cord |
| **Foot:** | transparent embroidery, narrow braiding, or standard buttonhole |
| **Feed dogs:** | up |
| **Needle position:** | left if using transparent embroidery or buttonhole foot; center if using narrow braiding foot |
| **Thread:** | all-purpose to match cord or nylon monofilament |

## GATHERING OVER A CORD

To gather fabric, pattern instructions usually say to stitch two rows of straight basting stitches, which you then pull (Fig. 8.20). Often these threads break while you are pulling up the gathers. To prevent this, zigzag over a cord.

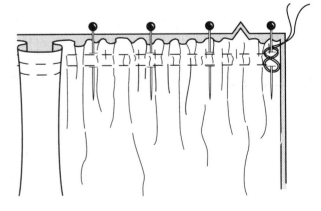

Fig. 8.20

Fig. 8.21
Zigzag over cord and
pull gathers up.

**Machine Readiness Checklist**

**Stitch:** zigzag

**Length:** 2–3; 9–13 spi

**Width:** 2–3 or wide enough to clear cord

**Foot:** transparent embroidery, standard buttonhole, or narrow braiding

**Feed dogs:** up

**Needle position:** left for embroidery and buttonhole feet; center for braiding foot

**Accessories:** size #8 or #5 pearl cotton or nylon fishing line

1. Place cord under groove of the foot on the wrong side of a single layer of fabric so 2–3" (5–7.5cm) extends behind it.

2. Guiding 1/2" (1.3cm) from the raw edge and on the wrong side of the fabric, zigzag over cord, being careful not to catch cord in the stitching (Fig. 8.21).

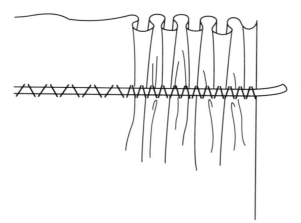

Fig. 8.21

3. Pull gathers up and adjust from both ends. Once fabric has been gathered to desired length, knot or anchor cord so gathers don't pull out. Although it is not necessary, you may remove the cord after stitching.

**Sew-How:** *If gathering a long ruffle, cut the cord or pearl cotton the length of the finished ruffle plus 4" (10cm). Mark the finished length of ruffle on the cord by pinning 2" (5cm) from the end of the cord at both ends of the ruffle. Then mark the cord into fourths between the pins. Mark ruffle fabric into fourths. Your cord is anchored by pins at the beginning and end. Zigzag over cord as described above. While stitching, guide cord with your right hand while pushing gathers down the cord with your left, matching the marks on the fabric with the marks on the cord. This way, the ruffle is gathered to the exact length needed without wasting a lot of cord.*

## 5/8" (1.5CM) KNIT SEAM

If a straight stitch is used to construct a knit, the thread often breaks. To prevent this, stitch the seam with a tiny zigzag stitch.

**Machine Readiness Checklist**

**Stitch:** zigzag

**Length:** 1–2; 13–24 spi

**Width:** 1

**Foot:** transparent embroidery

**Needle:** 70/10 or 80/12 universal

**Thread:** all-purpose

**Tension:** normal

1. Place right sides together and stitch seam at the 5/8" (1.5cm) seamline (Fig. 8.22).

2. Press seam flat and together to blend the stitches. Then press seam open.

**Fig. 8.22**
Use tiny zigzag to sew a 5/8" (1.5cm) seam on a knit.

**Fig. 8.23**
Zigzag over curled edge, holding fabric in front of and behind the foot.

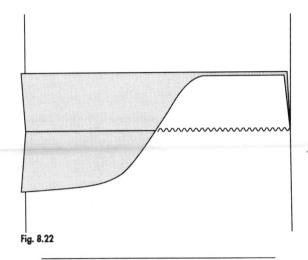

Fig. 8.22

---

**Sew-How:** *This stitch is difficult to rip, so baste the seam together first (see Speed Basting on page 161) to check the fit.*

---

## LETTUCE OR ROLLED EDGE

The lettuce edge looks like the edge of a lettuce leaf when stitched on a knit. It's used on lingerie, ribbing edges, and children's clothing. When used on a woven, it looks like a rolled hem found on the edge of placemats, napkins, and scarf edges. When worked on the bias and stretched, it becomes a lettuce edge, too.

| Machine Readiness Checklist | |
|---|---|
| **Stitch:** | zigzag |
| **Length:** | 0.5–0.8; 60 spi |
| **Width:** | widest |
| **Foot:** | transparent embroidery, standard buttonhole |
| **Feed dogs:** | up |
| **Thread:** | all-purpose |
| **Fabric:** | single knits (e.g., interlock, jersey, tricot, ribbings) |
| **Tension:** | top, loosened slightly |
| **Accessories:** | round-nosed scissors |

## Method One

This technique works beautifully on nylon tricot or any single knit. When stretched across the grain, single knits curl to the right side.

1. To make the fabric roll, stretch the raw edge across the grain. Place rolled edge under the foot, right side up, holding the fabric in front of and behind the foot (Fig. 8.23). **Note:** When using the buttonhole foot, place the roll under the left groove for easy guiding.

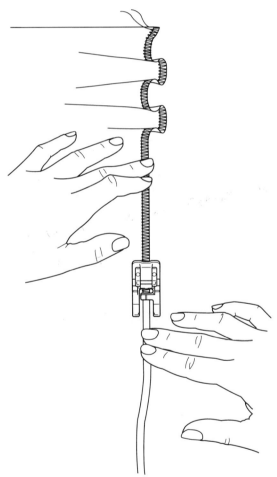

Fig. 8.23

2. Guide fabric so the needle stitches over the roll on the left and off the raw edge at the right.

Fig. 8.24
Finish raw edge with a
zigzag and overcast
guide foot.

## Method Two

This is recommended for woven fabrics and single knits that run or are very stretchy (e.g., ribbing, interlock, wool jersey, Lycra spandex, etc.).

1. Fold and press under at least a 1/2" (1.3cm) hem.

2. Place fold halfway under the foot, right side up, so the needle catches the fabric on the left and swings off the fold at the right. Do not stretch the fabric while sewing. The stitches automatically push the fabric out of shape, creating a ripple.

3. Carefully trim the excess fabric to the stitching line.

4. After trimming, stretch the fabric across the grain. The evenness of the stitches creates even lettuce "leaves."

## OVERCAST A RAW EDGE

Although it isn't always necessary to finish the seams, overcasting a raw edge prevents raveling and looks more professional. The zigzag stitch can be used to overcast a raw edge, however, many fabrics curl or tunnel under the stitch. To minimize this curling, try this.

| Machine Readiness Checklist | |
| --- | --- |
| **Stitch:** | zigzag |
| **Length:** | 1–1.5; 15–24 spi |
| **Width:** | 3–4 |
| **Foot:** | standard zigzag |
| **Needle:** | appropriate for the fabric |
| **Thread:** | all-purpose |
| **Tension:** | top, loosened slightly; bobbin, normal |

Place the raw edge halfway under the foot, so half of the stitch forms on the fabric, and half of the stitch forms off the raw edge.

If you have an overcast guide foot, you can overcome the tunneling by using the following method (also see Fig. 9.38).

## Zigzag Overcast with the Overcast Guide Foot

To overcast an edge with the zigzag stitch and to prevent tunneling, set your machine as follows:

| Machine Readiness Checklist | |
| --- | --- |
| **Stitch:** | zigzag |
| **Length:** | 1.5–2; 12–15 spi |
| **Width:** | widest |
| **Foot:** | overcast guide |
| **Needle:** | appropriate for fabric |
| **Thread:** | all-purpose |

1. Place single layer of fabric under the foot so the raw edge is even with the wire or guide.

2. Overcast edge, guiding the fabric so the needle swings off the edge on the right (Fig. 8.24).

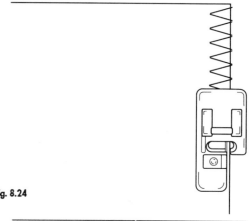

Fig. 8.24

**Sew-How:** *The three-step zigzag or double overlock are preferred stitches for overcasting. If you have any of these available, skip ahead to pages 170 and 174 and read how to use them for overcasting.*

**Fig. 8.25**
Varying widths of
satin stitching.

## SATIN STITCH

The satin stitch looks like a narrow satin ribbon stitched around appliqués and is used to monogram and embroider. Stitch different widths of satin stitches for your notebook.

Fig. 8.25

| Machine Readiness Checklist | |
|---|---|
| Stitch: | zigzag |
| Length: | 0.5–0.8; 60 spi |
| Width: | 2, 3, 4, 5, 6 |
| Foot: | transparent or metal embroidery |
| Feed dogs: | up |
| Needle position: | center |
| Thread: | cotton or rayon embroidery |
| Fabric: | tightly woven cotton or cotton blend |
| Tension: | top, loosened slightly; bobbin, normal |
| Accessories: | iron-on freezer paper or tear-away stabilizer |

1. Iron freezer paper or pin stabilizer to the back of your fabric and set your machine for a 2 width satin stitch. Stitch and examine. Then adjust the stitch length so the stitches are next to, but not on top of, each other.

2. Repeat for 3, 4, 5, and 6 stitch widths (Fig. 8.25).

## SPEED BASTING

This method is a fast, easy method of basting knits together. Seams stretch without breaking the stitches, making it easier to check the fit. Then the stitches pull out quickly after fitting.

| Machine Readiness Checklist | |
|---|---|
| Stitch: | zigzag |
| Length: | longest |
| Width: | widest |
| Foot: | transparent embroidery |
| Feed dogs: | up |
| Needle position: | center |
| Thread: | top, all-purpose; bobbin, contrasting color to top thread |
| Fabric: | knits |
| Tension: | top, very loose; bobbin, normal |

1. Stitch seam at seamline indicated on pattern.

2. Check fit and remove stitches by pulling bobbin thread (Fig. 8.26).

---

**Sew-How:** *Use water-soluble basting thread on the bobbin as a temporary seam. The bobbin stitches dissolve in water.*

---

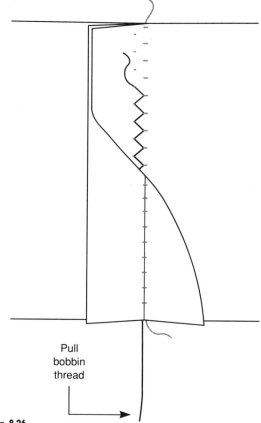

**Fig. 8.26**
Remove speed basting by pulling bobbin thread.

**Fig. 8.27**
Attaching a ribbon or yarn with thread tack.

Pull bobbin thread

Fig. 8.26

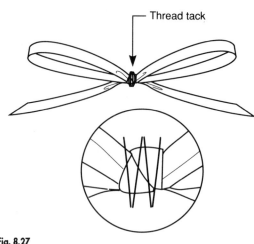

Thread tack

Fig. 8.27

## THREAD TACKS

Tack a facing, bow, or small appliqué like this:

**Machine Readiness Checklist**

| | |
|---|---|
| **Stitch:** | zigzag |
| **Length:** | 0 |
| **Width:** | 3–5; 0 |
| **Foot:** | transparent or metal embroidery |
| **Feed dogs:** | down |
| **Needle position:** | left |
| **Thread:** | all-purpose or cotton embroidery |
| **Accessories:** | Fray-Check |

1. Place item to be tacked under the foot. Take four to five zigzag stitches. Move the width to 0 (Fig. 8.27).

2. Stitch a few locking stitches, remove the fabric, and pull threads to the back. Clip threads close to the fabric and dab them with Fray-Check.

Now you know a little about the utility straight and zigzag stitches. The next section on automatic stitches will give you even more understanding of stitches. Continue to document your findings by making stitch samples for your notebook.

## AUTOMATIC STITCHES

- Blind Hem Stitch
- Blind Hem (Stretch) Stitch
- Scallop Stitch
- Three-Step Zigzag Stitch

Automatic stitches are variations on the zigzag stitch. The blind hem stitch, for example, takes a few straight stitches, then zigzags to the left. The stretch blind hem stitch looks like the blind hem but has narrow zigzags between the wider ones.

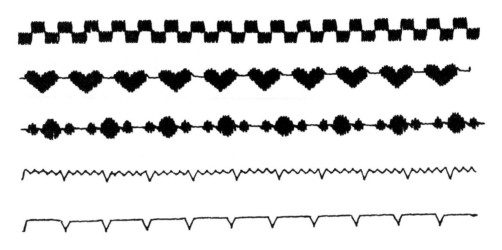

**Fig. 8.28**
Automatic stitches, from bottom to top: blind hem, stretch blind hem, ball, hearts, and domino.

Closed embroidery stitches such as the ball, hearts, and domino, are also automatic zigzag stitches (Fig. 8.28).

The following automatic stitches are found on most sewing machines and are listed and described here in alphabetical order.

### BLIND HEM STITCH

- Blind Hemming
- Shell Tuck and Corded Shell Tuck
- Couched Saddle Stitch

#### Blind Hemming

This technique takes some practice but, once mastered, will save you a lot of time.

| Machine Readiness Checklist | |
| --- | --- |
| **Stitch:** | blind hem |
| **Length:** | 2–3; 10–12 spi |
| **Width:** | 1–2 |
| **Foot:** | blind hem |
| **Needle:** | 70/10 universal |
| **Tension:** | top, loosened; bobbin, normal |

**Sew-How:** *Rather than using hem tape, overcast the hem edge with the three-step zigzag or double overlock stitch. It saves time, minimizes bulk, and it's one less thing you need to find to match your fabric (see Figs. 8.24, 8.41, and 8.48).*

1. Pin hem up desired amount, placing pins perpendicular to and 1/4" (6mm) from hem edge (Fig. 8.29).

2. Press hem without pressing over pins.

3. Fold hem allowance to the outside, folding the hem back to where the pins enter the fabric. Place hem under foot so the body of the garment is to the left and

**Fig. 8.29**
Place pins perpendicular to and 1/4" (6mm) from hem edge.

**Fig. 8.30**
Fold hem back to where the pins enter the fabric. Needle stitches on extension, then takes a small bite into the fold.

**Fig. 8.31**
Couched saddle stitch.

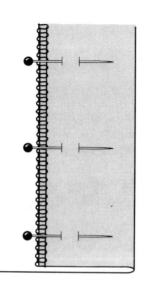

Fig. 8.29

the 1/4" (6mm) extension is to the right of the needle.

4. Begin stitching so the needle takes a few stitches on the extension, then a small bite into the fold, picking up a thread or two at the left (Fig. 8.30).

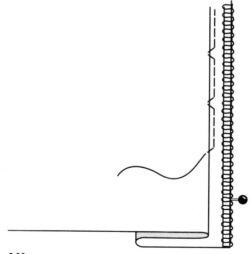

Fig. 8.30

---

**Sew-How:** *The less fabric the needle catches, the more invisible the hem, so use the narrowest width possible and loosen the upper tension. On lightweight fabrics, loosen the bobbin tension as well.*

---

Although it's not necessary, the finer the thread used when hemming, the more invisible the results. I like a size #50 weight cotton embroidery thread (see Sources of Supply).

## Couched Saddle Stitch

This topstitching technique is commonly used on ready-to-wear coats and suits and is easy to duplicate.

| Machine Readiness Checklist | |
|---|---|
| **Stitch:** | blind hem |
| **Length:** | 1–1.5; 20–24 spi |
| **Width:** | 1.5–2 |
| **Foot:** | narrow braiding or transparent embroidery |
| **Feed dogs:** | up |
| **Needle position:** | center |
| **Thread:** | nylon monofilament |
| **Fabric:** | wool coating, fleece, or suiting |
| **Tension:** | normal |
| **Accessories:** | #3, #5 pearl cotton or six-strand embroidery floss |

Clip pearl cotton or floss into the braiding foot or slide under the embroidery foot and topstitch. The straight stitches bury themselves in the fabric next to the floss while the zigzag creates an indentation so each stitch looks 1/4" (6mm) long (Fig. 8.31).

Fig. 8.31

Fig. 8.32
To shell tuck, place
folded edge under foot
with bulk to the right.

Fig. 8.33
Stretch blind
hem stitch on three
stitch lengths.

## Shell Tuck and Corded Shell Tuck

Shell tuck the edge of a half slip, skirt lining, neck edge, facing, or trim with the blind hem stitch.

### Machine Readiness Checklist

**Stitch:** blind hem

**Length:** 1.5–2; 13–20 spi

**Width:** widest

**Foot:** standard zigzag for lightweight fabrics; transparent embroidery for medium to heavy fabrics

**Thread:** all-purpose or nylon

**Feed dogs:** up

**Fabric:** nylon tricot, cotton knits, lining fabrics

**Tension:** top tightened slightly; bobbin, normal

**Accessories:** #3 or #5 pearl cotton

1. Turn up a hem and press. **Note:** If shell tucking a ribbing edge, do not press over folded edge.

2. Place folded edge under the foot so the bulk of the fabric is to the right. Place fold under the left toe of the foot and stitch (Fig. 8.32). **Note:** To prevent skipped stitches, the needle must swing completely off the folded edge.

   To cord the tuck, lay a strand of pearl cotton at the fold and stitch. Again, the needle must swing off the fabric and over the cord.

3. You can trim the excess fabric to the stitch; however, the edge may curl. To avoid this, run a row or two of decorative stitching or a twin needle tuck a presser foot width from the shell tuck; then trim excess fabric to the stitch.

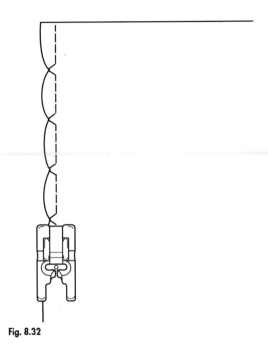

Fig. 8.32

**Sew-How:** *Stitching a shell tuck with the bulk of the fabric to the right can be awkward. Instead, use the reverse blind hem stitch and guide the fabric so the bulk is to the left.*

## BLIND HEM (STRETCH) STITCH

• Blind Hemming Knits

• Decorative Treatment

### Blind Hemming Knits

The stretch blind hem stitch works like the blind hem but is designed for use on knit fabrics. Notice the narrow zigzag stitches between the wider ones (Fig. 8.33). This

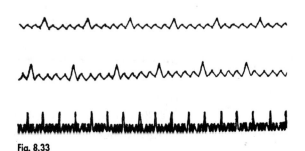

Fig. 8.33

Fig. 8.34
Corded stretch blind
hem stitch as an edge
finish.

enables the stitch to stretch with the fabric so you are less likely to catch your heel in a knit hemline and rip it out.

To blind hem with the stretch blind hem stitch, follow the instructions above for blind hemming.

## Decorative Treatment with Stretch Blind Hem Stitch

The stretch blind hem stitch can also be used on a shorter stitch length and a wider width to create a stitch that looks like an eyelash or hand buttonhole stitch. Use it to topstitch an appliqué, create eyelashes on a puppet or toy (see Chapter 6), or make a two-toned decorative effect by cording it (Fig. 8.34).

Fig. 8.34

### Machine Readiness Checklist

**Stitch:** stretch blind hem
**Length:** 0.5–0.8; 60 spi
**Width:** widest
**Foot:** transparent or metal embroidery
**Feed dogs:** up
**Needle:** 70/10 or 80/12 universal
**Thread:** all-purpose or cotton machine embroidery
**Accessories:** #5 or #8 pearl cotton contrasting to the fabric

For an edge finish, fold under at least a 1/2" hem and press. Guide cord under the left side of the foot, and place the fabric under the foot so the stitches zigzag off the fold on the right.

## SCALLOP STITCH

• Corded Scallop Edge Finish
• Scallop Edge Finish
• Tracery Scallop

## Corded Scallop Edge Finish

This decorative treatment is lovely on the edge of a collar, front tab, sleeve hem, or anywhere you would like a hand-crocheted look to an edge.

### Machine Readiness Checklist

**Stitch:** closed scallop
**Length:** 0.4–0.6; 60 spi
**Width:** widest
**Foot:** transparent embroidery, narrow braiding or rolled hemmer
**Thread:** cotton machine embroidery
**Fabric:** closely woven cotton or linen
**Tension:** top, loosen slightly; bobbin, normal
**Accessories:** construction paper to match fabric and thread, or tear-away stabilizer, #5 pearl cotton to match

1. Thread pearl cotton through the guide or groove in the foot so about 2" (5cm) is behind the foot.

2. Place a strip of construction paper partly under folded edge, with the right side of the fabric up. Place folded edge of fabric under the foot so half of the foot is resting on the fabric and half of the foot is resting on the paper (Fig. 8.35).

3. Begin sewing so that the point of the scallop catches on the edge of the fold and the rest of the scallop forms off the fabric on the paper or tear-away, over the cord.

4. Remove the stabilizer by carefully ripping it off the stitches. Scallops should look like a hand-crocheted edge. **Note:** Depending on how large a scallop your machine

Fig. 8.35
Guide so the point of the scallop catches on fold and the rest of scallop forms off the fabric on the adding machine tape.

Fig. 8.36
Two styles of closed scallop stitches used as a hem finish on skirt lining or other hem edge. Trim fabric to the stitch.

Fig. 8.37
Twin needle tracery scallop hem finish on sheer fabric.

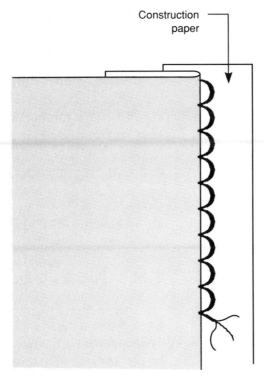

Fig. 8.35

1. Fold hem up desired amount. Stitch scallop on the folded edge, guiding so the needle zigzags off the edge on the right.

2. On the underside, trim excess fabric carefully to the stitch (Fig. 8.36).

Fig. 8.36

## Tracery Scallop

I use the twin needles to create this stitch for a hem finish on sheer fabrics. The bobbin thread shows through the sheer fabric, creating a delicate shadow effect (Fig. 8.37).

Fig. 8.37

makes, the space created between the fabric and scallop may be large enough to slip over a small button.

## Scallop Edge Finish

Use a scallop stitch to finish the edge of a half slip, skirt lining, sleeve hem, ruffle, or trim. There are many places to use a scallop. Understand these basics; then use your imagination in your next project.

### Machine Readiness Checklist

| | |
|---|---|
| **Stitch:** | closed scallop |
| **Length:** | 0.4–0.6; 60 spi |
| **Width:** | widest |
| **Foot:** | transparent or metal embroidery |
| **Thread:** | cotton machine embroidery |
| **Fabrics:** | closely woven or stabilized knit |
| **Tension:** | top, loosened slightly; bobbin, normal |

### Machine Readiness Checklist

| | |
|---|---|
| **Stitch:** | tracery scallop or scallop variation |
| **Length:** | varies (first test for desired length on a scrap) |
| **Width:** | 3 |
| **Foot:** | standard zigzag |
| **Needle:** | twin 2.0/80(12)–2.5/80(12) universal |
| **Suggested fabrics:** | organdy, organza, batiste, sheer tricot |
| **Tension:** | top, loosened; bobbin, normal |

**Sew-How:** *If you want a flat shadow hem, loosen bobbin tension or bypass it altogether. Otherwise, the fabric may be drawn into a slight tuck.*

1. Fold hem up desired width and press.

2. Stitch tracery scallop at least 1" (2.5cm) above folded edge so the foot rests on a double layer of fabric.

3. Trim away excess fabric to the stitch.

# THREE-STEP ZIGZAG STITCH

- Attaching Elastic
- Tacking
- Mending
- Twin Needles
- Overcasting a Raw Edge
- Patching
- Understitching

Next to the straight and zigzag stitches, I feel the three-step zigzag (also called serpentine or multiple zigzag) is the most useful. Use it for attaching elastic, mending, overcasting a raw edge, patching, tacking down facings or trims, twin needle cable stitching and understitching, and much more.

## Attaching Elastic

Pattern instructions usually say to stretch the elastic while attaching it to the fabric. When the needle stitches through the elastic, it causes the rubber to break down and the elastic to stretch out of shape. With the following method, for knits only, you can avoid this pitfall.

### Machine Readiness Checklist

**Stitch:** three-step zigzag

**Length:** 1–1.5; 15–24 spi

**Width:** 4–widest

**Foot:** transparent embroidery

**Thread:** all-purpose

**Fabric:** sweatshirt fleece, velour, stretch terry, and other knit fabrics

**Needle:** 70/10 or 80/12 universal

**Accessories:** vanishing marker, pencil with an eraser on the end

**Note:** To do this technique properly, you must have about 1/2" (1.3cm) fabric on either side of the elastic. Therefore, when cutting fabric out, add 1/2" (1.3 cm) to the top opening where elastic is to be stitched. This method also works the same no matter where elastic is applied. However, for this example, the instructions are written as if you were applying elastic to a waistline.

1. Cut elastic 3–5" (7–12.5cm) shorter than waistline measurement. Mark it into eighths with the vanishing marker. Mark garment waistline into eighths.

**Sew-How:** *Double-check the length of waistline elastic before cutting to be sure it stretches over your hips.*

2. Pin elastic to wrong side of fabric, matching eighth-marks and placing it 1/2" (1.3cm) from cut edge. Do not join elastic ends.

3. Place work under the foot and sew a couple of stitches to anchor elastic. Using index finger of both hands simultaneously, start sewing while pulling the fabric out sideways, exactly where the needle enters the fabric. Take four or five stitches, reposition your fingers, and repeat until the fabric is eased in place and elastic ends overlap (Fig. 8.38).

**Sew-How:** *For a firmer grip at the right, pull on the fabric using the eraser end of a pencil.*

4. Fold fabric over elastic so the three-step zigzag shows on the inside.

**Fig. 8.38**
Pin elastic to wrong side, 1/2" (1.3cm) from cut edge. Pull fabric out sideways where the needle enters the fabric, and sew four to five stitches. Repeat until fabric is eased into elastic.

**Fig. 8.39**
"Wiggle" fabric into place with left index finger.

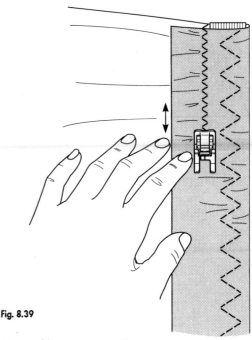

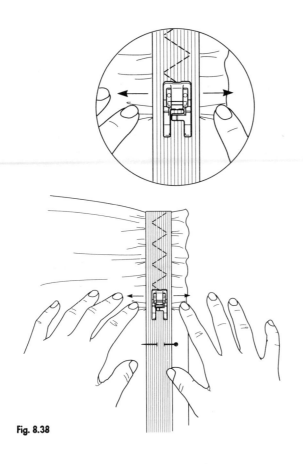

Fig. 8.38

Fig. 8.39

### Mending

Mend a run or tear with the three-step zigzag.

**Machine Readiness Checklist**

**Stitch:** zigzag

**Length:** 1.5; 20 spi

**Width:** 1

**Foot:** transparent or metal embroidery

5. Place waistline under foot, wrong side up. Place index finger to the left side of the foot. Sew to the left of the elastic while wiggling the fabric back and forth (Fig. 8.39). The using the index finger of your left hand to "wiggle" to fabric forward and back. This prevents elastic from stretching out and eliminates unnecessary puckers, tucks, or gathers from being stitched in the right side of the work.

6. Trim excess fabric away up to the stitch.

**Machine Readiness Checklist**

**Stitch:** three-step zigzag

**Length:** 0.4–0.8; 60 spi

**Width:** widest

**Foot:** transparent embroidery on medium to heavy fabric, standard zigzag foot on lightweight fabrics

**Thread:** all-purpose or 100% polyester thread one shade darker than fabric

**Accessories:** fusible interfacing

**Sew-How:** *I mend old denim jeans using a gray color thread on the bobbin and a blue to match the fabric on the top. Then I tighten the upper tension slightly. The mend is almost invisible because the gray thread pulls slightly to the surface of the fabric, giving the mend a faded look like the denim.*

**Fig. 8.40**
Center run or tear
under foot and mend
with the three-step
zigzag stitch.

**Fig. 8.41**
To save time, butt one
pattern piece up to the
next when overcasting.

1. Fuse a strip of interfacing to underside of tear. Center the run or tear under the foot and sew (Fig. 8.40). The stitches form over and across the tear, keeping the fabric flat and helping pull raveled threads in place.

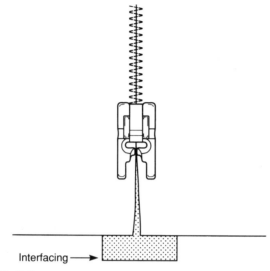

Interfacing →

**Fig. 8.40**

2. If necessary, turn the fabric around and stitch another row of three-step zigzags next to the first until tear is repaired.

## Overcasting a Raw Edge

Overcasting a raw edge with the zigzag stitch often causes tunneling. Because the three-step zigzag takes three stitches over and back, it keeps raw edges flat.

| Machine Readiness Checklist |
|---|
| **Stitch:** three-step zigzag |
| **Length:** 0.8–1.5 (use shorter length on fine fabrics; use longer length on heavy fabrics); 20–60 spi |
| **Width:** widest |
| **Foot:** standard zigzag on fine fabrics; transparent embroidery on medium to heavy fabrics |

Test for best stitch length on fabric scrap. Place raw edge under the foot so the right swing of the stitch is just off the edge.

---

**Sew-How:** *After cutting, overcast raw edges before putting the project together. To overcast quickly, butt one pattern piece up next to the other without lifting the foot. When you're done, pattern pieces will look like a kite tail (Fig. 8.41). Then cut threads between the pieces before construction.*

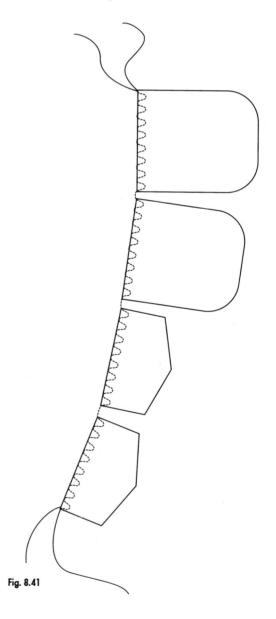

**Fig. 8.41**

Fig. 8.42
For extra
reinforcement, stitch
patch so three-step
zigzag stitches cross
each other at the
corners.

## Patching

The old-fashioned way to patch was to turn the raw edges in on the patch and stitch it over the hole by hand. This method is so slow, I found my mending pile getting unmanageable. Save time and put a patch on to stay.

**Machine Readiness Checklist**

**Stitch:** three-step zigzag

**Length:** 0.5–1; 24–60 spi

**Width:** widest

**Foot:** standard zigzag or Teflon-coated zigzag

**Feed dogs:** up

**Needle:** 90/14 jeans for medium to heavy fabrics; 80/12 universal for lightweight fabrics

**Thread:** all-purpose sewing or cotton darning (see Sources of Supply)

**Accessories:** glue stick

1. Cut patch large enough to cover the hole so the frayed fabric is covered. Don't turn under edges. Because the mending stitches are so close, the edges won't fray. This method cuts down on bulk.

2. Pin or glue-stick patch over hole. Starting at one corner, guide fabric so the right swing of the needle clears the raw edge of the patch. Sew to the corner, stopping with the needle on the far right side of the stitch (Fig. 8.42).

3. Pivot patch and stitch second side. The stitches should cross each other in the corner for extra reinforcement.

4. Repeat for other two sides. Pull threads to the back and tie them off. Trim damaged fabric from the wrong side of the patch.

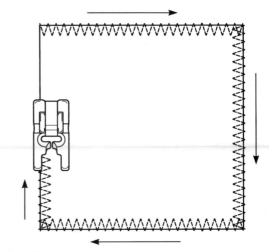

Fig. 8.42

**Sew-How:** *If you have a freearm machine, you can patch a knee or elbow without ripping out the seam, as long as your stitch length has the continuous reverse feature (see your instruction book). To do this, sew the first two sides of the patch as described above, then use the continuous reverse to sew the second two sides of the patch. When a knee or elbow is over the free arm of your machine, the continuous reverse allows you to patch it without removing the fabric.*

## Tacking

Tack down a facing, ribbon, or yarn tie when tying a quilt, or attach a small appliqué.

**Machine Readiness Checklist**

**Stitch:** three-step zigzag

**Length:** 0

**Width:** 3–widest

**Foot:** transparent embroidery

**Feed dogs:** down (if they can be lowered)

**Needle position:** left

**Fig. 8.43**
Stitch across and back
a few times to tack
down a facing, ribbon,
or yarn tie in a quilt.

**Fig. 8.44**
Use twin needles with
the three-step zigzag
to create a cable on a
soft knit.

1. Place facing, yarn, ribbon, or appliqué on background or fashion fabric and under the foot.

2. Stitch across and back in the same place five or six stitches (Fig. 8.43). Move width to 0 and stitch in one place a few stitches.

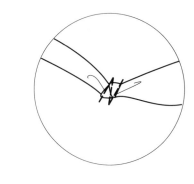

**Fig. 8.43**

3. Pull threads to the back and either cut or tie them off.

## Three-Step Zigzag with Twin Needles

Use thread matching the fabric to create a cable in a solid-colored fabric. I've used five to seven rows of cable stitching down the front of a stretch terrycloth sweatshirt and centered down each sleeve.

| **Machine Readiness Checklist** |
| --- |

| | |
| --- | --- |
| **Stitch:** | three-step zigzag |
| **Length:** | 1–2; 13–24 spi |
| **Width:** | 3 (wide enough for needles to clear the hole in the foot and needle plate) |
| **Foot:** | transparent embroidery |
| **Feed dogs:** | up |
| **Needle position:** | center |
| **Needle:** | twin, size 2.0/80(12) or 2.5/80(12) |
| **Thread:** | all-purpose |
| **Fabric suggestions:** | stretch terry, velour, wool jersey, some medium weight T-shirt knits |
| **Accessories:** | vanishing marker or dressmaker's chalk |

1. Using the vanishing marker or dressmaker's chalk, mark the center of the garment where the cables are to be stitched.

2. Sew the first row of cable stitches over the line marked in Step 1. Turn the fabric around and stitch the second row next to the first about a presser foot-width away (Fig. 8.44). (If you were to sew every line the same way, the fabric would distort.)

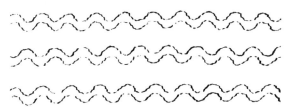

**Fig. 8.44**

3. Continue to sew row after row of cable stitching, working from the center row of cable stitches out, until you have the desired effect.

**Fig. 8.45**
Match twin needle,
three-step zigzag
cable stitches back to
back.

**Fig. 8.46**
Understitch facings
with the three-step
zigzag to prevent them
from rolling out of
place.

---

**Sew-How:** *Once you have mastered this technique, match the stitches, back to back, and use this design as the center row of cabling (Fig. 8.45).*

---

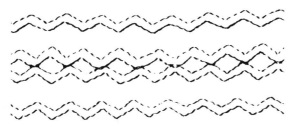

**Fig. 8.45**

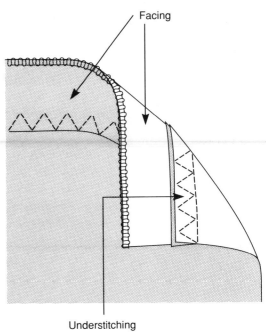

Facing

Understitching

**Fig. 8.46**

## Understitching

Understitching prevents the inside layer of fabric from rolling to the outside and is generally worked on a facing edge. You can understitch with the straight stitch, but the three-step zigzag flattens the bulk of a faced edge better and it's not always necessary to topstitch.

| Machine Readiness Checklist | |
|---|---|
| **Stitch:** | three-step zigzag |
| **Length:** | 1–1.5; 20–24 spi |
| **Width:** | widest |
| **Foot:** | standard zigzag for lightweight fabrics; transparent embroidery for medium and heavy fabrics |

1. After stitching and trimming the seam, press seam allowance toward the facing.

2. With the right side up, place the foot so the right edge of the needle hole is at the seamline, and understitch (Fig. 8.46).

In this section you have tried a few practical stitch applications and techniques. This is only the beginning. Keep experimenting to come up with your own innovations; take notes on what you do and store them with your samples in your notebook.

In the next section you will learn the basics of another type of stitch commonly available on today's sewing machines—the forward and reverse feeding stitch.

# FORWARD AND REVERSE STITCHES

- Double Overlock Stitch
- Smocking Stitch
- Elastic Straight Stitch
- Super Stretch Stitch
- Overlock Stitch

As you remember, we added width to a straight stitch to create a zigzag and automatic stitches, such as the blind hem and three-step zigzag.

Forward and reverse stitches, often referred to as stretch, Tri-motion™, or super-automatic stitches, are created by the feed dogs moving the fabric forward and backward as the needle zigzags from side to side. The combination of the needle swing and feed dog action creates stitches such as the double overlock (flatlock), feather, overlock, and smocking stitches, to name a few. Look at your machine and match the stitches available with those pictured in Fig. 8.47. Write in the names or numbers your machine uses.

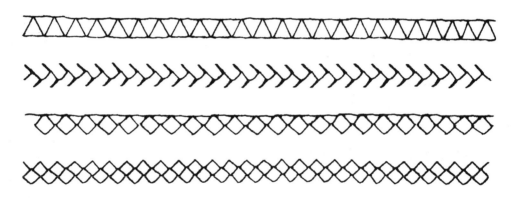

**Fig. 8.47**
From top to bottom: double overlock (flatlock), feather stitch, overlock, and smocking stitch.

The following forward and reverse feeding stitches are common to most brands and are listed alphabetically by their most common name.

## DOUBLE OVERLOCK STITCH

- Edge Finish
- 1/4" (6mm) Seams

Sometimes called a flatlock, the double overlock stitch emulates a 3-thread serger overlock. It is used on knits and wovens to overcast raw edges and to stitch and finish a 1/4" (6mm) seam in one operation. It is also used to topstitch T-shirts, sweatshirts, swim wear, and other active sportswear.

### Edge Finish

This edge finish is recommended for loosely woven fabrics.

| Machine Readiness Checklist | |
|---|---|
| **Stitch:** | double overlock |
| **Length:** | varies with brand; see instruction book |
| **Width:** | 4–widest |
| **Foot:** | overcast guide (overedge) |

Place raw edge under foot so the needle catches into the fabric on the left and swings just off the edge and over the guide in the foot on the right (Fig. 8.48; also see Fig. 9.38).

**Fig. 8.48**
Finish edge of loosely woven fabric with the double overlock (flatlock) stitch.

**Fig. 8.49**
Stitch 1/4" (6mm) seam allowance so the stitch on the right swings off raw edges.

**Fig. 8.50**
Guide seam allowance by the 1/2" (1.3cm) line in the needle plate and trim the fabric up to the stitch.

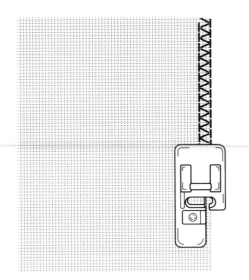

Fig. 8.48

## 1/4" (6mm) Seams

Use this method on most knits and medium-weight wovens. As always, test on a swatch first.

| Machine Readiness Checklist | |
| --- | --- |
| **Stitch:** | double overlock |
| **Length:** | varies with brand; see instruction book |
| **Width:** | 4–widest |
| **Foot:** | transparent embroidery for knits; overcast guide or standard zigzag for wovens |

1. For a project cut with 1/4" (6mm) seam allowances, place right sides together so raw edges are to the right inside edge of the needle hole in the presser foot. The needle stitches into the seam allowance on the left and off the raw edge on the right (Fig. 8.49; also see Fig. 9.38).

2. Trim excess fabric up to the stitch.

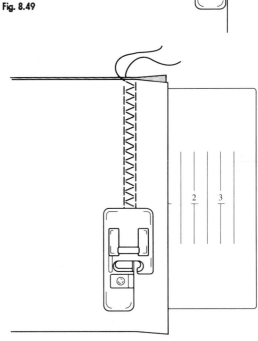

Fig. 8.49

Fig. 8.50

**Sew-How:** *For a project with 5/8" (1.5cm) seam allowances, place fabric under foot, guiding the raw edge by the 1/2" (1.3cm) line in the needle plate (Fig. 8.50). If you guide by the 5/8" (1.5cm) line in the needle plate, the stitch cheats you out of 1/8" (3mm) at each seam allowance. That doesn't sound like much, but multiply 1/8" (3mm) by eight cut edges and you have taken 1" (2.5cm) out of the total circumference. Your garment may be too snug for comfort.*

Fig. 8.51
Elongated elastic
straight stitch as a
topstitch on jeans.

Fig. 8.52
Elongated elastic
straight stitch used
with the wing needle
as a hem finish on
linen collar.

## ELASTIC STRAIGHT STITCH

• Reinforce Stress Seams

• Topstitch

• Hemstitch

Sometimes called the straight stretch stitch, this stitch takes two stitches forward and one back and is used to reinforce areas of stress such as underarm and crotch seams. It is not recommended for sewing straight seams on knits because it is almost impossible to rip if you make a mistake.

Lengthen it, and you get a beautiful topstitch, like those seen on jeans and leather goods (Fig. 8.51).

Fig. 8.51

### Hemstitch

Still another application is for linen collar, cuff, napkin, and tablecloth hems.

| Machine Readiness Checklist |
| --- |

| | |
| --- | --- |
| **Stitch:** | elastic straight |
| **Length:** | 4 or longest; 4–6 spi |
| **Width:** | 0 |
| **Foot:** | standard metal or Teflon zigzag |
| **Needle:** | 70/10 universal; wing |
| **Thread:** | all-purpose; darning 70 or 120 weight (see Sources of Supply) |
| **Fabric:** | tightly woven cotton or linen |

1. Finish hem edge with the three-step zigzag (length, 1; width, widest) using all-purpose thread and a 70/10 universal needle. Fold hem up desired amount and press.

2. Using a wing needle, rethread top and bobbin with darning thread. Topstitch hem so the foot is resting on a double layer of fabric.

**Sew-How:** *This stitch is made by taking two stitches forward and one stitch back. It's important that your machine is adjusted properly so the needle stitches back into the same hole, creating the look in Fig. 8.52. If your stitching line is rough and the holes created by the wing needle are uneven, check your instruction book to see how the stitch length can be fine-tuned.*

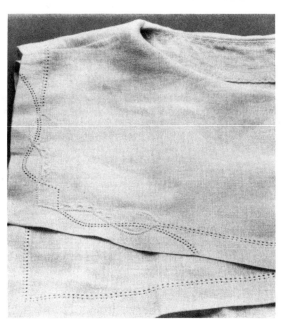

Fig. 8.52

## OVERLOCK STITCH

• One-Step Elastic Application

The overlock is sometimes used to overcast a raw edge or sew a 1/4" (6mm) seam, described in the double overlock techniques above. However, it often causes fabric to tunnel and the seams to ripple. My favorite application for the overlock is a one-step method of elastic application for lingerie.

**Fig. 8.53**
Place work so left side of stitch falls on the fabric and right side swings onto elastic. Pull fabric sideways where needle enters fabric and take four or five stitches. Repeat until fabric is eased into elastic. Trim excess fabric from behind elastic. Sew ribbon over elastic join.

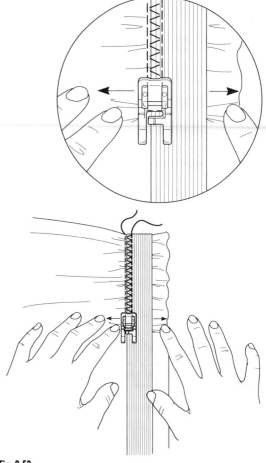

Fig. 8.53

**Machine Readiness Checklist**

**Stitch:** overlock

**Length:** varies with brand; see instruction book

**Width:** widest

**Foot:** transparent embroidery or standard zigzag

**Needle:** 70/10 or 80/12 universal

**Thread:** all-purpose or nylon

**Fabric:** nylon tricot or cotton single knit

**Accessories:** 1/2" (1.3cm) lingerie elastic, vanishing marker

**Note:** To do this technique properly, leave about 1/2" (1.3cm) of fabric on either side of the elastic. It works only on knits or loosely woven fabrics cut on the bias. Therefore, cut lingerie with 1/2" (1.3cm) extra fabric at the top of waistline and at panty legs where elastic is to be sewn.

1. Measure elastic to fit comfortably around the waist and or legs (usually 2–5") (5–12.5cm) smaller than garment opening. Mark elastic and opening into eighths using the vanishing marker.

2. Pin elastic to opening on the right side, 1/2" (1.3cm) down from the raw edge. Overlap and pin elastic ends at the side seams.

**Sew-How:** *Lingerie elastic wears longer when sewn on the outside of the garment because the fabric underneath protects it from perspiration and body oils.*

3. Place work under presser foot so the left side of the stitch falls on the fabric and the right side swings onto the elastic (Fig. 8.53). Take a couple of stitches to anchor elastic.

4. Using index fingers of both hands simultaneously, start sewing while pulling the fabric out sideways, exactly where the needle enters the fabric. Take four or five stitches, reposition your fingers, and repeat until the fabric is eased in place and elastic ends overlap.

5. Trim away excess fabric to the stitch. Stitch a ribbon over elastic ends to cover the overlap.

## SMOCKING STITCH

• 1/4" (6mm) Seam Finish

This stitch is often called the honeycomb and can be used to stitch and finish a 1/4" (6mm) seam in one step, for reverse embroidery, and for overlapped seams in lacy fabrics. See Part II, The World of Sewing, for stitch application to specific projects (Fig. 8.54).

Fig. 8.54

## SUPER STRETCH STITCH

• 1/4" (6mm) Seam Finish

• 1/4" (6mm) Stabilized Seam Finish

This practical stitch, sometimes called the overlock, is designed for use on super stretchy fabrics. Use it for 1/4" (6mm) seams on sweater knits, stretch terry cloth, ribbing, Lycra spandex swim wear, and biking fabrics.

Often these fabrics require stabilizing so seams will not droop or stretch out of shape.

| **Machine Readiness Checklist** | |
|---|---|
| **Stitch:** | super stretch |
| **Length:** | varies with brand; see instruction book |
| **Width:** | 4–widest |
| **Foot:** | transparent embroidery |
| **Needle:** | 80/12 universal |
| **Thread:** | all-purpose |
| **Fabric:** | very stretchy knits |
| **Accessories:** | elastic thread, yarn, or pearl cotton |

1. For a project cut with 1/4" (6mm) seam allowances, place right sides together so raw edges are to the right inside edge of the needle hole in the presser foot. Put needle in fabric and raise the foot.

2. Cut a length of elastic thread, yarn, or pearl cotton the length of the seam and place it under the foot. Put the foot down and stitch (Fig. 8.55). The needle stitches into the seam allowance on the left and off the raw edge at the right.

Fig. 8.55

Now you should have a general understanding of the practical forward and reverse stitches available, and a notebook of stitch samples to help you remember what stitch is best for the job. But there is a world of creative possibilities awaiting you with the decorative stitches. Read on to understand the basics; then make the projects in Part II to practice, invent, and create.

## DECORATIVE STITCHES

Decorative stitches vary greatly from brand to brand, so I will address them only from a general way. (Watch for Chilton's brand specific **Teach Yourself to Sew Better** books for information on utility and decorative stitches specific to your machine.) The specifics and some applications are found in your instruction book; in educational materials developed by the sewing machine companies and made available through your local dealer; and in Part II, The World of Sewing, in this book.

There are two types of decorative stitches—closed and open. Closed means the stitches are close together and variations of a satin stitch, like the ball, diamond, arrow head, and heart. Open decorative stitches are those where the beauty of the stitch is seeing the stitch and the fabric under it (Fig. 8.56). Use decorative stitches to create borders on a front tab, pocket top, belt, or pair of suspenders. Decorate a napkin, placemat, or table cloth. Use them on children's clothes, gifts, toys, and games.

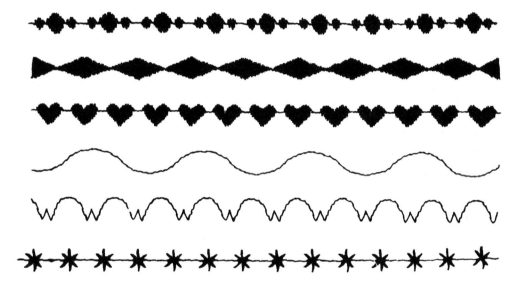

**Fig. 8.56**
Closed decorative stitches, from top to bottom: ball, diamond, heart. Open decorative stitches, from top to bottom: wave, scallop variation, daisy.

One of the most valuable samples in my notebook is a piece of pillow ticking where I stitched row after row of decorative stitches, using varying lengths and widths and experimenting with the twin needle.

In the next chapter, you will investigate what I call the "undiscovered treasures of sewing"—the presser feet. You'll see what the tops and undersides look like to better understand why and how each foot works. You'll see how a presser foot used with different stitches creates different effects. The information is also cross-referenced with the stitches in this chapter. So find that dusty box of accessories and start your treasure hunt.

# ENCYCLOPEDIA OF PRESSER FEET

MOST SEWING MACHINES COME WITH FIVE TO TEN standard presser feet, but there are up to fifty-eight presser feet and/or accessories available for some brands. Using the correct presser foot helps you stitch better and with more perfection. This encyclopedia suggests a number of ways to use each foot in both practical and decorative applications. But first, you need to understand the anatomy of the presser foot.

There are two parts to a presser foot—the shank and the foot or sole. The shank holds the foot in place and may be fixed to the foot or may have a clamp so the foot can snap on and off.

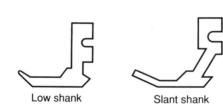

**Fig. 9.1**
Presser feet with high, low, and slant needle shanks.

High shank     Low shank     Slant shank

Fig. 9.1

There are three types of shanks: high, low, and slant needle (Fig. 9.1). Learn what type you have. The high shank measures 1" (2.5cm) from the needle clamp to the bottom of the foot. The low shank measures 1/2" (1.3cm) from the needle clamp to the bottom of the foot. The slant needle shank angles from the machine toward you. Once you know your machine's type of shank, you can put on presser feet not specifically designed for your machine, as long as they, too, are high, low, or slant needle shanks. This variety of presser feet opens a new world in sewing.

The purpose of a presser foot is to hold the fabric firmly against the feed dogs during stitch formation and to help complete a particular technique. It also protects your fingers from the needle.

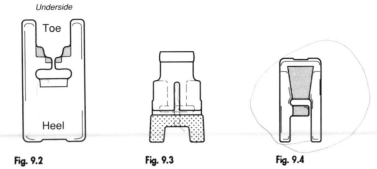

**Fig. 9.2**
Underside of toe and heel of presser foot.

**Fig. 9.3**
Underside of button sewing foot.

**Fig. 9.4**
Underside of the embroidery foot with wide channel at the heel.

**Fig. 9.2**  **Fig. 9.3**  **Fig. 9.4**

The foot or sole has a toe and heel (Fig. 9.2). The underside is the most important part because it helps guide the fabric and stitches so they feed smoothly over the feed dogs. The toe or toes are on the front of the foot in front of the needle. The heel is on the back of the foot behind the needle. Let me show you how important the presser foot can be.

When I taught machine embroidery, I showed the class a satin stitch—a wide zigzag stitch sewn very close together. When finished, satin stitching should look like a narrow strand of satin ribbon and have a smooth, rounded appearance, like the stitches you see on monogrammed towels.

Everyone tried it. But one of the students used her button sewing foot and wondered why the fabric wouldn't move. Look at the underside (Fig. 9.3). Notice the flat bottom, short toes, and the rubber sleeve or grip put there so the button will not slip out. You can imagine why this woman was having some difficulty—the foot could not move over the satin stitches.

The proper foot to use is the embroidery foot (Fig. 9.4). The underside has a wide channel behind the needle. This allows the stitches to form and the fabric to move smoothly under it without flattening the stitches into the fabric. Before we get ahead of ourselves, let's take a look at the five best, and most common, feet; the standard zigzag, embroidery, buttonhole, blind hem, and zipper foot.

## THE FIVE BEST FEET

- Standard Zigzag
- Embroidery
- Buttonhole
- Blind Hem
- Zipper

### STANDARD ZIGZAG FOOT

This foot is generally made of metal and is sometimes Teflon-coated. When you look at the underside, notice the smooth, flat bottom—no grooves or ridges (Fig. 9.5). This foot is designed to stitch very fine or heavy fabric because it holds the fabric firmly against the feed dogs.

Has your machine ever "eaten" the fabric? This foot helps prevent the problem. It offers support around the needle to prevent it from pulling and pushing fabric up and down with every stitch. On fine fabrics it also helps prevent puckering. On heavy fabrics it helps prevent skipped stitches.

**Application:** Most inexperienced sewers leave this foot on all the time, but that makes sewing harder. When you teach

**Fig. 9.5**
Standard zigzag foot with smooth, flat underside.

**Fig. 9.6**
In left or right needle position, the needle hole provides support around three sides of the needle to prevent puckering and skipped stitches.

**Fig. 9.7**
Metal embroidery, utility, or appliqué foot with wide channel on the underside.

**Fig. 9.8**
Open toe embroidery foot, sometimes called an appliqué or decorative stitching foot, is open in the front with a wide channel in the heel.

yourself to sew better, you will use this foot for about 30% of garment construction.

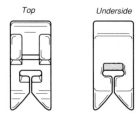

Top    Underside

**Fig. 9.5**

---

**Sew-How:** *If you have puckering or skipped stitches even with the appropriate needle size for the fabric, use the standard zigzag foot and decenter the needle to the far left or right (Fig. 9.6). This way, the needle hole in the foot and the needle plate provide support around three sides of the needle, rather than two sides, as is the case when the needle is in the center position.*

---

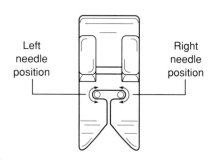

Left needle position    Right needle position

**Fig. 9.6**

# EMBROIDERY FEET

## Metal Embroidery Foot

Sometimes called a utility foot, the metal embroidery foot has a wide channel carved out of the heel on the underside (Fig. 9.7). This channel allows decorative stitches (e.g., satin stitch, scallop, ball, diamond, etc.) to be sewn and the fabric to move smoothly without flattening the stitches into the fabric.

The channel is also curved at the heel to help turn smooth curves and corners.

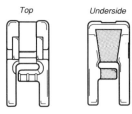

Top    Underside

**Fig. 9.7**

**Application:** Use this foot on lightweight fabrics because it provides more pressure on the fabric than the transparent embroidery foot described below. Also available for some brands with a Teflon coating or runners, this foot is helpful in embroidering on leather, vinyl, suede, or other sticky fabrics.

## Open-Toe Embroidery Foot

The open-toe embroidery foot, sometimes called an appliqué or decorative stitching foot, has the wide channel in the heel on the underside and two long toes in the front. Available in transparent or metal, it provides an excellent view of your work, but offers no support in front of the needle which may cause skipped stitches or puckering (Fig. 9.8).

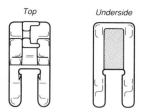

Top    Underside

**Fig. 9.8**

---

**Sew-How:** *If this foot is not available for your machine, buy another metal or transparent embroidery foot and cut out the section in front of the needle with a jigsaw or scissors.*

---

**Fig. 9.9**
Transparent
embroidery foot,
sometimes called an
appliqué foot, has a
wide channel in the
heel and one or two
grooves in front of the
foot on the underside.

**Fig. 9.10**
Sliding buttonhole feet
enable you to make all
the buttonholes the
same size. This type
has a lock screw
and stop. Snug stop
against the edge of the
button, remove the
button, and make
buttonhole to fit the
button.

**Application:** Use it on medium-weight fabrics for machine quilting and appliqué. Quarter-inch (6mm) elastic also fits perfectly under the foot and between the toes for elastic application.

## Transparent Embroidery Foot

Sometimes referred to as an appliqué foot, the transparent embroidery foot is made of a synthetic material that allows you to see through it. Some transparent embroidery feet also have two narrow channels in front of the needle on the underside—excellent for guiding cord or stitching over a narrow row of satin stitching (Fig. 9.9).

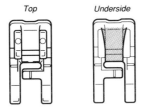

Top      Underside

**Fig. 9.9**

**Application:** Use this foot for most of the embroidery stitches sewn with a presser foot. Also use it for seaming techniques in medium and heavy wovens and knits.

## BUTTONHOLE FEET

### Sliding Buttonhole Foot with Guide

This type of foot is popular because it's designed to make a buttonhole as short as 1/4" (6mm) or as large as 1-1/4" (3cm), and it enables you to make all the buttonholes the same size without a lot of elaborate measuring.

One type is designed with a slide and lock screw. To use it, loosen the screw, set the button in place, slide the guide up to the button, then tighten the screw back down. Remove the button. The foot then moves the distance necessary to make a buttonhole to fit the button (Fig. 9.10).

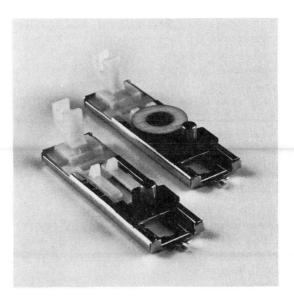

**Fig. 9.10**

Another type looks similar but does not have a lock screw. To use it, slide the foot shank to the back. Place the button on the foot so one edge of the button is against the foot shank. Cut a cardboard template to fill the space from the other edge of the button to the front of the foot. Snap the template into the slide, remove the button, and make a test buttonhole. Cut it open to be sure the button fits. Then mark each template with the correct buttonhole length for future use. **Note:** Both types of feet have bars on the front and/or back to cord buttonholes.

**Application:** Use this foot to make buttonholes or corded buttonholes on medium to heavy fabrics (see Fig. 8.13).

**Sew-How:** *When making a buttonhole on an uneven surface, such as over a hidden seam allowance, hold the foot with your index finger and thumb on top of the slide and in front and back of the shank. This levels the foot so you don't get a buildup of stitches going up or a space between the stitches coming off a bump.*

## Standard Buttonhole Foot

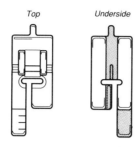

Fig. 9.11

**Fig. 9.11**
The standard buttonhole foot has two narrow channels in the heel and one wide channel in front on the underside. Some buttonhole feet have a bar in front or back for cording.

This foot has two narrow channels in the heel on the underside (Fig. 9.11). After the first column of stitches is made, the foot rides on the narrow column of stitching while the second side of the buttonhole is made, so the two sides of stitching are parallel.

Some feet have a bar in the front or back for cording. Corded buttonholes are more durable and generally better looking than uncorded buttonholes (see Figs. 8.12, 8.13).

**Application:** This foot works well on lightweight fabrics because the needle is supported around three sides. However, it is difficult to get all the buttonholes the same size without marking them accurately first.

## BLIND HEM FOOT

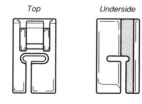

Fig. 9.12

**Fig. 9.12**
The underside of the blind hem foot is higher on the left than on the right. When fabric is folded for blind hemming, the double layer of fabric guides smoothly under it.

If this foot did not come with your machine, buy one. It saves time and helps guide the fabric so the needle won't pick up too much fabric when blind hemming. If used properly, the blind hem foot ensures invisible results on most fabrics. The underside of the foot is higher on the left

than the right (Fig. 9.12). This way, when the fabric is folded for blind hemming, there is enough room under it for the double layer of fabric (see Figs. 8.29, 8.30).

**Application:** Besides blind hemming, use this foot for edgestitching, topstitching, or making traditional pintucks. Snug the right toe or guide against the edge of the fabric. Move the needle position as far left as desired and stitch (Fig. 9.13).

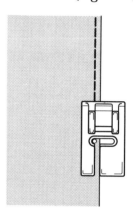

Fig. 9.13

**Fig. 9.13**
Use the blind hem foot for edge stitching, topstitching, or making traditional pintucks. Snug right toe or guide against edge of fold and stitch.

Some blind hem feet have a long guide in front. To stitch-in-the-ditch, center the guide down the seamline and stitch in the crack of the seam. Use this method to tack down facings or to final stitch waistbands (see Fig. 8.7).

### Zigzag Foot with Blind Hem Guide

Some machines come with a metal blind hem guide used in conjunction with the zigzag foot. It is a little awkward, but once in place, makes blind hemming much easier.

Fold fabric for blind hemming (see Figs. 8.29 and 8.30). Snug fold against the inside edge of the guide and blind hem.

**Application:** Blind hemming.

## ZIPPER FOOT

Fig. 9.14

Zipper feet adjust by a screw or clamp, or can be snapped on and off to move from side to side.

Fig. 9.15

Use the zipper foot to cover and attach piping in a seam on clothing, pillows, or slip covers.

If you have avoided a pattern because it called for a zipper, the zipper foot will help. It adjusts by screw or clamp, or can be snapped off and moved to sew both sides of the zipper without riding over the zipper coil (Fig. 9.14).

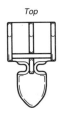

Top          Underside

Fig. 9.14

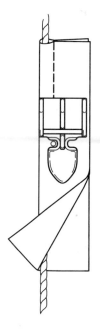

**Application:** Use the zipper foot for zipper insertions, and to cover cord or piping for the edges of pillows or slip covers (Fig. 9.15).

Fig. 9.15

# EXTRA PRESSER FEET AND ACCESSORIES

| | | |
|---|---|---|
| • Bias Binder | • Edge Guide | • Overcast Guide |
| • Button Reed | • Eyelet Plate | • Pintucking |
| • Button Sewing | • Felling | • Quilting Guide |
| • Braiding | • Fringe | • Roller |
| • Carpet Fork | • Gathering | • Ruffler |
| • Circle Maker | • Hemstitch Fork | • Straight Stitch |
| • Cording | • Hemmer | • Walking |
| • Darning | • Multiple Cord | • Weaver's Reed |

Some of these presser feet and accessories come standard with your machine; some don't. In this section, the most common name for each accessory is listed and illustrated to help you identify it. Alternate names are also listed, along with suggested applications. As you read through this section, check off those you own and make stitch samples for your notebook.

## BIAS BINDER

A bias binder is used for applying flat or prefolded bias tape, binding, or trim. Available for most machines, the bias binder has a funnel and guide to fold the binding over the base fabric before it reaches the needle (Fig. 9.16).

Some bias binders are used only with a straight stitch; others can be used with a zigzag or decorative stitch. Others are even adjustable to accommodate varying widths of tape or binding.

### Machine Readiness Checklist

| | |
|---|---|
| **Stitch:** | straight, zigzag, or decorative |
| **Length:** | varies |
| **Width:** | varies |
| **Foot:** | bias binder |
| **Thread:** | all-purpose |
| **Fabric:** | prequilted or medium to heavy woven |
| **Tension:** | normal |
| **Needle position:** | varies |
| **Accessories:** | 1/2" (1.3cm) flat or prefolded bias tape |

1. Unfold 3" (7.5cm) of one end of a length of bias tape and press flat.

2. On the pressed end, fold tape in half the long way and make a V-shaped cut so the point of the cut is at the fold (Fig. 9.16).

3. With the binder off the machine, thread tape through the funnel so the point of the cut is to the right. **Note:** If you are having trouble threading the funnel, use a hand needle and doubled thread to stitch through the point of the V and pull the point through the funnel.

4. Put binder on the machine and pull the feed end of tape so it extends about 2" (5cm) behind the foot.

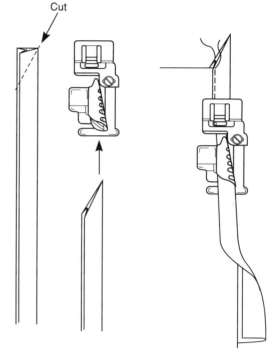

Cut

**Fig. 9.16**

5. Slip the base fabric into the slot in the center of the funnel.

6. Adjust your needle position so the needle stitches inside the folded edge of the tape.

**Application:** Bind the edges of double-faced quilted fabric for placemats or an unlined jacket. Stitch on bias tape or Seams Great™ for a Hong Kong seam finish or hem.

## BUTTON REED

### Button Reed for Sewing on Buttons

This accessory, sometimes called a clearance plate, is made by Viking but can be used on any machine. It has two ends, one thicker than the other, which provide space for a shank so the button stands away from the fabric. A button shank prevents the buttonhole from gapping and pulling too hard on the button and fabric. Use the thicker end of the button reed for heavy fabrics. Use the thinner end for medium-weight fabrics.

Fig. 9.17
With reed and button
in place, stab needle
into the left hole, lower
presser bar, and stitch.

### Machine Readiness Checklist

**Stitch:** zigzag

**Length:** 0

**Width:** 3–6 ( may vary with button)

**Foot:** none or transparent embroidery (**Note:** If your feet snap on, remove the foot and leave the foot shank on)

**Feed dogs:** dropped (if possible)

**Needle position:** left

**Accessories:** glue stick

1. Mark button placement. Dab glue stick on the back of the button and place it on button reed.

2. Place reed and button on fabric under the foot or foot shank. Stab the needle into the left hole and lower the presser bar lever (Fig. 9.17).

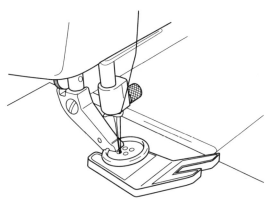

Fig. 9.17

3. Move the flywheel by hand to check needle clearance, adjust the stitch width if necessary, then stitch four to five zigzag stitches. If sewing a four-hole button, lift presser bar and move the fabric to stitch the back two holes.

4. Move stitch width to 0 and stitch two to three stitches to lock them off. Remove

fabric by pulling off enough thread to wrap the shank between the button and fabric.

5. Poke top and bobbin threads between button and fabric then thread them through a hand needle. Wrap the shank (see Fig. 8.17). Pull free ends through to the back of the fabric and tie them off.

---

**Sew-How:** *To eliminate the need to tie off threads, bring threads to the back, snip them close to the back of the fabric, and dab them with a spot of seam sealant.*

---

**Did You Know?** Regardless of button size, 90 percent of the holes are the same distance apart. Why? Button manufacturers use the same equipment to make the holes in most buttons, whatever the diameter.

### Button Reed as a Wedge

Sewing up and over heavy seams on a jean hem or attaching a belt loop is tough because the foot stalls on the way up and coasts on the way down the thickness. This happens because the foot is not level with the feed dogs.

Use the button reed as a wedge under the heel of the foot as you approach a thickness and under the toes as you come off the thickness.

1. As the toes tip up, stop with the needle in the fabric and lift the foot. Slip the wedge under the heel and lower the presser foot (Fig. 9.18A).

2. Stitch across the thickness until the toes begin to tip down. Stop with the needle in the fabric and lift the foot again.

3. Slip wedge under the toes and take a few stitches until the back of the foot is off the thickness (Fig. 9.18B). Remove wedge.

**Fig. 9.18**
Use button reed as a wedge under toes as you approach and come off a thickness. To start sewing on a thick edge, place needle in fabric, and wedge button reed under heel, then lower presser foot.

**Fig. 9.19**
Button sewing foot.

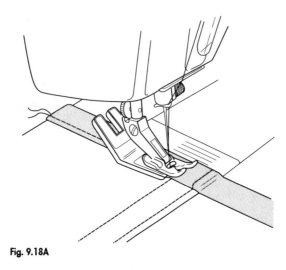

Fig. 9.18A

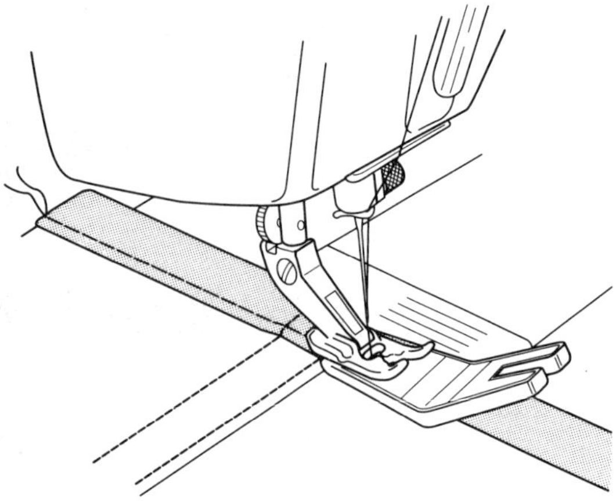

Fig. 9.18B

This technique prevents stitch distortion and keeps the needle from breaking on the foot as it pivots on and off the thickness.

When starting a seam or topstitching a heavy fabric, place needle at the edge of the fabric and the reed under the heel of the foot. This way the foot doesn't have to climb uphill to start sewing.

---

**Sew-How:** *Even though it may look as if the foot is down, remember to lower the presser foot on the wedge to engage the upper tension. Otherwise the stitches will not form properly.*

---

## BUTTON SEWING FOOT

Sometimes you need a button sewn with a thread shank, so use a button sewing foot. Some have a rubber sleeve with a channel underneath for a heavy needle to slip into to form the thread shank (see Fig. 8.17). Others have a plastic gripper to firmly hold button in place (Fig. 9.19). To use the foot:

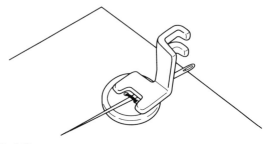

Fig. 9.19

1. Slip a needle under the foot between the toes.

2. Mark button placement and set your machine as described above for the button reed.

3. Dab glue stick on the back of the button; then place it on the fabric. Stitch button as described above.

### Button Sewing Foot with Guide

This foot has an adjustable guide that can be raised or lowered, depending on the length of thread shank needed. It is available in a low shank, so it fits most low-shank machines (see the beginning of this chapter). To use this foot, set your machine as described above for the button reed. Mark button placement and use glue stick to hold the button on the fabric. Stitch as described for the button sewing foot above.

**Did You Know?** The three buttons on jacket sleeves were stitched there to discourage soldiers from wiping their mouths and noses on their sleeves.

**Fig. 9.20**
Narrow braiding foot, sometimes called a narrow cording foot, has a narrow channel on the underside behind the needle and a clip or guide on top to guide yarn, pearl cotton, or narrow cord.

**Fig. 9.21**
Couch interesting yarn in a plaid, stripe, or scrolled design using the narrow braiding foot.

**Fig. 9.22**
Child's art work enlarged and appliquéd as a wall hanging. The outline is done with the narrow braiding foot threaded with black yarn and couched with a straight stitch using nylon monofilament thread top and bobbin.

# BRAIDING FEET

## Narrow Braiding Foot

Sometimes referred to as a narrow cording foot, this foot is not usually standard, but I feel it's a necessity. The top of the foot has a guide to hold narrow cord, such as pearl cotton, yarn, or cordonnet. The underside has a narrow channel behind the needle which flairs out at the heel, enabling you to stitch around curves and corners smoothly (Fig. 9.20).

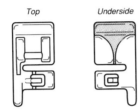

Top    Underside

**Fig. 9.20**

**Applications:** Use this foot to cord an edge that will be satin-stitched later. To gather, use this foot to zigzag over a cord so you don't catch the cord in the stitch (see Fig. 8.21). Create your own fabric by using

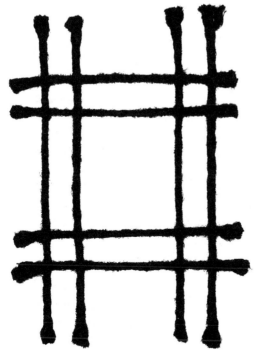

**Fig. 9.21**

a solid base fabric and couch interesting yarn in a plaid, stripe, or scrolled design (Fig. 9.21).

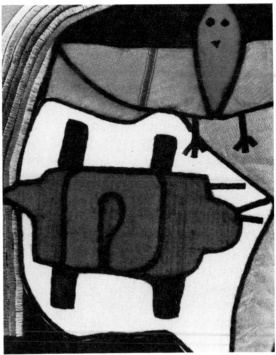

**Fig. 9.22**

Outline an appliqué with yarn or cord by straight stitching through it (Fig. 9.22). Because the clip or guide holds the cord in place, you can stitch in any direction and be assured of stitching through the cord to anchor it properly. For truly invisible results, use nylon monofilament thread top and bobbin. This way all you see is the cord or yarn and not the stitches used to attach it to the fabric.

### Standard Braiding Foot

The standard braiding foot has an opening in front of the needle large enough to accommodate middy or soutache braid. Some braiding feet have an adjustable guide or hole for varying weights of braid, yarn, or cord (Fig. 9.23).

The standard braiding foot works on the same principle as the narrow braiding foot but the channel on the underside is wider and feeds the braid straight.

Top        Underside

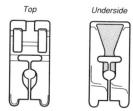

**Fig. 9.23**

Fig. 9.23
The underside of the standard braiding foot has a channel wider than that on the narrow braiding foot to feed braid straight.

**Applications:** Embellish jackets, children's clothing, and costumes with braid, or couch over heavy yarn, cord, or trim (Fig. 9.24).

Fig. 9.24
Embellish jackets or children's clothing and costumes with braid, heavy yarn, cord, trim, or soutache braid.

**Fig. 9.24**

Fig. 9.25
Wrap yarn around toes toward the bend. Anchor free end in V-shaped clip. Sew to the bend in the fork, pull fork toward you, then wrap again and stitch.

**Fig. 9.25**

## CARPET FORK

This accessory is designed to make fringe and can be used with any machine, even an old treadle straight stitch. Another accessory designed for a similar use is called the weaver's reed. (See end of this chapter).

To use the carpet fork, wrap yarn around the toes at the end of the fork, wrapping yarn toward the bend. Anchor yarn in the V-shaped clip at the top (Fig. 9.25). Do not cut the yarn.

| Machine Readiness Checklist | |
|---|---|
| Stitch: | three-step zigzag |
| Length: | 2.5–3; 9–12 spi |
| Width: | widest |
| Foot: | transparent embroidery |
| Feed dogs: | up |
| Needle position: | center |
| Thread: | polyester or nylon |
| Fabric: | rug backing, denim, or pillow ticking |
| Tension: | normal |
| Accessories: | carpet fork, adding machine tape, wide bias tape, transparent or masking tape |

Fig. 9.26
Tape thumbtack
upside-down on the
bed of your machine
the radius distance
away from the needle.

**Sew-How:** *To prevent the toes of the presser foot from catching in the loops of the yarn, wrap over both of them with transparent or masking tape to form a bar.*

1. Center the foot and wrapped fork over fabric or bias tape and stitch. Backstitch at the beginning. Sew to the bend in the fork, and stop with the needle down (Fig 9.25).

**Sew-How:** *Jackie Dodson, author of 20 Easy Machine-Made Rugs (Chilton, 1990), uses pillow ticking as a rug backing because the fabric is sturdy and the stripes are easy to follow so the rows of fringe are evenly spaced.*

2. Pull the fork toward you until the end of its toes are about 1-1/2" (3.8cm) behind the needle. Wrap yarn again and stitch to the bend. Pull fork toward you, wrap, then stitch, until you have stitched to the end of the fabric or tape. Backstitch, clip off the yarn, and remove fork.

3. Leave fringe looped or cut loops for a shaggier look.

**Sew-How:** *Robbie Fanning makes fringe by stitching the yarn to a measured strip of adding machine tape. This way, she makes the exact length of fringe needed and, when applied, the fringe won't twist. The paper tears off easily afterwards.*

**Applications:** Make fringe stitched to a strip of wide bias tape to set in a hood or pocket top or to sandwich between a jacket and front facing. Use it for doll or clown hair, or for animal fur on a stuffed toy.

For finer fringe, wrap fork with pearl cotton or baby yarn. For heavier fringe, wrap fork with 1/4" (6mm) ribbon, heavy yarn, or fabric strips cut on the bias. Heavier fringe can be used to make rugs and textured fringe for home decorating projects.

## CIRCLE MAKER

Sometimes referred to as a circular sewing or circular embroidery device, the circle maker is used to stitch perfect circles for patches or buttons, to aid in circular embroidery and appliqué, and to make scallops.

Some types clip to or over the feed dogs; others clamp on behind the presser foot like a quilting or edge guide. Some sewing machines may have evenly spaced holes in the bed of the machine used as pivot points to make circles. In this case, the point of the compass is a pivot point to the right or left of the needle. All circle makers work like the compass you may have used in geometry class.

Circle makers are available for some brands and not for others. A good substitute is a piece of tape and a thumbtack, used as follows:

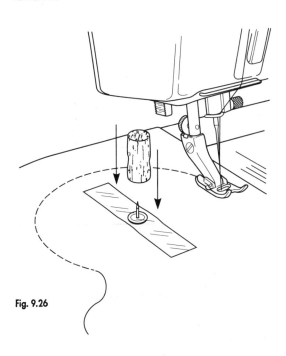

Fig. 9.26

**Fig. 9.27**
The cording foot, sometimes called the knit edge or bulky overlock foot, has a wide groove on the underside to hold and cover cord used for upholstery, pillows, or slip covers.

**Fig. 9.28**
Darning foot.

1. Tape a thumbtack upside-down on the bed of your machine, the radius distance away from the needle. Be sure the point of the tack is exactly opposite the needle (Fig. 9.26). I find it's easier to position the tack correctly if I remove the foot.

2. Iron plastic-coated freezer wrap to the wrong side of the fabric or stretch it in a hoop. If you are using a heavy, closely woven fabric, this may not be necessary. At the center of the circle, pierce the fabric with the point of the tack. Put a cork over the point snugging it down to the surface of the fabric. Put the presser foot down.

3. Stitch around the circle, matching stitches at the beginning and end. Use a straight stitch, zigzag or other decorative stitch.

---

**Sew-How:** *When using this method to make a lot of circles, use a sturdy tape that will not tear. Silk surgical tape works well and should be available through your local hospital or hospital supply store. A friend who's a doctor or nurse may be able to get you some.*

---

**Applications:** Outline a perfect circle used as an appliqué, stitch concentric circles of decorative stitching on a round belt buckle, or make scallops.

## CORDING FOOT

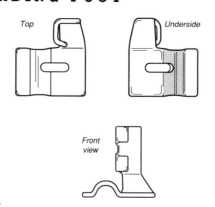

Top  Underside

Front view

**Fig. 9.27**

This foot goes by a number of names—e.g., knit edge and bulky overlock. The underside has a wide groove designed to cover the cord used to edge upholstery and pillow seams (Fig. 9.27). It is also used to insert piping. Although you can use the zipper foot for either purpose, the cording foot makes it easier and the stitching is more accurate.

To cover cord, cut the fabric on the bias the width of the cord plus 1-1/4" (3.2cm) or unfold bias tape. Sandwich cord in the bias tape or fabric; then place it under the foot so the cord fits in the groove. Decenter the needle, so the line of stitching snugs up against the cording, and stitch.

To attach the finished cord or piping evenly without catching it in the seam, this foot is a must.

**Applications:** Cord yokes and pockets, tote bags, handbags, backpacks, pillows, hemlines, or upholstering projects—almost anywhere there is a seam.

## DARNING FOOT

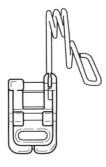

**Fig. 9.28**

As the name implies, the darning foot is used for free-machine darning (Fig. 9.28). If your machine does not have a darning foot, a darning spring may be available instead. The purpose of the foot or spring is to insure proper stitch formation, minimize skipped stitches and puckering, and protect your fingers while moving the fabric freely under the needle.

**Fig. 9.29**
Edge guide slips behind the foot shank and adjusts out 3" (7.5cm) to the right of the needle.

**Fig. 9.30**
Eyelet plates in 2mm and 4mm widths make eyelets of varying size. Place hole over tube, then zigzag while turning fabric slowly to overcast hole.

To use the foot or spring, drop the feed dogs or cover them with a darning plate. When you put the foot or spring down and the needle is out of the fabric, the foot or spring rests about 1/8" (3mm) above the fabric. When the needle is in the fabric, the foot or spring rests on the surface during stitch formation.

**Applications:** Use the darning foot or spring to gain confidence when learning free-machine embroidery or for darning heavy or very fine fabrics.

## EDGE GUIDE

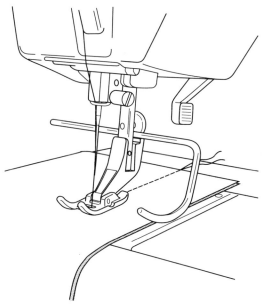

Fig. 9.29

Do you have trouble sewing straight? The edge guide will help. It slips in behind the foot shank and adjusts out 3" (7.5cm) to the right of the needle (Fig. 9.29).

**Applications:** Use as a seam guide or anytime you are stitching farther from the edge of the fabric than what is marked on the needle plate. The edge guide also is helpful for stitching deep hems or cuffs and for topstitching and quilting.

## EYELET PLATES

Eyelet plates come in a few sizes, commonly 2mm and 4mm, and are used with an awl to make thread eyelets (Fig. 9.30).

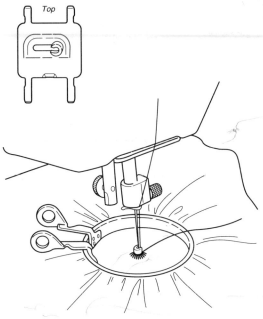

Fig. 9.30

1. Place the eyelet plate over feed dogs. Some machines require you to drop the feed dogs; others don't. (See your instruction book.)

2. Place the fabric in a hoop and poke a hole with the awl where the eyelet is to be sewn. Push the hole over the tube in the plate, so the fabric fits snugly over the tube.

3. Set your machine for a zigzag stitch, length 0 (or drop feed dogs), width 2–4. Begin sewing and turn the fabric slowly to overcast the hole.

**Applications:** Thread ribbon, lacing, or trim through eyelets. Use them to create designs like a bunch of grapes or flower centers. Create your own eyelet fabric. Once you have perfected making eyelets with the zigzag stitch, use closed embroidery stitches like a triangle or half circle to create a decorative eyelet.

# FELLING FOOT

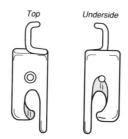

Top    Underside

**Fig. 9.31A**

**Fig. 9.31A**
The felling foot, sometimes called a lap hemmer, has a round hole and is completely flat on the underside behind the needle to minimize puckering on lightweight shirt cottons.

**Fig. 9.31B**
Turn and press top seam allowance under, then edgestitch, guiding the fold to the inside edge of the curl.

**Fig. 9.32**
The fringe foot, sometimes called a special marking, tailor tacking, or looping foot, has one or two raised bars in front, causing the thread to stand away from the fabric. The underside has a high, deep groove. Pull fabric apart so thread loops are between two layers of fabric, then clip thread to mark.

If you are going to make a lot of men's shirts or other projects requiring flat-felled seams, the felling foot is a must (Fig. 9.31A). It has a round hole, which offers support around the needle, and the underside is completely flat behind the needle, which minimizes puckering on fine shirt- weight cottons. Sometimes called a lap hemmer, the felling foot has a curl in it, which keeps the fabric turned under when topstitching the second step of a flat-felled seam. To make a flat-felled seam:

1. Put wrong sides together and sew a 5/8" (1.5cm) seam, using a 2–2.5 (10–12 spi) straight stitch. Press seam to one side. Trim the underneath seam allowance to 3/8" (1cm).

2. Turn top seam allowance under 1/4" (6mm) and press. Pin folded edge over the trimmed seam allowance.

3. Edgestitch, guiding the fold to the inside edge of the curl in the felling foot (Fig. 9.31B).

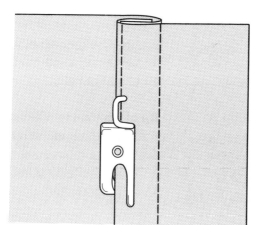

**Fig. 9.31B**

**Applications:** Use it for flat-felled seams and for turning narrow edges and hems on light- to medium-weight wovens.

# FRINGE FOOT

Sometimes called a special marking, tailor tacking, or looping foot, the fringe foot has a bar or two in the front that stick up off the fabric (Fig. 9.32). When used with the zigzag stitch, the bar causes the thread to stand away from the fabric. The underside has a high, deep groove, which allows the thread loops to stand up once stitched.

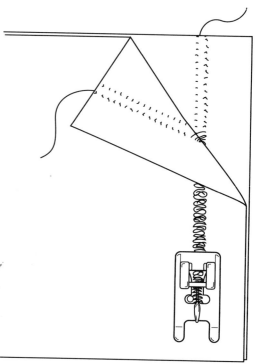

**Fig. 9.32**

**Applications:** Use for pattern marking and making chenille fringe.

## Fringe Foot for Marking

For tailor tacking, set your machine as follows:

**Fig. 9.33**
The underside of the gathering foot is raised behind the needle and has a slot in front of the needle. To gather and attach a ruffle at the same time onto a flat piece, place ruffle under foot right side up. Slip flat piece into slot, right side down, and straight stitch.

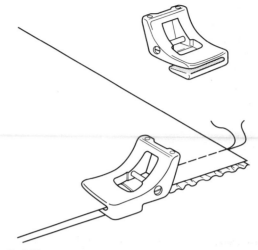

**Fig. 9.33**

### Machine Readiness Checklist

**Stitch:** zigzag

**Length:** 1–2; 13–24 spi

**Width:** 3-4

**Foot:** fringe

**Feed dogs:** up

**Needle position:** center

**Thread:** all-purpose or embroidery

**Fabric:** medium-weight woven or knit

**Tension:** top, loosened slightly; bobbin, normal

1. Place right sides together and stitch.

2. Pull fabric apart so the thread loops are between the two layers of fabric, then clip threads. The threads accurately mark both pieces of fabric.

### Fringe Foot for Chenille Fringe

Make chenille fringe for flowers, eyelashes, or grass or to texture an existing piece of fabric. Use it also for appliqués or a freely embroidered design.

Set your machine as described above, but shorten the stitch length to 0.4–0.5 (60 spi). If you are covering a large area on one layer of fabric, fill it in faster by using two threads through the same needle and lengthen the stitch to about 0.8.

To make a circle or square, start in the middle and work out.

## GATHERING FOOT

This foot gathers light- to medium-weight fabric automatically while sewing. The underside is raised behind the needle and there is a slot in front of the needle (Fig. 9.33).

To use it, set your machine for a straight stitch. The amount the fabric gathers is determined by the stitch length and upper thread tension. Use a long stitch and a tighter tension for a lot of heavy gathers. Use a short stitch and normal tension for finer gathers.

To gather and sew a ruffle onto a flat piece of fabric, place the fabric to be gathered under the foot, right side up, and put the foot down. Slip the flat piece into the slot with the right side down and stitch. Everything is stitched in one step. However, the stitching may not be straight and even. Therefore, you may want to gather the fabric first and attach it in a second step.

To determine how much gathering you need, stitch a test piece. Start with a strip of fabric 10" (25.5cm) long. This way, if the fabric gathers to 5" (12.5cm), you know to use a two to one ratio—or use a 50" (125cm) length of ruffle to attach to a 25" (62.5cm) waistband.

**Applications:** Gather ruffles for children's clothing, curtains, dust ruffles, tablecloths, or blouses.

## HEMSTITCH FORK

This accessory is available through your local Viking dealer and can be used on any

**Fig. 9.34**
Hemstitch fork works on all brands and ages of machines. Pin fabric together. Slip fork between fabric with loop toward you. Put needle down between the tines, put foot down, and stitch slowly. Remove fork and press seam open.

**Fig. 9.35**
Pieced collar made with the hemstitch fork. Decorative stitching on either side of fagoting keeps seams flat during cleaning and pressing.

**Fig. 9.36A**
The rolled hemmer has a scroll-shaped feeder on the top and a straight groove the width of the finished hem on the underside.

brand of sewing machine. It looks like a large bobby pin and is used for fagoting with the straight stitch (Fig. 9.34).

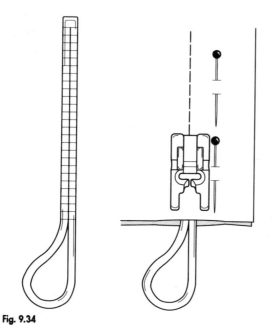

Fig. 9.34

**Machine Readiness Checklist**

**Stitch:** straight
**Length:** 3–4; 9–13 spi
**Width:** 0
**Foot:** standard zigzag
**Needle:** 80/12 universal
**Thread:** all-purpose or cotton sewing
**Feed dogs:** up
**Tension:** top, loosened slightly; bobbin, normal

1. Pin your fabric, right sides together, placing pins parallel to, and 1/8" (3mm) from, the raw edge.

2. Slip the fork between the layers of fabric so the loop of the fork is toward you and the fork is snugged up to the pins.

3. Place the fork under the needle, put the needle down between the tines, then put the foot down. Stitch slowly to the loop in

the fork. Stop with the needle down, lift the foot, and pull the fork toward you.

4. Put the foot back down, stitch to the loop, pull the fork toward you. Continue until the line of stitching is complete.

5. Remove the fork and press the seam open. The folds will separate and you will see a thread ladder between them. If desired, topstitch seam allowances on either side of the ladders (Fig. 9.35).

Fig. 9.35

**Applications:** Use this method to join seams on baby clothes, French hand-sewn (by machine) blouses, collars, pocket tops, yokes, or anywhere you may want an interesting seam. Piece fabrics together for a collar, tablecloth, or front tab.

## HEMMER

Sometimes referred to as a rolled hemmer, a hemmer is used to stitch the narrow, rolled hems commonly found on shirttails. The top has a scroll-shaped feeder—the underside, a straight groove (Fig. 9.36A). This is a common foot, so you may have one with your machine.

*Underside*

Fig. 9.36A

**Fig. 9.36B**
Overlap a square of tear-away to the starting end of the hem and start rolling stabilizer in the scroll. Hold fabric up and slightly to the left of center, curling the edge before it enters the scroll.

**Fig. 9.37**
The multiple cord foot has five or seven holes in front of the needle and a wide groove on the underside behind the needle. Create trims and decorative hemlines using the multiple cord foot and one or more of the decorative stitches available on your machine.

The width of the groove on the underside determines how wide the finished hem will be. Hemmers are available in 2, 3, 4, and 5mm. Use the 2 and 3mm hemmers on lightweight fabrics. Use the 4 and 5mm hemmers on mid- to heavy-weight fabrics. **Note:** The wider the finished hem, the easier a hemmer is to use.

**Sew-How:** *For stitches that start at the very edge of the rolled hem, overlap a 3" (7.5cm) square of tear-away stabilizer and stitch it to the raw edge of the fabric. Start rolling the stabilizer into the scroll of the hemmer (Fig. 9.36B). The stitches attaching the stabilizer to the fabric will be inside the roll. Remove the tear-away after stitching.*

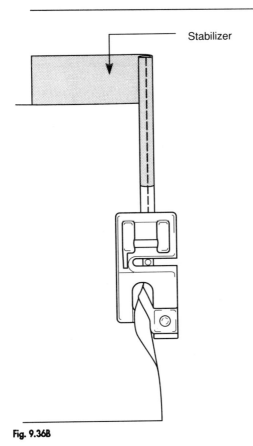

Stabilizer

**Fig. 9.36B**

1. Roll and press a few inches of the hem to get started.

2. Feed the stabilizer into the scroll and begin sewing. With your right hand, hold the fabric up and slightly to the left of center, curling the edge of the fabric before it enters the scroll.

3. Stitch slowly and carefully to finish hem. Remove stabilizer. **Note:** This takes some practice, so try it on a scrap first.

**Applications:** Roll hems on shirt and ruffle hems. Use the scroll to guide cord, yarn, pearl cotton, or narrow trim for a corded edge finish.

## MULTIPLE CORD FOOT

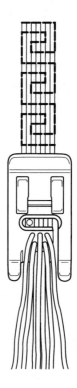

**Fig. 9.37**

The multiple cord foot is sometimes called a 5-hole or 7-hole foot, depending on how many holes are in front of the needle (Fig. 9.37). The underside looks like the embroidery foot, with a wide groove behind the needle.

**Fig. 9.38**
The overcast guide foot, sometimes called an overedge, overlock, or edging foot, has a wire or bar on the top and is either flat or has a narrow channel behind the wire or bar on the underside.

**Fig. 9.39**
The pintucking foot, also referred to as a cording, tucker, or raised seam foot, is used with twin needles to stitch multiple rows of pin tucks. The underside has between three and nine grooves. After the first tuck is stitched, the remaining rows are parallel to the first.

To use it, thread pearl cotton, embroidery floss, metallic thread, baby yarn, or any fine cord through two or more holes and stitch over them using an open embroidery stitch (daisy, wave) or a closed pattern (ball, diamond, triangle). The holes keep the cords in line and untangled, regardless of the direction you sew.

**Applications:** Create your own trims; decorate hemlines, pockets and placemats; or use short lengths to texture a solid fabric with a yarn or corded plaid, or with small motifs.

## OVERCAST GUIDE FOOT

Have you overcast a raw edge with a zigzag stitch and ended with the fabric tunneled under it? The overcast guide foot, often referred to as an overedge, overlock, or edging foot, has a wire or bar in the center (Fig. 9.38). The underside is either flat or has a narrow channel behind the wire or bar. When the zigzag stitch is used on a 4-6 width, the stitch forms over the bar, which keeps thread tension even during stitch formation to prevent tunneling.

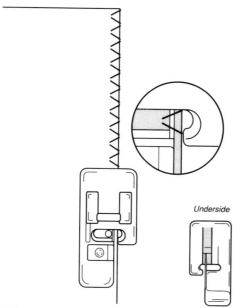

**Fig. 9.38**

**Applications:** Use this foot with the zigzag, overlock, double overlock, rickrack, or any stitch that causes tunneling on a 4 width or wider. Use it not only for overcasting seam allowances, but for making 1/4" (6mm) seams with the above mentioned stitches.

## PINTUCKING FOOT

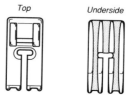

*Top*  *Underside*

**Fig. 9.39**

The pintucking foot is also known as a cording foot (3, 5, 7, or 9 grooves), tucker foot, or a raised seam foot. It's used with twin needles to duplicate the multiple rows of pintucks found on dressy blouses or shirts, christening gowns, and French hand-sewn garments. The underside can have three to nine grooves in it (Fig. 9.39). Twin needles with the needles close together (1.6–2.0mm) create a narrow tuck and are used with a 7- to 9-groove pintucking foot. Twin needles with needles farther apart (2.5–3.0mm) are used with the 3- to 5-groove pintucker. The grooves of the foot make it easy to stitch all the rows parallel and evenly spaced from one another. If you want to buy one size, buy the 5-groove type.

**Fig. 9.40**
Stitch multiple rows of tucks starting from the center row out.

**Fig. 9.41**
The quilting guide adjusts out to the right or left of the needle to keep many rows of quilting straight and even.

### Machine Readiness Checklist

**Stitch:** straight

**Length:** 2–2.5; 10–12 spi

**Width:** 0

**Foot:** pintucking

**Feed dogs:** up

**Needle position:** center

**Thread:** 100% cotton or all-purpose

**Fabric:** light- to medium-weight cotton, cotton blend, wool jersey, cotton T-shirt knit

**Tension:** for more pronounced tuck, tighten upper tension

**Accessories:** vanishing marker or dressmaker's chalk

1. Mark tuck placement with vanishing marker or dressmaker's chalk, marking center row only.

2. Stitch the first tuck on the line marked in Step 1.

3. Stitch second row next to first, guiding the fabric so the first tuck rides in one of the channels in the foot. Stitch as many rows of tucking as desired, working from the center row out (Fig. 9.40).

**Fig. 9.40**

**Applications:** Pintuck blouses, shirts, or children's clothing. Use this method to create texture on a solid fabric, matching the thread to the fabric.

**Sew-How:** *If you plan a lot of tucks on a pattern that doesn't call for them, stitch rows of tucks first; then center the pattern on top of the tucks and cut out the project. This ensures the garment will not be too tight.*

## QUILTING GUIDE

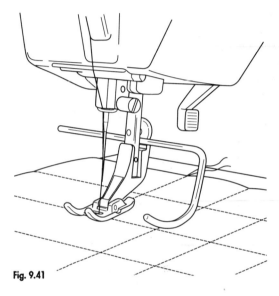

**Fig. 9.41**

A quilting guide will help you keep many lines of quilting straight and evenly spaced from one another. As with the edge guide, the quilting guide slips behind the foot shank and adjusts to the right or left of the needle (Fig. 9.41). Quilt your own fabric using the straight stitch, zigzag, three-step zigzag, or other decorative stitches.

**Sew-How:** *If you are quilting many rows, the underlayer of fabric may pucker or come out shorter than the rest of the piece. You can prevent this by using the walking foot (see walking foot instructions), but then you can't use the quilting guide. When using the walking foot, use removable transparent tape to mark your quilting lines.*

Fig. 9.42
The roller foot has textured rollers that roll against the fabric and act like a track on a bulldozer for sewing heavy fabrics.

Fig. 9.43
Ruffler.

Fig. 9.44
The hole in the straight stitch foot supports the needle to prevent puckering and the foot may have a narrow groove struck on the underside to keep stitching straight.

**Applications:** Use for even quilting, and/or as an edge guide for topstitching deep cuffs and hems.

## ROLLER FOOT

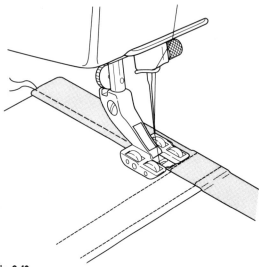

Fig. 9.42

The roller foot has textured rollers that roll against the fabric and act like the track on a bulldozer for sewing heavy fabrics (Fig. 9.42). The rollers move freely between the foot and feed dogs, so the foot rides easily over varying thicknesses.

**Applications:** Use this foot when sewing heavy fabrics such as denim, upholstery, and drapery fabrics. Use it also to sew sticky leather and vinyl.

## RUFFLER

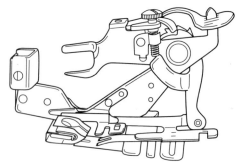

Fig. 9.43

Rufflers haven't changed much from the days of the treadle machine (Fig. 9.43). They are adjustable and designed to ruffle or pleat the fabric to the desired fullness. Remember to stitch a sample first, because once stitched, ruffles or pleats are not adjustable.

I have found rufflers differ greatly from one another even within the same brand. So if you plan to purchase one, take your own fabric and test it in the store before buying it.

**Applications:** Stitch ruffles for square dance dresses, costumes, tablecloths, curtains, and children's clothing.

## STRAIGHT STITCH FOOT

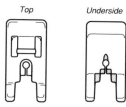

Fig. 9.44

The straight stitch foot is often used on very fine or very heavy fabrics. The reason? It's flat and may have a narrow channel on the underside (Fig. 9.44). The channel keeps the stitching straight and the hole in the foot surrounds the needle, minimizing puckering and skipped stitches.

Some machines come with a straight stitch foot. If yours does, it should be wide enough to cover the feed dogs. Narrow feet make only partial contact with the feed dogs, which causes the fabric to slip.

**Note:** It is not necessary to use a straight stitch foot when straight stitching, provided you are using the appropriate needle for the fabric and the proper stitch length.

**Fig. 9.45**
The walking foot, sometimes called a dual feeder or even-feed foot, has a top set of feed dogs to prevent fabric from shifting or slipping and the under layer from coming up short. Use the walking foot for matching plaids and stripes, for quilting, or for sewing long drapery seams and hems.

**Fig. 9.46**
Use the 30mm or 45mm weaver's reed and straight stitch carefully down open channel. Slide yarn off reed. Leave yarn looped or cut loops for shaggier look.

To achieve similar results, use the flat-bottomed standard zigzag foot and decenter your needle to the left or right (see Fig. 9.5).

---

**Sew-How:** *Use a fine needle and short stitch length for fine fabrics. Use a heavier needle and longer stitch length for heavier fabrics.*

---

**Applications:** Use this foot if you have tried everything else and are still experiencing skipped stitches and puckering. Also use it to topstitch difficult fabrics and to piece quilts.

**Did You Know?** If your fabric puckers, shorten the stitch length. If your fabric waves out of shape, lengthen the stitch. This rule works with straight stitch, zigzag, or any other stitch available on your sewing machine.

## WALKING FOOT

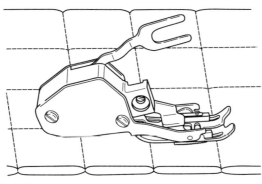

Fig. 9.45

Often referred to as a dual feeder or even-feed foot, the walking foot has a top set of feed dogs to feed the fabric without shifting or slipping and to keep the under layer from coming up short (Fig. 9.45). It works best with the straight stitch; however, it can be used with other stitches, providing the needle hole is wide enough to accommodate the swing of the needle.

**Applications:** Use the walking foot for matching stripes and plaids, napped, and slippery fabrics. It's also wonderful for quilting.

Use the walking foot when sewing long seams and hems for draperies and curtains.

## WEAVER'S REED

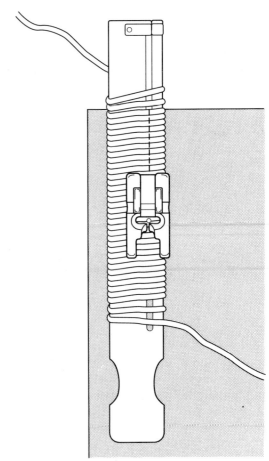

Fig. 9.46

The weaver's reed works much like the carpet fork but the line of stitching is to one side, rather than in the middle (Fig. 9.46; see carpet fork instructions, page 190). It is also available in two sizes, 30mm and 45mm, is available through your local Viking dealer, and will work on any brand of machine. To use it:

1. Close the clip at the end of the toes and wrap the reed with yarn. Do not cut the yarn. Place wrapped reed on a piece of fabric or bias tape. Using a straight stitch length 3–4 (6–9 spi), carefully stitch down the open channel. Stop with the needle in your work.

2. Open the clip on the reed. Lift the foot and slide yarn off the reed, pulling the reed toward you and stopping with the toes of the reed 1-1/2" (3.8cm) behind the needle. Wrap the reed again. Stitch down the channel, slide yarn off, wrap, and stitch to the end of the fabric or tape.

3. Leave yarn looped or cut loops for a shaggier look.

**Applications:** Use this reed to make fringe for doll or clown hair, or for animal fur for a stuffed toy. Make fringe stitched to a strip of wide bias tape or adding machine tape to set in a hood or pocket top, or sandwiched between a jacket front and front facing. For finer fringe, wrap fork with 1/4" (6mm) ribbon, heavy yarn, or fabric strips cut on the bias. Heavier fringe can be used to make rugs and textured fringe for home decor projects.

# SOURCES OF SUPPLY

This list tells where you can find or write for information on sewing machines, threads, and other sewing supplies your local sewing store may not have. For a more extensive list and specific sewing needs, see *Sew, Serge, Press—Speed Tailoring in the Ultimate Sewing Center*, by Jan Saunders, Chilton, 1989, and *Innovative Sewing*, by Gail Brown and Tammy Young, Chilton, 1990.

## SEWING MACHINE COMPANIES

If you're in the market for a sewing machine or serger, write to these companies for dealer referrals and brochures. (Brand names are in parentheses following each company name.)

Allyn International, Inc. (Necchi)
1075 Santa Fe Drive
Denver, CO 80204

baby lock U.S.A
P.O. Box 730
Fenton, MO 63026

Bernina of America
(Bernina and Bernette)
534 West Chestnut
Hinsdale, IL 60521

Brother International Corp.
(Brother and Homelock)
8 Corporate Place
Piscataway, NJ 08854

Elna, Inc.
(Elna and Elnalock)
7642 Washington Ave. South
Eden Praire, MN 55344

Fabric-Centers of America, Inc.
(Sonata Compusew)
23550 Commerce Park Road
Cleveland, OH 44122

J.C. Penney Co., Inc. (Penney)
1301 Avenue of the Americas
New York, NY 10019

Juki Industries of America (Jukilock)
421 North Midland Ave.
Saddlebrook, NJ 07662

Sears, Roebuck (Kenmore)
Sears Tower
Chicago, IL 60607

Montgomery Ward (Ward's)
P.O. Box 8339
Chicago, IL 60680

New Home Sewing Machine Co.
(New Home and Mylock)
100 Hollister Rd.
Teterboro, NJ 07608

Pfaff American Sales Corp.
(Pfaff and Hobbylock)
610 Winters Ave.
Paramus, NJ 07653

Riccar America (Riccar)
14281 Franklin Ave.
Tustin, CA 92680

Simplicity Sewing Machines (Simplicity)
P.O. Box 56
Carlstadt, NJ 07072

Singer Sewing Co. (Singer and Ultralock)
North American Sewing Products Division
135 Raritan Center Parkway
Edison, NJ 08837

V.W.S., Inc. (Viking and Huskylock;
White and White Superlock)
11760 Berea Road
Cleveland, OH 44111

# THREADS

Ask your local retailer or send a preaddressed, stamped envelope to the companies below to find out where to buy their threads.

## Extra-fine

• *Assorted threads*

Robison-Anton Textile Co.
175 Bergen Blvd.
Fairview, NJ  07022

• *DMC 100% cotton, Sizes 30 and 50*

The DMC Corp.
107 Trumbull St.
Elizabeth, NJ  07206

• *Dual-Duty Plus Extra-fine, cotton-wrapped polyester*

J & P Coats/Coats & Clark
Consumer Service Department
P.O. Box 1010
Toccoa, GA  30577

• *Iris 100% rayon*

Art Sales
4801 W. Jefferson
Los Angeles, CA  90016

• *Iris 100% silk*

see Zwicky

## Madeira threads

Madeira Co.
56 Primrose Drive
O'Shea Industrial Par
Laconia, NH  03246

• *Mettler Metrosene fine machine embroidery cotton, size 60/2*

Swiss-Metrosene, Inc.
7780 Quincy St.
Willowbrook, IL  60521

• *Natesh 100% rayon, lightweight*

Aardvark Adventures
P.O. Box 2449
Livermore, CA  94550

• *Paradise 100% rayon*

D & E Distributing
199 N. El Camino Real #F-242
Encinitas, CA  92024

• *Sulky 100% rayon, sizes 30 and 40*

Speed Stitch, Inc.
P.O. Box 3472
Port Charlotte, FL  33949

• *V.W.S., Inc.*
11760 Berea Road
Cleveland, OH  44111

• *Zwicky 100% cotton, size 30/2; white and black darning thread*

V.W.S., Inc.
11760 Berea Rd.
Cleveland, OH  44111

• *Zwicky 100% silk*

see V.W.S., Inc., above

## Ordinary

• *Dual-Duty Plus, cotton-wrapped polyester*

see Dual-Duty Plus Extra-Fine

• *Natesh heavyweight, Zwicky in cotton and polyester, Mettler Metrosene in 30/2, 40/3, 50/3, and 30/3, and Metrosene Plus*

see addresses under Extra-fine, above.

## Metallic

YLI Corp.
45 West 300 North
Provo, UT  84601

Troy Thread & Textile Co.
2300 W. Diversey Ave.
Chicago, IL  60647

# MACHINE-EMBROIDERY AND SEWING MACHINE SUPPLIES

*Marking and cutting tools, hoops, threads, patterns, books, etc.*

Aardvark Adventures
P.O. Box 2449
Livermore, CA 94550
    *also publishes "Aardvark*
    *Territorial Enterprise"*

Clotilde, Inc.
1909 S.W. First Ave.
Ft. Lauderdale, FL 33315
*Clo-Chalk, Needle Lube*

Craft Gallery Ltd.
P.O. Box 8319
Salem, MA 01971

D & E Distributing
199 N. El Camino Real #F-242
Encinitas, CA 92024

June Tailor, Inc.
2861 Highway 175
Richfield, WI 53076
    *tailor boards, hams, mits,*
    *press cloths, etc.*

Nancy's Notions
P.O. Box 683
Beaver Dam, WI 53916

National Thread & Supply Corp.
695 Red Oak Road
Stockbridge, GA 30281

Patty Lou Creations
Rt. 2, Box 90-A
Elgin, OR 97827

Sew-Art International
P.O. Box 550
Bountiful, UT 84010

Sew/Fit Company
P.O. Box 565
LaGrange, IL 60525

Sewing Emporium
1087 Third Ave.
Chula Vista, CA 92010

Speed Stitch, Inc.
P.O. Box 3472
Port Charlotte, FL 33952

The Fabric Carr
P.O. Box 32120
San Jose, CA 95152

The Perfect Notion
566 Hoyt Street
Darien, CT 06820

Treadleart
25834 Narbonne Ave.
Lomita, CA 90717

# ASSOCIATIONS

American Sewing Guild
P.O. Box 50967
Indianapolis, IN 46250
    *chapters in major cities*

4-H
    *for information on sewing programs, contact your county Cooperative Extension Agent*
    *(listed in the phone book or ask your public librarian)*

# MISCELLANEOUS

Applications
871 Fourth Ave.
Sacramento, CA 95818
*release paper for appliqué*

Berman Leathercraft
145 South St.
Boston, MA 02111
*leather*

Boycan's Craft and Art Supplies
P.O. Box 897
Sharon, PA 16146
*plastic needlepoint canvas*

Clearbrook Woolen Shop
P.O. Box 8
Clearbrook, VA 22624
*Utrasuede scraps*

Folkwear Patterns
The Taunton Press
63 South Main St.
Box 5506
Newtown, CT 06470-5506
*timeless fashion patterns*

KidSew Patterns
1176 Northport Drive
Columbus, OH 43235
*children's patterns and teaching materials*

Kids Can Sew
P.O. Box 1710
St. George, UT 84771-1710
*children's patterns and teaching materials*

To Sew
P.O. Box 974
Malibu, CA 90265
*beginning sewing kits for children of all ages*

---

# MAGAZINES

Aardvark Adventures
P.O. Box 2449
Livermore, CA 94550
*newspaper jammed with information about all kinds of embroidery, design, and things to order*

Fiberarts
50 College Street
Ashville, NC 28801
*gallery of the best fiber artists, including those who work in machine stitchery*

Sew It Seams
P.O. Box 2698
Kirkland, WA 98083-2698

Sew News
P.O. Box 1790
Peoria, IL 61656
*monthly tabloid, mostly of fashion garment sewing*

Threads
Box 355
Newton, CT 06470
*glossy magazine on all fiber crafts*

Treadleart
25834 Narbonne Ave.
Lomita, CA 90717
*bimonthly publication about machine embroidery*

Update Newsletters
2269 Chestnut #269
San Francisco, CA 94123
*two excellent newsletters on sewing and on serging*

# BIBLIOGRAPHY

Ambuter, Carolyn, *The Open Canvas*, Workman Publishing, New York, 1982.

Betzina, Sandra, *Power Sewing* and *More Power Sewing*, Sandra Betzina, San Francisco, CA, 1985, 1990.

Bishop, Edna Bryte, Arch and Marjorie Stotler, *The Bishop Method*, W & W Publishing Company, Memphis, TN, 1966.

Brown, Gail, and Pati Palmer, *The Complete Handbook for Overlock Sewing*, Palmer/Pletsch Inc., Portland, OR, 1985.

Coffin, David Page, *The Custom Shirt Book*, David Page Coffin, c/o Threads Magazine (see page 206)

Dodson, Jackie, *Know Your Bernina*, Chilton Book Company, Radnor, PA, 1987

Dodson, Jackie, *Know Your Sewing Machine*, Chilton Book Company, Radnor, PA, 1988.

Hazen, Gale Grigg, *Owner's Guide to Sewing Machines, Sergers, and Knitting Machines*, Chilton Book Company, Radnor, PA, 1989.

Fanning, Robbie and Tony, *The Complete Book of Machine Quilting*, Chilton Book Company, Radnor, PA, 1980.

Griffin, Barb, *Pizzazz for Pennies* and *Petite Pizzazz*, Chilton Book Company, Radnor, PA, 1986, 1990.

Griffin, Barb, *St. Nick's Knacks*, Country Thread Designs, 1988.

Habeeb, Virginia, *Ladies' Home Journal Art of Homemaking*, Simon & Schuster, New York, 1973.

Jabenis, Elaine, *The Fashion Director*, John Wiley & Sons, New York, 1972.

Maddigan, Judi, *Learn Bearmaking*, Open Chain Publishing, Menlo Park, CA, 1989.

Palmer, Pati, Gail Brown, and Sue Green, *Creative Serging Illustrated*, Chilton Book Company, Radnor, PA, 1987.

Reader's Digest, *Complete Guide to Sewing*, The Reader's Digest Association, Inc., Pleasantville, New York, 1976.

Saunders, Jan, *Illustrated Speed Sewing*, Speed Sewing Ltd., Centerline, MI, 1985.

Saunders, Jan, *Sew, Serge, Press: Speed Tailoring in the Ultimate Sewing Center*, Chilton Book Company, Radnor, PA 1989.

Shaeffer, Claire, *The Complete Book of Sewing Shortcuts*, Sterling Publishing, New York, 1981.

Shaeffer, Claire, *Claire Shaeffer's Sewing S.O.S.*, Open Chain Publishing, Menlo Park, CA, 1988.

Shaeffer, Claire, *Claire Shaeffer's Fabric Sewing Guide*, Chilton Book Company, Radnor, PA, 1989.

*Singer Instructions for Art Embroidery and Lace Work*, Foreword by Robbie Fanning, Open Chain Publishing, Menlo Park, CA, 1989.

Simplicity, *New Simplicity Sewing Book*, Simplicity Pattern Company, New York, 1979.

Simplicity, *Simply the Best Sewing Book*, Simplicity Pattern Company, New York, 1988.

Singer, *Singer Sewing Update 1988*, Cy DeCosse Inc., Minnetonka, MN, 1988.

Vogue, *The New Vogue Sewing Book*, Butterick Publishing, New York, 1980.

Zieman, Nancy, with Robbie Fanning, *The Busy Woman's Fitting Book*, Open Chain Publishing, 1989.

Zieman, Nancy, with Robbie Fanning, *The Busy Woman's Sewing Book*, Open Chain Publishing, 1989.

# VIDEO TAPES

Betzina, Sandra. "Power Sewing," available in BETA or VHS. Write: Power Sewing, P.O. Box 2702, San Francisco, CA 94126.

Clotilde. Clotilde's T.V. Teaching Segments Series numbers 1 through 6, available in BETA or VHS. Write: Clotilde, Inc., 1909 S.W. First Ave., Ft. Lauderdale, FL 33315.

———. Clotilde's Seminar Videos, "Sew Smart for the $500 Look," "Smart Tailoring," "Ultrasuede and Other Leather-like Fabrics," available in BETA or VHS. Write: Clotilde, Inc., 1909 S.W. First Ave., Ft. Lauderdale, FL 33315.

Salyers, Donna. "Sew a Wardrobe in a Weekend," "Re-Do a Room in a Weekend," "Super Time-Saving Sewing Tips," "Craft and Gift Ideas." Write: Congress Video Group, 10 East 53rd St., New York, NY 10022.

Tailor, June. "Pressing Matters." Write: June Tailor, P.O. Box 208, Richfield, WI 53076.

Zieman, Nancy. Nancy has devoted five pages in her current catalog to her video tape list, which is too extensive to list here. Write: Nancy's Notions, P.O. Box 683, Beaver Dam, WI 53919.

# Index

Accessories
  bias binder, 186
  blind hem foot, 13, 184
  braiding feet, 189-190
  buttonhole feet, 12-13, 183-184
  button reed, 186-188
  button sewing foot, 13, 188
  carpet fork, 190-191
  circle maker, 191-192
  cording foot, 192
  darning foot, 192-193
  edge guide, 13, 193
  embroidery feet, 12, 182-183
  eyelet plate, 193
  felling foot, 194
  fringe foot, 194-195
  gathering foot, 195
  hemmer, 196-197
  hemstitch fork, 195-196
  metal zigzag foot, 12
  multiple cord foot, 197-198
  overcast guide foot, 198
  pintucking foot, 198-199
  quilting guide, 13, 199-200
  roller foot, 200
  ruffler, 200
  straight stitch foot, 200-201
  walking foot, 201
  weaver's reed, 201-202
  zipper foot, 13, 185
All-purpose cotton-wrapped polyester thread, 11
American needle sizes, 9, 10
Appliqué and embroider
  for Compass Tote
    label, 73-76
    pocket, 67-73
  definition of, 61
  for Envelope Placemats, 86-87
  fabric selection for, 62-63
  planning for, 62-64
  supplies needed for, 63-64
  thread selection for, 62-63
Appliqué feet. See Embroidery feet
Automatic buttonholes, 154-155
Automatic stitches
  blind hem stitch, 163-165
  blind hem (stretch) stitch, 165-166
  scallop stitch, 166-168
  three-step zigzag stitch, 168-173
  warm-up exercises for, 24-25

Backgammon Board, 131-133
Backing, 95, 100
Basting, 148, 161-162
Batting, 95, 96
Belt loops, 156-157
Bias binder, 186
Blind hem foot, 13, 184
Blind hemming knits, 165-166
Blind hem stitch, 163-165
Blind hem (stretch) stitch, 165-166
Bobbin, 4, 7, 8
Bobbin case, 4, 8
Bobbin winding, 7
Body measurements, 37
Books, 207
Braiding feet, 189-190
Buttonhole feet, 12-13, 183-184
Buttonholes, 31, 153-155
Buttonhole Sampler, 29-30
Buttonhole stitch, 29-30
Button loops, 156-157
Button reed, 186-188
Button sewing, 155-156
Button sewing foot, 13, 188

Carpet fork, 190-191

Checker Board, 133-135
Circle maker, 191-192
Cleaning sewing machine, 13
Closed decorative stitch, 179
Color selection, 83-84
Compass Tote
  appliqué and embroider for
    label, 73-76
    pocket, 67-73
  constructing, 76-79
  fabric selection for, 62-63
  label for, 73-76
  pocket for, 67-73
  supplies needed for, 65
  thread selection for, 62-63
  tracing and transferring design for, 65-66
  transferable learnings from, 81
  variations of, 80-81
Corded buttonholes, 154-155
Corded scallop edge finish, 166-167
Corded shell tuck, 165
Cording foot, 192
Cotton darning thread, 63
Cotton embroidery thread, 11
Cotton sewing thread, 11
Couched saddle stitch, 164
Couching with zigzag stitch, 157
Cutting area, 35
Cutting tools, 15-16

Darning foot, 192-193
Decorative stitch, 179
Doodle cloth, 62
Double needle, 10, 172-173
Double overlock stitch, 174-175
Dressmaker's chalk, 17

Easestitching, 148-149
Easiest Pin Cushion, 28

Edge finish, 174-175
Edge guide, 13, 193
Edgestitching, 149
Elastic, 51-53, 168-169
Elastic straight stitch, 176
Embellishments. See Appliqué and embroider
Embroider, 61, 205. See also Appliqué and embroider
Embroidery feet, 12, 182-183
Envelope "Lapkins", 91-94
Envelope Placemats
  appliqué and embroider for, 86-87
  constructing, 90-91
  cutting of, 85-86
  fabric selection for, 83-84
  flap for, 87-89
  supplies needed for, 85
  thread selection for, 84
  transferable learnings from, 94
  variations of, 91-94
European needle sizes, 9, 10
Eyelet plate, 193

Fabric Game Board and Pouch
  backgammon, 131-133
  checker board, 133-135
  fabric selection for, 125-126
  game pieces for, 138-139
  pouch for, 135-138
  preshrinking fabric for, 126
  supplies needed for, 131
  thread selection for, 126
  transferable learnaings from, 140
Fabric guide, 5
Fabric selection
  for appliqué and embroider, 62-63
  for Compass Tote, 62-63
  for Envelope Placemats, 83-84

# Index

for Fabric Game Board and Pouch, 125-126

for Hobbyhorse, 109-110

for Jumbo Fabric Blocks, 109-110

machine needle selection and, 9-10

for quilt, 96

for Quilted Wall Hanging, 96

for Woven Pull-On Shorts, 40-41

Fabric stabilizers, 19, 64

Feed dogs, 5

Felling foot, 194

Figure types, 38-39

Finishing stitch, 28

5/8" (1.5cm) knit seam, 158-159

Flywheel, 6

"Fob" Key Ring, 128-130

Foot, 180-181

Forward and reverse stitches
   double overlock stitch, 174-175
   elastic straight stitch, 176
   hemstitch, 176
   overlock stitch, 176-177
   smocking stitch, 178
   super stretch stitch, 178
   warm-up exercises for, 26-28

Free-arm, 6

Fringe foot, 194-195

Fusible interfacing, 31, 64

Game Piece Pouch, 135-138

Game Pieces, 138-139

Gathering foot, 195

Gathering over a cord, 157-158

Gifts. See Fabric Game Board and Pouch; Key Rings

Glue stick, 17

Grab-It, 16

Grainlines, 40

Hand iron, 18

Hand needle, 17

Hand wheel, 6

Hemmer, 196-197

Hemming
   blind hem stitch in, 163-165
   blind hem (stretch) stitch in, 165-166
   hemstitch in, 176
   Knit Top with Ribbing, 59
   Woven Pull-On Shorts, 53

Hemstitch, 176

Hemstitch fork, 195-196

High shank, 180-181

Hobbyhorse
   constructing, 117-123
   fabric selection for, 109-110
   pattern for, 115-117
   supplies needed for, 114-115
   thread selection for, 109-110
   transferable learnings from, 124

Holding tools, 16

Inside and outside curves, 31

Instant T-shirts, 59-60

Interfacing, 19

Interfacing selection, 20-21

Iron, hand, 18

Ironing, 30-31. See also Pressing

Ironing board, 19

Jumbo Fabric Blocks
   constructing, 113-114
   fabric selection for, 109-110
   square decoration for, 110-112
   supplies needed for, 110
   thread selection for, 109-110

Key Rings
   "Fob", 128-130
   Monogrammed, 127
   Round, 127-128
   thread selection for, 125

KidsCanSew patterns, 42

KidSew patterns, 42

Knit Top with Ribbing
   hemming, 59
   layout and cutting of, 53-54
   marking of, 53-54
   neck band for, 57-58
   seams and seam finishes for, 54-57

Lapkins, 91-94

Layout and cutting, 44-45, 53-54

Lettuce edge, 159-160

Lining, 95

Liquid fabric sealant, 17, 64

Low shank, 180-181

Machine. See Sewing machine

Machine needle, 4, 5

Machine needle guide, 5

Machine needle point types, 10

Machine needle selection, 9-10

Magazines, 206

Manual buttonholes, 153-154

Manufacturers of sewing machines, 203

Markers, 16-17, 64

Marking, 45-46, 53-54

Marking tools, 16-17

Mat, 15-16

Measurement and ease chart, 38

Measuring tools, 14-15

Medallion, for quilt, 98, 99

Mending, 169-170

Men's figure types, 39

Metal embroidery foot, 182-183

Metal zigzag foot, 12

Monogrammed Key Ring, 127

Multiple cord foot, 197-198

Narrow braiding foot, 189

Neck band, 57-58

Needle. See Hand needle; Machine needle

Needle plate, 4

Needle threader, 18

Notions. See Accessories; Tools

Nylon monofilament thread, 11, 63

Oiling sewing machine, 13

1/4" (6mm) seam, 175

One hundred percent cotton sewing thread, 11

Open arm, 6

Open decorative stitch, 179

Open-toe embroidery foot, 182-183

Outside curves, 31

Overcast guide foot, 198

Overcasting a raw edge, 160, 170

Overlock stitch, 176-177

Paper-backed fusible web, 19

Patching, 171

Pattern selection, 41-43

Pattern symbols, 43

Pattern weights, 16

Pin cushion, 16, 28

Pins, 16

Pintucking foot, 198-199

Pintucks, 152

Pivoting, 31

Placemats. See Envelope Placemats

Plastic-coated freezer wrap, 19, 64

# Index

Pockets
  for Compass Tote, 67-73
  embellishment for, 80
  for Woven Pull-On Shorts, 47-49
Preshrinking, 41, 96, 126
Press cloth, 19
Pressed Fabric Leaves, 23-24
Presser feet
  blind hem, 13, 184
  braiding, 189-190
  buttonhole, 12-13, 183-184
  button sewing, 13, 188
  cording, 192
  darning, 192-193
  description of, 5
  embroidery, 12, 182-183
  felling, 194
  fringe, 194-195
  gathering, 195
  guide, 5
  metal zigzag, 12
  multiple cord, 197-198
  overcast guide, 198
  pintucking, 198-199
  pressure of, 9
  for quilt, 97
  roller, 200
  standard, 12-13, 180
  standard braiding, 189-190
  standard buttonhole, 184
  standard zigzag, 181-182
  straight stitch, 200-201
  walking, 201
  zipper, 13, 185
Pressing, 30-31, 46
Pressing area, 36
Pressing tools, 18-19
Pressure, 9
Puckers, 6

Quilt, 94-97. *See also* Quilted Wall Hanging

Quilted Wall Hanging
  backing for, 100, 105-106
  border for, 101-103
  fabric selection for, 96
  frame border for, 103-104
  last border for, 105-106
  medallion for, 98, 99
  quilt border for, 104-105
  straight-stitch quilting and, 107
  supplies needed for, 98
  thread selection for, 97
  tie a quilt and, 107
  transferable learnings from, 108
Quilting guide, 13, 199-200

Race area, 4, 13
Rayon embroidery thread, 11
Reverse stitch. *See* Forward and reverse stitch
Rolled edge, 159-160
Rolled hemmer, 196-197
Roller foot, 200
Rotary cutter, 15-16
Round Key Ring, 127-128
Ruffler, 200
Ruler, see-through cutting, 15

Satin stitch, 31, 161
Scallop edge finish, 167
Scallop stitch, 166-168
Scissors, 15
Sealant, liquid fabric, 17, 64
Seam ripper, 17
Seams and seam finishes, 46-47, 54-57
Sewing. *See also* specific names of sewing projects
  figure types for, 38-39
  measurement and ease chart for, 38

planning before, 37-38
  pressing during, 46
  in straight line, 31
  work space for, 35-36
Sewing area, 35-36
Sewing gauge, 14
Sewing machine
  care and maintenance of, 13-14
  cleaning, 13
  companies, 203
  needle selection and, 9-10
  oiling, 13-14
  parts of, 4-7
  pressure and, 9
  standard presser feet and, 12-13
  threading, 7-9
  thread selection and, 11-12
  tools with, 14-19
  transferable learning from, 30-31
Sewing projects. *See* specific names of
Sewing tools, 17-18. *See also* Sewing machine
Shank, 180-181
Shears, 15
Shell tuck, 165
Shorts. *See* Woven Pull-Up Shorts
Slant shank, 180-181
Sliding buttonhole foot with guide, 183
Smocking stitch, 178
Sole, 180-181
Speed basting, 161-162
Spring hoop, 18
Standard braiding foot, 189-190
Standard buttonhole foot, 184
Standard zigzag foot, 181-182
Staystitching, 149-150

Stitches. *See also* Automatic stitches; Forward and reverse feeding stitches; Straight stitches; Zigzag stitches
  buttonhole, 29-30
  decorative, 179
  finishing, 28
  forming, 4
  length of, 6, 31
  satin, 31
  tapered satin, 68-71
  width of, 6, 31
Stitch-in-the-ditch, 150
Stitch length, 6, 31
Stitch-n-Tear fabric stabilizer, 64
Stitch Sampler, 26-28
Stitch selector, 6
Stitch width, 6, 31
Straight seams, 150
Straight stitches
  basting, 148
  easestitching, 148-149
  edgestitching, 149
  formation of, 146
  paper patterns for, 22
  purpose of, 31
  staystitching, 149-150
  stitch-in-the-ditch, 150
  straight seams, 150
  topstitching, 150-151
  twin needle hem, 151-152
  twin needle tucks, 152
  understitching, 152
  uses of, 146-147
  warm-up exercises for, 23-24
Straight stitch foot, 200-201
Straight-stitch quilting, 107
Super stretch stitch, 178
Supply sources
  books, 207
  machine-embroidery, 205
  magazines, 206

# Index

miscellaneous, 206

sewing machine companies, 203

sewing machine supplies, 205

threads, 204

video tapes, 208

Tacking, 171-172

Tailor's ham, 19

Take-up lever, 6-7

Tape, transparent, 17

Tape measure, 14

Tapered satin stitch, 68-71

Tapestry needle, large-eye, 17

Tear-Away fabric stabilizer, 19, 64

Tension, 8-9

Thimble, 17

Thread, 204

Thread control, 6, 8-9

Thread guide, 5

Threading, 7-9

Thread selection

for appliqué and embroider, 62-63

for Compass Tote, 62-63

for Envelope Placemats, 84

for Fabric Game Board and Pouch, 126

for Hobbyhorse, 109-110

for Jumbo Fabric Blocks, 109-110

for Key Rings, 125

for quilt, 97

for Quilted Wall Hanging, 97

rules for, 11-12

Thread tacks, 162

Thread types, 11-12, 204

Three-step zigzag stitch, 168-173

Three-step zigzag with twin needles, 172-173

Throat plate, 4

Tie a quilt, 107

Tools

cutting, 15-16

fabric stabilizers, 19

holding, 16

marking, 16-17

measuring, 14-15

pressing, 18-19

sewing, 17-18

Topstitching, 150-151

Top thread tension, 6

To Sew Kits, 42

Tote. See Compass Tote

Toys. See Hobbyhorse; Jumbo Fabric Blocks

Tracery scallop, 167-168

Transparent embroidery foot, 183

T-shirts, 59-60, 80-81

Tweezers, 16

Twin needle, 10, 172-173

Twin needle hem, 151-152

Twin needle tucks, 152

Understitching, 152, 173

Upper threading, 7

Vanishing markers, 16-17, 64

Video tapes, 208

Walking foot, 201

Wall hanging. See Quilted Wall Hanging

Water-erasable markers, 16, 64

Water-soluble stabilizer, 19

Waves out of shape, 6

Waxed paper, 18

Weaver's reed, 201-202

Women's figure types, 39

Wonder-Under paper-backed fusible web, 31

Wonder-Under Transfer Web, 64

Work space, 35-36

Woven Pull-On Shorts

constructing, 50-51

elastic application for, 51-53

fabric selection for, 40-41

hemming, 53

layout and cutting of, 44-45

marking of, 45-46

pattern selection for, 41-43

pockets for, 47-49

preshrinking fabric for, 41

seams and seam finishes for, 46-47

top for, 53-59

transferable learnings from, 60

variations of, 59-60

Zigzag foot with blind hem guide, 184

Zigzag stitches

button and belt loops, 156-157

buttonholes, 153-155

button sewing, 155-156

couching with, 157

5/8" (1.5cm) knit seam, 158-159

gathering over a cord, 157-158

lettuce or rolled edge, 159-160

overcast a raw edge, 160

satin stitch, 161

speed basting, 161-162

thread tacks, 162

Zipper foot, 13, 185